# SACRAMENTS OF LIBERATION

## The Poor, Creation, and the Church's Prophetic Call

Henry Walter Spaulding III

DIVINITY&
DISCOURSE

Divinity & Discourse
19 East 34th Street
New York, NY 10016
www.churchpublishing.org

Divinity & Discourse is an imprint of Church Publishing Incorporated.

Cover design by Newgen
Typeset by Apex CoVantage

ISBN 978-1-64065-894-3 (paperback)
ISBN 978-1-64065-895-0 (eBook)

Library of Congress Control Number: 2026936182

For Ellen Baker
(1997-2025)

A student, an advocate for justice, a lover of creation, a friend.
I think (hope) you would have liked this book.

*requiescat in pace*

*There is a place called "heaven" where the good here unfinished is completed; and where the stories unwritten, and the hopes unfulfilled, are continued. We may laugh together yet.*

*J. R. R. Tolkien*

# Table of Contents

## INTRODUCTION

# The Crisis of Space and the Recovery of Place

*Sacraments of Liberation* is a response to the economic and political forces that have rendered both people and land disposable, and to the theological drift that has relegated sacraments to the realm of personal piety rather than communal transformation. It calls for a sacramental theology rooted in the preferential option for the poor and the flourishing of creation.

Thus, in a world where both people and land are becoming increasingly commodified, the Christian sacramental imagination can offer a radical alternative: a vision of reality where justice, grace, and belonging are not solely dictated by economic systems, but by the self-giving love of God. Lamentably, many contemporary Christian communities have distanced their sacramental practices from the struggles of the poor and the integrity of creation. The preferential option for the poor, a cornerstone of liberation theology, urges the church to reclaim its calling to justice. But this call cannot be separated from the material conditions of our world. The Eucharist, baptism, and other sacramental practices cannot be isolated religious rituals but are understood as deeply embedded in economic, social, and ecological realities. This book argues that the sacramental life of the church must be reoriented toward the most vulnerable—both human and non-human creation—if it is to embody God's justice and restoration.

The sacraments are sometimes viewed as timeless rituals of grace, sacred acts that connect the church to God's presence and promises. Yet, in a world marked by ecological devastation and systemic poverty, how can these sacred practices speak meaningfully to a world in crisis? *Sacraments of Liberation* argues that the sacraments must be more than static rituals and certainly more than a new mode of spiritual exchange. Rooted in the preferential option for the poor, this book proposes that the sacraments are not only divine acts of grace but also embodied practices that resist exploitation, heal creation, and proclaim God's justice.

To explore this vision, the book integrates insights from liberation theology, the metaphysical frameworks of Maximus the Confessor and Sergei Bulgakov, and philosophical reflections on the shift from space to place. It argues that the sacraments have the potential to transform abstract *spaces*—so often commodified and exploited by modern systems—into sacred *places* where justice, solidarity, and care are embodied. This transformation is not merely conceptual but profoundly practical, reshaping how the church lives, worships, and acts in the world.

To be clear, sacramental theology has been guilty of abstracting place into space. Therefore, this book offers a novel yet theologically orthodox reading of the sacraments in the ordering of creation. The Eucharist is not only the presence of Christ, but a meal that calls into question the world's economic order, a practice that grounds the church in the materiality of bread and wine, tying the sacred to the fruits of creation and human labor. Baptism is not only an initiation into the church but a reorientation of identity in solidarity with the suffering of the world, drawing the church into the waters of renewal, connecting our identity to the created order. Both sacraments invite the church to reclaim its mission of justice, resisting the disembodied monotonous logic of neoliberalism and rooting itself in the lived realities of the poor and the earth.[1]

## Locating this Work Among its Contemporaries

Admittedly, this project emerges within a broader contemporary movement in theology that seeks to recover sacramental, liturgical, and embodied accounts of human existence in response to the abstractions of late modernity and neoliberal capitalism. Across the fields of political theology, liberation theology, ecological theology, and sacramental theology, a growing number of theologians and scholars have argued that modern economic systems do not merely organize markets but fundamentally shape our moral imagination, social relations, and conceptions of human personhood. In response, these thinkers have increasingly turned toward themes such as embodiment, place, participation, communion, ecology, gift, and liturgical formation as theological resources capable of resisting processes of fragmentation and commodification.

Within sacramental theology specifically, many theologians have challenged modern accounts of reality that split spirit from matter, worship from politics, or theology from everyday life. Alexander Schmemann famously argued that the sacraments reveal the world itself as a site of communion with God rather than as raw material for technological or economic manipulation.[2] Likewise, John Zizioulas developed an ontology of communion in which personhood is constituted relationally rather than through isolated autonomy, thereby challenging many of the typical anthropological assumptions embedded within classical liberalism.[3] Similar concerns appear in the work of Catherine Pickstock and the broader Radical Orthodoxy movement, which critiques the secular fragmentation of reality and argues for the recovery of liturgical participation as a counter-formation to modern systems of abstraction and instrumental reason.[4] These theologians collectively insist that Christian worship is not reducible to private spirituality but forms a comprehensive vision of reality that reshapes how persons inhabit time, space, desire, and community.

At the same time, theologians working more explicitly in political theology and theological critiques of capitalism have examined how neoliberalism functions not merely as an economic arrangement but as a formative moral order. William T. Cavanaugh has argued that consumer capitalism mimics religious structures by shaping desire through rituals of consumption and promises of fulfillment.[5] Similarly, Vincent Miller has explored the commodification of culture and religion under global capitalism, showing how even religious symbols and practices become detached from the communities and traditions that originally gave them meaning.[6] John Milbank has likewise argued that supposedly secular social theories often conceal theological assumptions about violence, desire, and human flourishing.[7] Together, these thinkers illuminate the ways economic systems shape not only institutions and behavior but also imagination, hope, and moral perception.

This project also stands in conversation with liberation theology and ecological theology, both of which insist that theological reflection cannot be abstracted from questions of material existence, labor, land, poverty, and social power. Gustavo Gutiérrez famously argued that theology must begin from the lived realities of the poor and oppressed rather than from detached speculation.[8] Leonardo Boff extended these concerns into ecological theology by emphasizing the interconnectedness of social exploitation and environmental destruction under global capitalism.[9] These traditions have increasingly recognized that neoliberal systems not only produce economic inequality but also distort relationships between persons, communities, and creation itself.

Alternatively, this book is especially indebted to contemporary thinkers who have sought to recover place, creatureliness, and material belonging against the placelessness and abstraction of modern economic life. Norman Wirzba argues that modern industrial society conditions persons to view land, food, animals, and even human relationships primarily through utilitarian and consumptive categories.[10] Similarly, Wendell Berry repeatedly critiques the logic of industrial capitalism for severing persons from the land, from communal memory, and from forms of life shaped by restraint, care, and fidelity to place.[11] These concerns resonate deeply with sacramental theology insofar as sacramental practices resist abstraction by rooting human existence within embodied, communal, and material forms of life.

Sacramental theology alone cannot solve the crises generated by neoliberal modernity. Neither is this project an entirely unprecedented line of inquiry. Rather, this work participates in an expanding theological effort to recover thicker accounts of embodiment, participation, communion, and creatureliness in response to economic and technological systems that have reduced human life to optimization and productivity inputs. Its distinctive contribution lies, I hope, in bringing these sacramental, agrarian, and liberationist insights into sustained conversation with questions of neoliberal temporality, moral formation, and the theological meaning of place.

## A Roadmap of the Book

Each chapter contributes to a vision of sacramental life that integrates theological depth with practical action. Chapter 1 explores how modern culture is shaped by economic systems from mercantilism to neoliberal capitalism, highlighting human complicity in economic exploitation and the theological implications of debt, land ownership, and labor. This lays the foundation for the theological framework that follows in chapter 2, which examines the preferential option for the poor as a central practice of sacramental theology. This chapter demonstrates how sacraments embody God's justice by rooting the church in the material realities of the oppressed.

With this foundation laid, chapter 3 examines Christian complicity in neoliberalism and the theological rationale that undergirds neoliberalism. It will set up how sacraments function as acts of embodied resistance against the commodification of life. It presents the Eucharist as a counter-narrative to consumerism and individualism, emphasizing the communal and economic implications of breaking bread together. Baptism, too, is reframed as a radical act of solidarity with the suffering world and a reorientation toward creation.

These themes are further deepened in chapter 4, which engages the metaphysical insights of Maximus the Confessor and Sergei Bulgakov. Here, the book argues that sacramental theology must be grounded in a robust doctrine of the incarnation and creation, integrating the divine presence within the material world and affirming that creation itself participates in God's salvific work.

Expanding this theological vision, chapter 5 extends the preferential option for the poor to include creation itself, showing how ecological degradation and systemic poverty are entwined. Highlighting the urgent need for ecological justice within sacramental theology, the chapter explores practical ways in which the church can enact justice for both the poor and the environment through liturgical practices, land stewardship, and economic resistance.

The book concludes by reaffirming that sacraments, when deeply integrated with the preferential option for the poor and creation, have the power to transform communities, challenge economic and ecological injustice, and offer a prophetic witness to the world. Through this vision, the church can rediscover its mission as a people rooted in place, embodying God's grace and restoration for all creation. By recovering a sacramental imagination attuned to the cries of the poor and the suffering earth, the church can become an agent of justice, reconciliation, and hope in a world desperately in need of transformation.

## Notes

1. The terms *market*, *capitalism*, *globalization*, and *neoliberalism* are often employed interchangeably in both popular and scholarly discourse, yet they describe distinct phenomena. Markets refer to mechanisms of exchange that have existed across diverse economic systems and are not inherently capitalist. Capitalism denotes an economic order organized around private ownership of capital, wage labor, and the accumulation of profit. Globalization describes the increasing integration of economic, political, technological, and cultural systems across national boundaries. Neoliberalism, as employed throughout this study, refers not simply to free-market economics but to a broader political, cultural, and anthropological rationality that extends market logic into every sphere of human life. While markets may generate genuine goods—including innovation, voluntary exchange, economic development, and certain protections against centralized power—this study argues that neoliberalism transforms these partial goods into a comprehensive metric of what counts as human flourishing, thereby subordinating political, ecclesial, and creaturely relationships to the logic of competition, efficiency, and

exchange. For this distinction see Friedrich Hayek, *The Constitution of Liberty*; Milton Friedman, *Capitalism and Freedom*; Angus Burgin, *The Great Persuasion*; Quinn Slobodian, *Globalists*; and Kevin Hargaden, *Theological Ethics in a Neoliberal Age.*

2. Alexander Schmemann, *For the Life of the World: Sacraments and Orthodoxy* (St. Vladimir's Seminary Press, 1973).

3. John D. Zizioulas, *Being as Communion: Studies in Personhood and the Church* (St. Vladimir's Seminary Press, 1985).

4. Catherine Pickstock, *After Writing: On the Liturgical Consummation of Philosophy* (Blackwell, 1998).

5. William T. Cavanaugh, *Being Consumed: Economics and Christian Desire* (Eerdmans, 2008).

6. Vincent J. Miller, *Consuming Religion: Christian Faith and Practice in a Consumer Culture* (Continuum, 2005).

7. John Milbank, *Theology and Social Theory: Beyond Secular Reason*, 2nd ed. (Blackwell, 2006).

8. Gustavo Gutiérrez, *A Theology of Liberation*, trans. Sister Caridad Inda and John Eagleson (Orbis Books, 1973).

9. Leonardo Boff, *Cry of the Earth, Cry of the Poor*, trans. Phillip Berryman (Orbis Books, 1997).

10. Norman Wirzba, *The Paradise of God: Renewing Religion in an Ecological Age* (Oxford University Press, 2003).

11. Wendell Berry, *The Art of Loading Brush: New Agrarian Writings* (Counterpoint, 2017).

## CHAPTER 1

# Neoliberalism: History and the Commodification of Creation

Neoliberalism, in its simplest sense, is the extension of market ways of thinking into areas of life that are not themselves markets. It is therefore neither synonymous with markets nor reducible to capitalism. Markets are mechanisms of exchange that have existed across many different economic systems and can facilitate genuine goods, including voluntary exchange, innovation, economic development, and certain protections against centralized power. Capitalism refers more specifically to an economic order organized around private ownership of capital, wage labor, and the accumulation of profit, while globalization describes the increasing integration of economic, political, technological, and cultural systems across national boundaries. Neoliberalism is different. As the term is used throughout this book, it names a broader political, cultural, moral, and anthropological rationality that takes principles associated with the market—competition, efficiency, profitability, exchange, and measurable value—and increasingly treats them as standards for organizing human life as a whole.

Neoliberalism thus becomes visible in familiar economic and political policies such as deregulation, privatization, austerity, and the upward redistribution of wealth, but it cannot be understood adequately as a collection of policies alone. Its deeper power lies in how it reshapes practical reason: how people learn to perceive what is valuable, what freedom means, what relationships are for, and what kinds of lives and communities are worth sustaining. Market rationality migrates beyond explicitly economic activity into politics, law, education, medicine, family life, religion, and humanity's relationship with creation. Persons are increasingly encouraged to understand themselves as competitors and entrepreneurs of their own lives; institutions are evaluated according to productivity and efficiency; relationships become susceptible to calculations of utility and exchange; and even goods that resist quantification are pressured to justify themselves according to measurable outcomes. The problem, then, is not the existence of markets themselves. It arises when the partial goods and limited logic of markets become a comprehensive moral anthropology—when market rationality exceeds its proper sphere and begins determining the meaning and value of human flourishing itself.

Against this neoliberal logic, this book develops the concept of *durable networks*. By durable networks, I mean forms of relationship and belonging capable of sustaining mutual obligation, shared life, and solidarity across time precisely because their value cannot be reduced to efficiency, profitability, individual preference, or exchange. Families, neighborhoods, churches, friendships, communities of care, relationships to place and land, and other forms of common life can become durable networks when persons understand themselves as bound to one another by obligations that endure even when those relationships become costly or inefficient. Durability does not mean permanence at all costs, nor does it romanticize communities that may themselves become oppressive. Rather, it names the capacity of relationships and institutions to resist disposability: to sustain forms of belonging in which persons and places are valued as more than interchangeable resources.

The relationship between neoliberalism and durable networks is therefore central to the argument that follows. Neoliberalism tends to weaken forms of belonging that cannot justify themselves according to competition, mobility, efficiency, and exchange, teaching us to regard relationships, institutions, places, and even people as replaceable when they cease to maximize value. Durable networks embody a different moral imagination. They locate human flourishing in forms of fidelity, mutual dependence, responsibility, and solidarity that cannot be adequately measured by the market. The central problem with neoliberalism is therefore not simply that it produces unjust economic outcomes, but that it reorganizes how human beings imagine value, freedom, community, and creation itself. The question running throughout this book is consequently not only how neoliberalism distributes material goods, but what happens to human solidarity when the logic of the market becomes the logic through which we learn to understand the world and one another.

To diagnose neoliberalism adequately, therefore, requires more than economic critique. It requires a theological analysis attentive to how systems of value form souls, bodies, and communities. This chapter approaches neoliberalism as a political theology, one that establishes its own idols, sacraments, and disciplines. Markets come to function as arbiters of truth; capital becomes the measure of worth; and freedom is redefined as the capacity to compete and accumulate without obstruction. Creation itself is rendered abstract: land becomes real estate, labor becomes human capital, relationships become networks, and the poor become risks to be managed rather than neighbors to be loved.

The chapter begins by tracing the rise of neoliberalism from a theoretical analysis of its twentieth-century intellectual origins through its global institutionalization, emphasizing how economic rationality overtakes and absorbs political, moral, and social life. It then examines the categories of public and private and the emergence of a single source principle that governs all domains of existence.

Drawing on analyses of capital, as Marx would term it, as "value in motion," the chapter shows how neoliberalism transforms not only material production but also social relations, affective attachments, and moral codes into sites of accumulation.

Ultimately, the chapter situates neoliberalism within a much longer Christian historical narrative of abstraction, one in which land, the poor, and even salvation itself have been progressively detached from material, communal life. From colonial theology to development economics and debt regimes, Christianity has often supplied the moral grammar that allows domination to appear as order, obligation, or even grace. Against this backdrop, the chapter argues that neoliberalism represents not a rupture with Christian history but an intensification of its most distorted tendencies.

## The Private and the Public: The Rise of Economic Practical Reason

As suggested, neoliberalism is not simply an economic policy model; it is a theological system. The market has taken on, as Marx himself describes, a metaphysical authority, displacing traditional theological claims about meaning, value, and communion.[1] Understanding how neoliberalism emerged and embedded itself in the global order is essential for diagnosing why sacraments, ecclesiology, and even our understanding of creation itself have become increasingly abstracted from materiality, place, and justice.

Neoliberalism emerged in the mid-twentieth century as a response to the perceived failures of collectivist and Keynesian models of economic regulation. Following the devastation of the Great Depression and World War II, the postwar consensus favored state-managed capitalism: full employment, labor rights, and government regulation were seen as the path to prosperity. However, by the 1970s, rising inflation, oil shocks, fiscal crises, and stagnating productivity generated growing dissatisfaction with the postwar Keynesian consensus. In response, a new political and economic vision emerged that came to be known as neoliberalism. Rather than using the state to manage economic outcomes through public ownership, industrial policy, robust welfare programs, and demand management, neoliberalism increasingly understood the state's primary task as creating, protecting, and extending competitive markets. Government did not disappear under neoliberalism; instead, its role was reoriented. The state became an architect of market competition through deregulation, privatization, trade liberalization, monetary discipline, and the restructuring of public institutions according to market principles. At the international level, this shift was reinforced by organizations such as the International Monetary Fund (IMF), the World Bank, and, later, the World Trade Organization (WTO), which promoted structural adjustment programs, fiscal austerity, and market liberalization as conditions for economic development. The result was not less governance but a new global orthodoxy in which political authority increasingly understood its purpose as facilitating markets rather than directing them.

By the 1980s and 1990s, neoliberalism had become a global orthodoxy through institutions like the IMF, World Bank, and WTO. Developing nations were subjected to "structural adjustment programs" that forced them to cut social spending, open markets to foreign investment, and sell off public assets, often in exchange for loans. These policies devastated local economies, especially agrarian ones, and deepened dependency on global capital. Furthermore, neoliberal globalization transformed the idea of poverty from a condition to be remedied into a risk to be managed. Meanwhile, "freedom" came to mean the freedom of capital—not people.

At its core, neoliberalism severs human life from place, labor from meaning, and relationships from reciprocity. It transforms human beings into economic actors whose worth is measured solely by productivity and consumption. David Harvey helps readers envision these central virtues of neoliberalism. "Neoliberalism . . . is in the first instance a theory of political economic practices that proposes that human well-being can best be advanced by liberating individual entrepreneurial freedoms and skills within an institutional framework characterized by strong private property rights, free markets, and free trade."[2] On the face of Harvey's description is the assumption that economic institutions lead to personal freedom. As such, neoliberalism influences every aspect of society, so much so that all institutions replicate its logic because it satisfies a central desire for freedom and autonomy. In the late twentieth century, this logic became especially visible through neoliberal political movements such as Thatcherism in the United Kingdom and Reaganomics in the United States, both of which emphasized deregulation, privatization, and market-driven approaches to social life.

The critique advanced so far should not be understood as a rejection of markets per se or as a denial of the genuine achievements associated with liberal political and economic traditions. Indeed, neoliberalism emerged in response to profound historical crises. The totalitarian regimes of the twentieth century were case studies in the devastating consequences of concentrated political power, while centrally planned economies frequently produced inefficiency, corruption, and widespread deprivation. Recent historians of neoliberalism, too, have also cautioned against reducing the movement to an ideology of laissez-faire economics or unrestricted markets, as espoused by critics Hayek and Friedman. Quinn Slobodian has suggested that many of neoliberalism's leading architects were less interested in eliminating the state than in redesigning political institutions capable of insulating markets from democratic interference.[3] Likewise, Angus Burgin has shown that neoliberalism emerged not as a monolithic doctrine but as a contested intellectual tradition forged through decades of debate among economists, political theorists, and policymakers who sought to reconcile economic liberty with political stability.[4] Such scholarship rightly complicates simplistic portrayals of neoliberalism and reminds us that some of its advocates were motivated by genuine concerns regarding freedom, coercion, and the preservation of liberal institutions.

Liberal societies have often secured important moral goods, such as freedom of conscience, constitutional government, legal equality, scientific innovation, entrepreneurial creativity, and opportunities for social mobility.[5] The difficulty, however, lies not in the existence of markets, which have long formed part of liberal societies, but in the neoliberal expansion of market rationality beyond its proper sphere. The concern of this study is therefore not with markets as institutions of economic exchange, but with the neoliberal expansion of market rationality into domains of life governed by moral, political, ecclesial, familial, and ecological goods.[6] Yet the historical development commonly identified as neoliberalism increasingly transformed these limited economic claims into a total system. The market ceased to be one institution among many and instead became the governing metaphor through which all human activity was interpreted.

The question, therefore, is not whether neoliberal markets possess genuine goods. They plainly do. Markets can facilitate cooperation among strangers, encourage creativity, distribute resources efficiently, and protect individuals from certain forms of centralized coercion. The theological question is whether these goods are capable of sustaining the fullness of human existence.

It is at precisely this point that neoliberalism exceeds the legitimate boundaries of economic theory and becomes a theological vision. As Kevin Hargaden argues, neoliberalism is not simply a set of economic policies but "a philosophical vision about what makes us human."[7] Kelly Oliver similarly observes that neoliberalism reshapes the subject itself by colonizing the psychic conditions through which agency is experienced.[8] What began as an effort to protect freedom from political domination gradually becomes an account of freedom that understands every sphere of life according to the logic of competition, efficiency, and exchange.

The argument of this chapter is therefore not that neoliberal market societies have produced no genuine goods. Rather, it is that neoliberalism mistakes partial goods for ultimate goods. Hence, the task of Christian theology is not to abolish neoliberal markets but to refuse their transformation into an ontology.

## Excursus: Modernity's Moral Achievement and Its Limits

Central to the genealogy traced throughout this chapter so far is that modernity is characterized by narratives of abstraction, commodification, and domination, but this does not exhaust the moral aspirations that animated the modern project. Many of modernity's leading interpreters have argued that its emergence also represents a profound expansion of moral consciousness. Charles Taylor, for example, argues that the modern age cannot simply be narrated as a story of secular decline. Rather, modernity represents the unfolding of new "moral sources" that increasingly affirmed the dignity of everyday life, the legitimacy of democratic participation, the importance of conscience, and the equal worth of every human being.[9] Likewise,

Larry Siedentop traces the emergence of liberal political institutions not primarily to Enlightenment rationalism but to Christianity itself. He contends that the Christian conviction that every person stands equally before God gradually transformed Western understandings of authority, equality, and individual responsibility, ultimately giving rise to the moral foundations of liberal democracy.[10]

These accounts provide a corrective to narratives that portray modernity as little more than a tragic tale of disenchantment or domination. They remind us that many of the freedoms contemporary liberal societies rightly cherish represent genuine moral achievements. Christian theology should neither dismiss nor minimize these developments.

Yet because these achievements are genuine, they also beg further theological questions. Can the institutions designed to protect human dignity also explain what human dignity ultimately is? Can political freedom sustain itself when detached from thicker accounts of the common good? Can autonomy alone generate the forms of communion upon which freedom itself depends?

Taylor himself repeatedly cautions against reducing modernity to what he famously calls an "exclusive humanism" in which transcendence gradually disappears from public imagination.[11] The result is not necessarily the disappearance of morality but its progressive flattening. Human dignity remains affirmed, yet increasingly without any shared account of why persons possess such dignity in the first place. Similarly, Siedentop's genealogy demonstrates that liberalism owes an incalculable debt to Christian anthropology. Nevertheless, once these theological foundations become detached from the practices and metaphysical vision that originally sustained them, liberal institutions increasingly struggle to provide a substantive account of the human good beyond procedural freedom and individual choice.[12]

The concern of this chapter is not that modernity failed to produce genuine moral goods. Rather, it is that these goods became progressively detached from the theological vision that first made them intelligible. From this perspective, neoliberalism should be understood not as the inevitable outcome of modernity nor as its simple fulfillment. It represents, instead, the conquest of one trajectory within modern thought—the expansion of market rationality into a comprehensive account of human existence. The theological task, therefore, is not to reject modernity wholesale but to retrieve and deepen its genuine moral insights within a richer account of creation, participation, and communion.

## Arendt and a Critique of Neoliberal Freedom

The categorical place of entrepreneurial freedom, free trade, free markets, and private property rights all serve one end, namely the ability to secure wealth or profit of some kind. However, this is a relatively new goal for society. Traditionally, humanity separated society into the public and private realms. Among the first to popularize this approach were the ancient Greek cultures of the Western world. The *polis* signified the public space where certain individuals were able to live and act among equals, while the household, *oikos*, remained a sequestered place of necessity.

The modern figure most known for this description of the public and private realms is Hannah Arendt.[13] Central to Arendt's description of the public and private is the underlying presupposition that life is always in the presence of others.[14] Natural life, according to the ancient world, is in the home (*oikonomia*), and one's public life only comes as a means of an unnatural, second association with the home.[15] The home is the place of the economic, where one must strive to survive for the accumulation of necessary resources for consumption.[16] For all intended purposes, the *oikos* served the good of the *polis* by providing necessities so that one could leave the home and engage in a second life, namely a life in addition to the one of necessity at home, of freedom in the public realm among equals.[17]

This "second life" in the political realm takes many forms and relates, in many ways, to the natural life of the home, according to Arendt, but her great contribution to the study of modern politics and economics is that private (*oikos*) interests now overtake the public sphere.[18] The place of necessity, namely the *oikos*, is the economic, which overtakes a free, public realm by making economic interest central to freedom as a desire unto itself. In short, freedom exists only insofar as one is released from the necessities of the oikos; when private interests dominate, they eclipse the political realm and thereby destroy the conditions for a free public space. The interests of *oikos* engender a society of individuals aimlessly pursuing their own private interests and accumulation of materials to be used up.[19] Individuals now seek to consume and accumulate as the purpose and meaning of life. However, as Arendt argues, this runs counter to the ancient, preferred order of divisions between politics and economics.

Much more can be said about Arendt's axiom, but the essence of her position pressed readers to think critically about the full shape of their lives. The private and public each have roles in shaping the individual toward the ends of creating a shared common space. However, later critics argue that her method troubles her ends. The bifurcation between public and private, but also political and economic, misdirects our attention from the overarching synthesis of all areas of life. The world emerging in Arendt's analysis, they contend, is far more connected. The economic and political are not two poles that need balance. Arendt helps us recognize the danger of subjecting every aspect of life (both public and private) to categories that are incapable of sustaining or defining the public good. Arendt's axiom struggles to articulate public and private well. Therefore, a different framework is needed that draws on Arendt's axiom and the division between public and private, while also describing the overarching place of neoliberalism and its ubiquity in our time.

At the same time, it is important not to press Arendt beyond the historical horizon of her own work. Writing before the full emergence of neoliberalism as a global political and economic order, Arendt did not directly confront the contemporary forms of privatization, deregulation, financialization, and technocratic governance that would define the late twentieth and early twenty-first centuries. She died just as neoliberalism was beginning to crystallize into a dominant social paradigm. For this reason, her account should not be read as a direct critique of neoliberalism in its contemporary form, but rather as providing conceptual categories that help illuminate its conditions of possibility. Indeed, many of her concerns—the reduction of politics to administration, the expansion of economic rationality into public life, and the eclipse of genuine political action—appear with even greater intensity under neoliberal conditions than in the world she herself inhabited.

Her work, therefore, functions less as a comprehensive diagnosis of neoliberalism than as a set of conceptual tools for understanding how economic necessity can gradually colonize political existence. If neoliberalism represents a historically distinct configuration of these dynamics, Arendt nevertheless helps explain the deeper anthropological and political shifts that made such a configuration conceivable in the first place.

Arendt's axiom was a pivotal idea for many working in the area of political philosophy for much of the twentieth century, but recent critics challenge the prominence of the axiom. For example, Adam Kotsko suggests that Arendt assumes that the division between economic and political is not "pregiven."[20] Arguing that this is a "idiosyncratic" reading, Kotsko shows how Aristotle, the one on whom Arendt bases most of her division between the economic and political, "takes issue with those who claim that the forms of rule present in the household and the city are simply the same, but his purpose is not to claim that the former are foreign or opposed to the latter."[21] Kotsko therefore argues that the distinction between public and private, or between the political and the economic, is itself a relatively late conceptual development that ultimately hinders an adequate understanding of neoliberalism. Instead, neoliberalism must be examined "without presupposing any normative boundaries between" politics, religion, economics, and philosophy. For Kotsko, then, Arendt's sharp division between these spheres must in some sense be overcome.[22]

Kotsko shows that Arendt's description of the economic seizure of the political is the exception and not the rule.[23] The axiom developed by Arendt, through a very specific reading of the ancient world, imposes a normative apparatus on the world rather than reflecting its true structure.[24] Following Kotsko's critique of Arendt, these spheres are not separable but operate together as a single, fluid—if uneven—configuration that ultimately privileges economic calculation. The economic and the political, then, exist in tension and constantly reconfigure one another in an ever-changing landscape of human self-discovery.

Therefore, the issue is not how to retrieve a dyad where the political and the economic are pushed into their separate spheres or to develop an account of one over and against the other. Rather, one must overcome the division and determine how economic and political forces, among others, structure the entirety of the human quest for the good and structure society as a larger struggle for power. Neoliberalism provides a lens through which to examine acute struggles for power that, while often articulated in economic terms, depend upon the interwoven forces of political and economic authority to shape and express the human condition.

The centrality of the making and remaking of our world according to free market logic and dogma cannot be underestimated. However, it is important to recognize the limit of the double movement, which Kotsko helpfully recognizes as a different form of Arendt's axiom. As self-regulating markets emerged and gained power, they reformed the institutions according to their logic by unequally privileging those most advantageously positioned to perpetuate their internal logic. As Kotsko writes, "neoliberalism does not simply destroy some preexisting entity known as 'the family,' but creates *its own* version of the family, one that fits its political-economic agenda, just as Fordism created the white suburban nuclear family that underwrote its political-economic goals."[25] The double movement is beyond economic and political institutions and involves reforming the social and moral spheres. These institutions, thus, become a vessel for the extension of neoliberal power by injecting neoliberal logic into the whole fabric of existence.

Neoliberal logic also reshapes the nuclear family by increasingly interpreting familial relationships through economic categories such as productivity, financial security, and upward mobility. Under these conditions, the family is no longer understood primarily as a moral, social, or relational good in itself, but as an economic unit responsible for maximizing stability, managing risk, and generating future success. Wealth and economic achievement, therefore, begin to function not merely as one good among many within family life, but as organizing principles capable of subordinating competing goods such as leisure, care, community, or even presence with one another.

Self-regulating markets, as Polanyi notes, produced an unheard-of material welfare for many.[26] Thus, as wealth increases, institutions adapt to the measures necessary for sustained economic growth. As Kotsko recognizes, "the state actively cultivates and maintains the conditions necessary for vigorous market competition, trusting in the price mechanism to deliver more efficient outcomes than direct state planning ever could."[27] The double movement, then, invests in every means to capitalize on this peace and secure wealth as a promised maxim of a just, peaceful society and only intervenes, as Polanyi argues, when it threatens society. The market forces that created freedom would ultimately have to be contained. The overarching aim, then, was to secure market conditions that maximized profitability while fostering a well-ordered, peaceful, and, above all, free society.

Although Kotsko insists that economic profitability and governmental power are not a dyad, he must nonetheless concede that economic profit is systematically advantaged within structures of state power. Where other theorists separate economics and politics, Kotsko points readers back to their allegiance, but he also sees so much more. Neoliberalism cannot be expressed as a mere "double-movement" between politics and economics because it is an entire social order.[28] As Kotsko argues, "it is an order of family and sexuality and an order of racial hierarchy and subordination. . .a totalizing world order, an integral self-reinforcing system of political theology."[29] The allegiance of these forces under neoliberalism relies on a matrix of powers that intends to shape and form citizens. In other words, the market not only provides a path to prosperity and thus freedom but also an internal matrix of desire that makes individuals crave profit itself.

Kotsko appeals to Michel Foucault's account of governmentality to clarify these formative aspects of neoliberalism. For Foucault, power is not always exerted by overt authorities violently and physically on the bodies of innocent people. Rather, the power of governmentality is the subversive influence that creates cooperation between individual citizens and the alliance of political and economic forces. Governmentality works by positively investing in a certain form of life (or icons in the market sense) as advantageous and, thus, structures codes of profitability (e.g., legal, social, moral) that cause humans to desire it while simultaneously demonizing other forms of life outside the realm of its parameters.[30]

To summarize thus far: Arendt proposed a framework through which the private and public spheres can be understood according to a shared logic. Neoliberalism, however, elevates profit to the status of the singularly dominant human desire. It is here that Arendt's axiom reaches its limit, as it fails to account for neoliberalism's pervasive and all-encompassing reach. Neoliberal logic consumes the entire fabric of society and reforms it in its own image. Therefore, certain institutions emerge as avenues toward the single principle of profit. They are protected by the order and, in exchange, either intentionally or not, perpetuate its existence. Perhaps no one institution better represents the neoliberal order than the nuclear family. The family has been the subject of intentional, dramatic shaping into the image of the neoliberal order (for example, the Aid to Families with Dependent Children). It is the desire for profit that creates durable structures (i.e., the family) that can create the conditions of untold profits. All that is left is for individuals to *choose* profit by choosing these structures. Therefore, Polanyi is correct when he postulates a great disruption, but he probably never grasped how great that disruption would be.

If, following Polanyi, disruption is driven by the ever-changing centrality of self-regulating markets, this would entail a corresponding reshaping of the political, legal, and social institutions that preserve free-market virtues and structure economic policy, judicial authority, and governance. This is one of the far-reaching implications of neoliberalism, which, as the great French sociologist Pierre Bourdieu argues, is "rooted in a system of beliefs and values, an ethos and a moral view of the world, in short, an *economic common sense,* linked, as such, to the social and cognitive structures of a particular social order."[31] In light of the great disruption, the social order becomes organized around an economic common sense (e.g., one based on the principles of free trade, free markets, and private property) that attempts to place the generating and accumulating of wealth within all social norms.

One way neoliberalism shapes value is through the very principle that earned its legitimacy in opposition to totalitarianism: freedom. Recalling Arendt, the realm of necessity is the realm of the economic (*oikos*) and, according to her account, the pursuit of necessity arises from one's private interests. The individual consumed with the life of the *oikos* desires ever greater to consume and accumulate. Thus, political freedom means freedom from external coercion in pursuing private interests, unhindered by state intervention. Ironically, the self-regulated markets created in response to totalitarianism would also perpetuate an inability for the state to intervene in any meaningful way without being accused of totalitarianism.

In modernity, freedom is often understood primarily in terms of individual autonomy, the ability to make choices for oneself without outside interference. This understanding became especially influential in response to political systems associated with tyranny and totalitarianism, where governments strictly controlled personal behavior, economic opportunity, and social mobility. Within neoliberal thought, autonomy is therefore consecrated as a central political and moral good because it appears to protect individuals from domination by the state or other external authorities.

This emphasis on autonomy also has deeper philosophical roots in Enlightenment thought, particularly in the distinction between autonomy and heteronomy. Enlightenment thinkers argued that moral action should arise from rational self-governance rather than from external coercion. Using this framework, a person is considered truly free when they are able to determine their own actions and pursue their own goals independently.[32] However, this freedom also includes one crucial feature when extended into the economic sphere: namely, the freedom from *dependence*. To be sure, the state preserves a specific capacity for autonomy, but neoliberalism hijacks the very description of autonomy and perpetuates an economic account of everything as freedom from external limits, coercion, and value. Every decision must be expressed as a spontaneous choice for a good among other goods. This creates markets of competition wherein labor must constantly invent new commodities that might attract new consumers.

However, this freedom is illusory. Freedom understood primarily as independence proves incapable of sustaining the very communities upon which freedom depends. The autonomous individual increasingly becomes detached from shared histories, communal obligations, and material relations until freedom itself is reduced to consumer choice within an ever-expanding market order.[33]

Kenneth Surin argues that this reduction is not accidental but intrinsic to the modern conception of the subject. Modern political philosophy gradually abandoned the ancient and medieval conviction that humanity participates within an ordered reality grounded beyond itself and instead relocated freedom within the self-grounding individual. The modern subject becomes sovereign precisely by imagining itself independent of prior relations and obligations. Yet this sovereign subject ultimately gives way to what Surin describes as the consumer subject, whose apparent autonomy masks a deeper captivity to the global logic of capital.[34] Freedom becomes participation in markets rather than liberation from domination.[35]

For Surin, liberation requires more than the removal of external constraints. Freedom demands the emergence of a different kind of subject altogether. Liberation occurs through what he calls a "truth event" or "singularity" that interrupts the prevailing order of capitalist existence and opens the possibility of new forms of communal agency.[36] Freedom is not simply freedom from coercion but freedom for participation in relationships capable of resisting the abstractions of market society.[37]

Neoliberal freedom offers the individual freedom from external coercion, contra totalitarianism, but only insofar as the individual deeply embraces participating in the market. Kotsko offers an example by way of the Affordable Care Act (ACA). A central tenet of the act mandated that all individuals possess and maintain health insurance. The alternative, posed by some of the Act's progressive critics, was a single-payer option that was affordable to the average American citizen and prohibited insurers from rejecting applicants with preexisting conditions. In the ACA's newly formed market, and individual could choose their provider from a list of many providers according to need, cost, and advantage. In short, it offered the allure of freedom to choose whatever they deemed pleasant. However, this new market is not entirely free. As Kotsko notes, the individual citizen "was not free to opt out of the market altogether."[38] Freedom, even freedom from external coercion, can only exist inside the market itself. Thus, as Kotsko states, either one exercises one's freedom as *for* the market and *inside* the market or one "must be forced to be free."[39]

Kotsko's insurance market example illustrates two key points. First, the Affordable Care Act is an example of a neoliberal legal order, in which laws support the creation and preservation of market space, which in turn creates the market "freedom." Second, it shows how neoliberal freedom is conditioned by and for the market itself. It is not freedom in the negative sense, wherein the individual can choose any choice as previously desired in the Enlightenment. Rather, freedom is only freedom to be in the market itself.

Freedom, thus, as the goal of law and economics, is tempered by a single source principle inimical to the market itself: profit. The neoliberal order offers "flexibility" in markets to allow individuals to make their own choices (e.g., career, housing).[40] This flexibility allows the individual to make the choices that are most advantageous for themselves. However, this flexibility also destabilizes security and, thus, propels the individual into "the sheer necessity for survival."[41] As Kotsko argues, the illusion that deregulation and laws lead to stability and freedom corrupts the possibility of one ever finding rest and security. For example, though individuals are free to choose advantageous and economically lucrative work, they are nevertheless required "to fight continually to keep it."[42] One must constantly seek upward mobility and greater resources to feel more secure in an ever-changing market. This is the bottom line, namely, *I am only free to pursue economic prosperity and not rest from the labor of the market.*

Considering the constant shifts and pressures of the market, companies are also "subjected to the more comprehensive and inescapable constraint of market discipline."[43] By way of illustration, a company can "move to a more compliant (or, to use the term of art, 'competitive') countries," but it is not free to treat its workers better and offer them job security.[44] This seems counterintuitive because, of course, companies are free to use their resources in ways they deem fit, but their freedom is quite simply limited by the logic of the market. The reason many companies do not offer better job security is, as Kotsko notes, because "the market would never allow it: a shareholder revolt or hostile takeover would lead to the removal of any management team that made such a scandalous proposal."[45] The freedom is the freedom for profit, and those who transgress must suffer the consequences.

Recent Indigenous theologians and scholars have argued that colonialism should be understood fundamentally as a rupture in relationships rather than merely the acquisition of territory. George Tinker, writing from an Indigenous theological perspective, argues that European colonization transformed land from a sacred relation into an object of possession, thereby disrupting the reciprocal relationships that had long ordered Indigenous life.[46] Likewise, Randy Woodley contends that Indigenous understandings of creation begin not with ownership but with kinship, where land, creatures, and human communities exist within robust networks of mutual responsibility rather than domination.[47] The violence of colonization, therefore, consisted not simply in territorial conquest but in the replacement of relational ontologies with possessive ones.

This displacement was not only material but epistemological. Leanne Betasamosake Simpson similarly describes Indigenous knowledge as emerging from lived relationships with particular places. Land is not a passive resource awaiting development but a teacher that forms identity, memory, and communal responsibility.[48] When colonial expansion removes people from these places, abstraction occurs not merely because property changes hands but because the very conditions through which persons come to know themselves are dismantled. Place becomes space; homeland becomes territory; relationship becomes ownership.

If Simpson demonstrates how colonization fragments the ways communities know the world, Steven Charleston shows that this fragmentation is ultimately theological, severing human beings from the web of relationships through which creation itself is encountered. Indigenous spiritual traditions resist precisely the fragmentation characteristic of modernity. Human beings do not stand over creation as autonomous subjects but participate within a living community that includes ancestors, future generations, creatures, and the land itself.[49] The loss of place, therefore, entails the erasure of memory, belonging, and ultimately identity.

This genealogy complements rather than replaces the economic account developed subsequently in this chapter, namely that of a Marxist account of the economy. Marx demonstrates how capitalism abstracts labor from the worker, transforming living activity into exchange value. Indigenous theologians remind us that a prior abstraction had already occurred: land itself had first to be detached from community, memory, and covenant before it could become property, commodity, or capital. Colonialism prepared the conceptual conditions under which neoliberalism could later universalize market rationality across the globe.

Seen in this light, neoliberalism should not be understood simply as an economic system but as the culmination of a much older logic of dislocation. The abstraction of labor presupposes the abstraction of place. The commodification of creation presupposes the severing of creation from covenantal relationships. What appears within neoliberalism as market efficiency often rests upon centuries of colonial practices that transformed gifts into property and communion into possession.

For Christian theology, this broader genealogy deepens rather than alters the argument of this chapter. The biblical witness consistently portrays land as a gift, a covenant, and a shared inheritance rather than absolute possession. Israel's relationship to the land is constituted through divine promise and communal responsibility, while the Jubilee traditions explicitly resist the permanent alienation of land from families and communities. Colonial abstraction, therefore, represents not merely a political injustice but a theological distortion that severs creation from the relational purposes for which it was given. Any sacramental retrieval of creation must therefore reckon not only with capitalism's commodification of the world but also with the colonial histories that first rendered the world available for commodification.

## Value in Motion: Capital

Though neoliberalism shapes the human soul to desire a single source of profitability, one must clarify the means to gain profit, which leads to the controversial role of capital in neoliberalism. Capital mobilizes and energizes neoliberalism by offering a clear measure of profitability grounded in the possession and accumulation of capital. Capital is not limited to money itself or to financial assets alone. Rather, capital encompasses anything the market recognizes as capable of generating additional value or profit. This can include property, machinery, education, social influence, or even personal skills when they can be leveraged for economic gain. For example, a university degree functions as a form of capital insofar as it increases a person's earning potential and competitiveness within the labor market. One must have capital to make money. In other words, money indeed, as Eugene McCarraher writes, "is the measure of all things," but capital is the measure of money.[50] Therefore, one must understand capital to fully grasp the social order established by neoliberalism.

One needs to look no further for a lucid and comprehensive study of capital than Karl Marx's work *Das Kapital*. The vastness and complexity of Marx's works require a guide in order not to become dizzy with possibility. Therefore, I turn to David Harvey as an aid for a succinct account of Marx's "capital" for our present discussion of neoliberalism.

Marx defines capital, according to Harvey, as "value in motion."[51] Capital is not all money but rather how money is mobilized in a particular way and the means by which one places value on labor, commodities, and even money.[52] However, capital only exists within systems of exchange and circulation.[53] In short, one can only circulate and exchange in a market developed alongside processes of valuation. "Value," as Harvey writes, "is produced and sustained by a movement that runs from things (commodities) to processes (the activities of laboring that congeal value in commodities) to things (new commodities)."[54] Labor is important to Marx because it is the production of a commodity whose value is determined by the amount of labor required to produce it. The value of a thing comes from the complex process of its production and pricing, determined by the means used to produce it. By selling their labor for wages, workers generate value embodied in the resulting commodity. Therefore, value (i.e., capital) moves through the market forces that price commodities.

Labor gives value to the commodities it produces, but the process is incomplete until those commodities are exchanged in the market. When a consumer purchases a commodity, its value is converted back into monetary form, allowing the producer to receive compensation for the labor embodied within it. Capital is therefore best understood as "value in motion" because it describes the continual movement of value through production, exchange, compensation, and reinvestment. In this way, capital encompasses the broader social process through which value is recognized, circulated, and expanded.

There is one element that ties capital, freedom, and neoliberalism together into a single concept: surplus value. Surplus value is the excess of value produced by the labor of workers over the wages they are paid. A commodity is given value equivalent to the value of the labor it costs to produce it.[55] However, the capitalist who owns the means of production earns more than the cost of producing a commodity. As Harvey writes,

> a point arrives in the working day when the labourer has produced the equivalent of [the value of labour] and transferred the value of [capital] into the new commodity. The labourer does not at this point cease to labour. His or her contract says he or she should work for the capitalist for ten hours. If the value of labour power has been covered in the first six hours then the labourer ends up working for capital for free for four hours.[56]

The four free hours constitute the value surplus. The employer receives the value of the labor for the commodity plus the extra capital gained from the extra hours.[57]

The surplus value shows that laborers and those who own the means of production are rewarded differently.[58] As Harvey continues,

> money that flows to labour in the form of wages returns to the overall circulation of capital in the form of an effective demand for those commodities produced in wage goods. . .In its return to circulation, however, the labourer takes on the persona of the buyer rather than worker while the capitalist becomes the seller.[59]

The laborer must reinvest his wages in the market to buy commodities, while the capitalist doubles their profit.

In Harvey's analysis, not only does the laborer work more than is required for the value to congeal into a commodity, but also a surplus.

Furthermore, the laborer must then purchase the commodity from the capitalist to gain the necessities of life. The capitalist and the laborer are rewarded differently. If the laborer wants to escape the vicious cycle of necessity, they must increase their capital, namely, their possession of value. The laborer must invest in commodities that will increase their capital. The commodification of higher education, for example, leads universities to influence students to treat their education as profit-generating commodities.[60] Education, thus, is a means to grant laborers greater access to higher-paying work, becoming less dependent on capitalists to generate capital for themselves in the marketplace. In short, investing wages in capital leads to more freedom from the necessities of labor (as Arendt would interpret).

This is the great promise of capital, namely that such an ascent is possible. However, it is largely an illusion, like all freedom in a neoliberal society. The laborer is free to invest in any commodity that appears to offer some freedom.[61] Yet, the laborer is not free to refuse to invest. In order to survive, one must invest and perpetuate value in motion (capital). The inescapability of "freedom" in neoliberalism depends on capital as it measures the value of work, things, and even people. Thus, capital creates "markets where none had previously existed."[62] Contemporary examples include the monetization of personal data through social media platforms, where ordinary human interaction becomes a commodity bought and sold for advertising profit. Similar dynamics can be seen in the rise of the "gig economy," where activities once considered informal acts of hospitality or personal transportation are transformed into market transactions through companies such as Uber or Airbnb. In both cases, areas of life that were not previously governed primarily by market exchange become newly integrated into systems of economic valuation and profit generation.

In sum, capital is a driving force in neoliberal culture, shaping the meaning of value in our world. Performing a moral action, choosing an economically advantageous action, constructing law, and even constructing government all rely on this economic thinking. Capital, thus, energizes the single source principle of profitability that judges all means, actions, and goals of human life. Therefore, its pursuit presents the possibility of the most morally developed and peaceful pursuit of our time.

## Alienation and the Loss of Place

Yet the dominance of capital as the organizing principle of value cannot remain confined to abstract systems of calculation. Marx's account of alienation already makes clear that when human activity is subordinated to the logic of capital, estrangement follows, not only from the products of one's labor, but from the very conditions of human life itself. What is at stake, then, is not simply a distortion of economic relations but a deeper dislocation of human existence. If capital governs what counts as meaningful action, it simultaneously severs the worker from the meaningful contexts in which such action might unfold. Alienation, in this sense, is not merely psychological or economic; it is spatial. The same forces that estrange workers from their labor also reshape the environments they inhabit, reorganizing the world according to the demands of accumulation rather than the rhythms of human flourishing.

If alienation describes the estrangement of workers from their labor, their products, and ultimately their own human nature, it also raises another question that Marx himself only partially explored: what happens to the places in which human life unfolds under the rule of capital? The circulation of capital does not merely reorganize labor; it reorganizes space. As value moves through markets, commodities, and financial systems, the environments in which human beings live and work are reshaped according to the requirements of accumulation. Capital, as value in motion, cannot remain confined to the factory or the market; it must continually transform the spatial conditions that make circulation possible.

In this sense, alienation extends beyond the worker to the environments that sustain human life. The same logic that estranges the laborer from the product of their labor also distances communities from the places in which they dwell. Land becomes property, property becomes investment, and investment becomes a vehicle for further circulation of capital. The result is a gradual detachment of human life from the places that once grounded it. There was a time when land was understood primarily as a shared environment of life: soil-fed communities, waters that sustained ecosystems, and landscapes that shaped communal identity. Now land increasingly appears as a commodity whose value is determined by the market.

This transformation reflects a deeper shift in how space itself is perceived. According to the logic of capital, space becomes increasingly abstract. It is measured, mapped, and reorganized according to its capacity to facilitate exchange and circulation. Cities are redesigned to maximize capital flows, infrastructure is built to accelerate mobility, and landscapes are reorganized according to their economic utility. In such a world, the significance of place gradually disappears behind calculations of profitability.

The consequences of this are not merely economic but existential. When the places that shape human life are reorganized to meet the demands of capital, individuals increasingly experience their environments as transient and unstable. Neighborhoods change rapidly according to the pressures of development, work requires constant mobility, and communities are reorganized around economic opportunity rather than the lives they share together.

Recognizing this dynamic prepares the ground for a deeper examination of the nature of place itself. If capital reorganizes not only labor but the spatial environments of human life, then any attempt to address alienation must also address the meaning of place. The question that emerges is not merely economic but philosophical: what is lost when human beings become estranged from the places they inhabit? And how might recovering a richer understanding of place help illuminate the forms of life capable of resisting the abstraction produced by capital?

## Conclusion

This chapter has argued that neoliberalism functions not merely as an economic system but as a comprehensive moral and theological order. Neoliberalism does not simply shape policies surrounding trade, labor, or finance; it also shapes how persons understand themselves, others, and the purpose of human life. Under neoliberal conditions, individuals increasingly come to view themselves as entrepreneurial subjects, and human identity is shorn of shared moral obligations, communal belonging, or even transcendent purpose.

In this sense, neoliberalism functions as a moral framework by establishing its own vision of virtue and vice. Discipline, flexibility, innovation, and self-sufficiency are praised as signs of responsible personhood, while dependence, inefficiency, and economic failure are often treated as moral shortcomings. Social problems such as poverty, unemployment, loneliness, or exhaustion are thus interpreted primarily through the lens of individual responsibility and market participation. Persons are expected to continually adapt themselves to changing economic conditions, treating even their own personalities, relationships, and education as forms of capital to be managed and improved.

The theological dimensions of neoliberalism become visible in its implicit account of salvation and hope. Rather than orienting persons toward reconciliation, communion, or transcendence, neoliberalism promises fulfillment through continual self-improvement and economic mobility. The "good life" becomes closely tied to accumulation, productivity, visibility, and the freedom to choose among competing consumer possibilities. Even ordinary practices of modern life, such as networking, personal branding, résumé building, productivity tracking, and algorithmic self-presentation, take on a formative role analogous to liturgical habits insofar as they train persons to imagine themselves according to market categories. Neoliberalism, therefore, functions not only as an external economic arrangement but also as a comprehensive vision of human flourishing that shapes our desires, imagination, and moral perception.

It is also important to note that neoliberalism itself may now be entering a period of instability and transformation. While this study has focused primarily on the emergence and consolidation of neoliberalism as a dominant moral, political, and economic order in the postwar West, contemporary political developments suggest that some of its central assumptions are increasingly contested. The resurgence of nationalist and populist movements across Europe and the United States, many of which reject aspects of globalization, free trade, and liberal internationalism, reflects growing dissatisfaction with the social and economic consequences of neoliberal governance.

Yet these movements should not be understood as simple departures from neoliberalism. Even where nationalist political rhetoric appears to oppose neoliberal globalization, such movements often remain deeply shaped by neoliberal assumptions regarding competition, market identity, media spectacle, privatization, and individualized political belonging. In many cases, neoliberalism has not disappeared so much as fragmented into new political configurations that combine economic nationalism with longstanding habits of market rationality and technological governance. The present moment may therefore represent less the end of neoliberalism than a transition into new forms of political and economic organization that continue to bear the marks of the neoliberal age. Persistence is especially significant for theology because the cultural and moral assumptions cultivated under neoliberalism have also shaped many contemporary forms of Christian thought and practice.

Christianity has not always resisted this formation. There are times when Christian language has been used to sanctify the very abstractions that sustain neoliberal order by spiritualizing injustice, moralizing debt, and disciplining the poor. When salvation is imagined primarily as the balancing of moral accounts, the gospel begins to mirror the logic of the market rather than challenge it.

Yet the biblical tradition offers a different vision. In Sabbath and Jubilee, in the prophetic condemnation of accumulation, and in Jesus' proclamation of release of the captive and recovery of sight to the blind, Scripture frames dispossession and debt as theological crises. Liberation in this tradition is not merely spiritual but material. It concerns land returned, bodies restored, and communities freed from systems of domination. Grace does not simply reconcile souls; it reorders the conditions of life.

This insight stands at the heart of liberation theology's preferential option for the poor. The gospel's promise of salvation cannot be separated from the concrete realities in which the poor struggle to live. Chapter 2 turns to the preferential option for the poor as the theological lens through which sacramental life must be reimagined in a neoliberal age. If neoliberalism abstracts life into markets, liberation theology insists that God's grace must take material form within the struggle for justice, restoration, and the renewal of creation.

## Notes

1. Karl Marx, *Capital: A Critique of Political Economy* Vol. 1, translated by Ben Fowkes (Penguin Books, 1976), 1000–1001.

2. David Harvey, *A Brief History of Neoliberalism* (Oxford University Press. 2005), 2.

3. Quinn Slobodian, *Globalists: The End of Empire and the Birth of Neoliberalism* (Harvard University Press, 2018), 5–21, 145–82.

4. Angus Burgin, *The Great Persuasion: Reinventing Free Markets since the Depression* (Harvard University Press, 2012), 1–20, 170–202.

5. Because the terms are often confused, it is important to distinguish liberalism from neoliberalism. Liberalism refers broadly to a political tradition that emphasizes constitutional government, the rule of law, individual rights, representative democracy, religious liberty, and limits on arbitrary state power. Liberal societies are therefore characterized by institutions designed to protect human freedom, mediate political disagreement, and secure the conditions for civic participation. Although liberal traditions encompass diverse and often competing schools of thought, they are not inherently committed to organizing every sphere of life according to market principles.

Neoliberalism, by contrast, is not simply a more market-oriented version of liberalism. It is a distinct rationality that increasingly understands both political institutions and human relationships through the logic of competition, efficiency, entrepreneurialism, and economic exchange. Rather than asking how political institutions should promote justice, cultivate the common good, or sustain democratic life, neoliberalism increasingly evaluates institutions according to whether they maximize market efficiency and economic growth. Liberal institutions remain in place under neoliberalism, but they are reoriented toward different ends. Universities become producers of human capital, hospitals become providers competing within healthcare markets, churches are tempted to measure success through metrics of growth and consumer satisfaction, and governments increasingly understand their role as creating and maintaining competitive markets rather than pursuing substantive visions of the common good.

This distinction is important for the argument that follows. The concern of this study is not with liberal democracy as such, nor with the constitutional institutions that protect freedom and human dignity. Rather, it is with the gradual transformation of those institutions by a neoliberal imagination that extends market rationality into domains of life governed by moral, political, ecclesial, and creaturely goods that cannot be adequately measured by efficiency, competition, or exchange.

6. Friedrich Hayek, *The Constitution of Liberty* (University of Chicago Press, 1960), 29–54.

7. Kevin Hargaden, *Theological Ethics in a Neoliberal Age* (Cascade Books, 2018), 11.

8. Kelly Oliver, *The Colonization of Psychic Space: A Psychoanalytic Social Theory of Oppression* (University of Minnesota Press, 2004), 27.

9. Charles Taylor, *Sources of the Self: The Making of the Modern Identity* (Harvard University Press, 1989), 211–302; Charles Taylor, *A Secular Age* (Belknap Press, 2007), 473–504.

10. Larry Siedentop, *Inventing the Individual: The Origins of Western Liberalism* (Belknap Press, 2014), 17–61, 332–57.

11. Taylor, *A Secular Age*, 539–93.

12. Siedentop, *Inventing the Individual*, 332–57.

13. Hannah Arendt, *The Human Condition.* 2nd Ed. (University of Chicago Press, 1958), 22–78.

14. Arendt, *The Human Condition,* 22.

15. Arendt, *The Human Condition,* 24.

16. Arendt, *The Human Condition,* 31–33.

17. Arendt, *The Human Condition,* 37.

18. For a fuller account of Arendt's distinctions between public and private, see my exploration of her work in *The Just and Loving Gaze of God with Us: Paul's Apocalyptic Political Theology* (Wipf and Stock Publishing 2019), 23–46.

19. Arendt, *The Human Condition,* 96.

20. Adam Kotsko, *Neoliberalism's Demons: On the Political Theology of Late Capital* (Stanford University Press, 2018), 10.

21. Kotsko, *Neoliberalism's Demons,* 51.

22. Kotsko, *Neoliberalism's Demons,* 53–54. Yet one may wonder whether Arendt herself would entirely reject this conclusion if confronted with the contemporary neoliberal condition. Given the extent to which economic rationality has come to shape both public and private life, it is possible that she would recognize the instability of the very distinctions she sought to preserve.

23. Kotsko, *Neoliberalism's Demons,* 65.

24. Kotsko, *Neoliberalism's Demons,* 67.

25. Kotsko, *Neoliberalism's Demons,* 71.

26. Polanyi, *The Great Transformation,* 3.

27. Kotsko, *Neoliberalism's Demons,* 12.

28. Kotsko, *Neoliberalism's Demons,* 94.

29. Kotsko, *Neoliberalism's Demons,* 94–95.

30. The creation of demons in neoliberalism is a central feature of its existence in Kotsko's work.

31. Pierre Bourdieu, *The Social Structures of the Economy,* trans. Chris Turner (Polity, 2005), 10. Emphasis in original.

32. Immanuel Kant, *Groundwork of the Metaphysics of Morals,* translated and edited by Mary Gregor (Cambridge University Press, 1996), 37–108.

33. Kenneth Surin, *Freedom Not Yet: Liberation and the Next World Order* (Duke University Press, 2009), 13–30.

34. Surin, *Freedom Not Yet*, 31–59. Here Surin traces the transition from the classical and medieval participatory understanding of subjectivity to the autonomous liberal subject and its culmination in neoliberal forms of personhood.

35. Surin, *Freedom Not Yet*, 40–59. Surin describes capitalism as an "order of orders" that shapes the entire social field and transforms political subjects into consumer subjects.

36. Surin, *Freedom Not Yet*, 59–72, 215–230. Surin argues that liberation requires a truth-event or singularity that interrupts the prevailing capitalist order and creates the conditions for emancipatory subjectivity.

37. Surin, *Freedom Not Yet*, 230–270. See also Adrian Pabst, review of *Freedom Not Yet: Liberation and the Next World Order*, by Kenneth Surin, *Modern Theology* 27, no. 1 (2011): 152–54, for a concise summary of Surin's account of agency, reciprocity, and participatory liberation.

38. Kotsko, *Neoliberalism's Demons,* 37.

39. Kotsko, *Neoliberalism's Demons,* 37.

40. Kotsko, *Neoliberalism's Demons,* 37.

41. Kotsko, *Neoliberalism's Demons,* 37.

42. Kotsko, *Neoliberalism's Demons,* 37.

43. Kotsko, *Neoliberalism's Demons,* 37–38.

44. Kotsko, *Neoliberalism's Demons,* 37–38.

45. Kotsko, *Neoliberalism's Demons,* 38.

46. George E. Tinker, *Missionary Conquest: The Gospel and Native American Cultural Genocide* (Fortress Press, 1993), 3–27.

47. Randy S. Woodley, *Shalom and the Community of Creation: An Indigenous Vision* (Eerdmans, 2012), 17–46.

48. Leanne Betasamosake Simpson, *As We Have Always Done: Indigenous Freedom through Radical Resistance* (University of Minnesota Press, 2017), 19–42.

49. Steven Charleston, *The Four Vision Quests of Jesus* (Morehouse Publishing, 2015), 15–33.

50. Eugene McCarraher, *The Enchantments of Mammon: How Capitalism Became the Religion of Modernity* (Belknap Press, 2019), 591.

51. David Harvey, *Marx, Capital, and the Madness of Economic Reason* (Oxford University Press, 2018), 4.

52. Harvey, *Marx, Capital, and the Madness of Economic Reason,* 7.

53. Harvey, *Marx, Capital, and the Madness of Economic Reason,* 8.

54. Harvey, *Marx, Capital, and the Madness of Economic Reason,* 8.

55. Harvey, *Marx, Capital, and the Madness of Economic Reason,* 10.

56. Harvey, *Marx, Capital, and the Madness of Economic Reason,* 10.

57. Harvey, *Marx, Capital, and the Madness of Economic Reason,* 10–11.

58. Harvey, *Marx, Capital, and the Madness of Economic Reason,* 14.

59. Harvey, *Marx, Capital, and the Madness of Economic Reason,* 14.

60. See Hargaden, *Theological Ethics in a Neoliberal Age,* 18–19.

61. Harvey, *Marx, Capital, and the Madness of Economic Reason,* 14.

62. Kotsko, *Neoliberalism's Demons,* 5.

## CHAPTER 2

# The Preferential Option for the Poor and the Sacramental Life

The preferential option for the poor has emerged as one of the most significant theological developments of twentieth-century Christian thought. It has helped reshape how doctrine, ethics, spirituality, and ecclesial practice are understood in relation to history. Born from the rising awareness of the concrete suffering of oppressed peoples in the Global South in the nineteenth and twentieth centuries and articulated within liberation theology, the option names not merely a moral emphasis but a fundamental orientation of faith, claiming that God's saving action is disclosed in a particular way among those rendered vulnerable by unjust social, political, and economic arrangements. To take the option seriously is to allow the reality of the poor to puncture theology's abstractions and to demand that Christian speech about God remain accountable to historical suffering.

The emergence of liberation theology within the Roman Catholic Church must also be understood within the broader tensions and transformations surrounding the Second Vatican Council and its aftermath. The reforms and global attentiveness encouraged by Vatican II created new space for theological reflection rooted in local histories of poverty, colonialism, and political violence, especially in Latin America. Yet the movement's rapid growth also generated deep internal conflict within the Roman Catholic Church, particularly over the use of Marxist social analysis and revolutionary political language, as well as questions about ecclesial authority. As accounts of the period have shown, liberation theology became a major point of contention during the pontificates of John Paul II and Benedict XVI, both of whom sought to discipline or redirect aspects of the movement even as they affirmed the church's obligation to the poor.[1] The latter rehabilitation of many liberationist concerns under Pope Francis reveals not only the enduring theological force of the preferential option but also the extent to which debates surrounding poverty, capitalism, political theology, and the mission of the church remained unresolved within modern Catholicism itself.

This chapter traces the emergence of that option, beginning with the historical and theological conditions that gave rise to liberation theology. It then assesses its methodological, ecclesiological, and soteriological claims. From its earliest articulations, liberation theology insisted that theology must be more than interpretation; it must be critical reflection on praxis oriented toward liberation. The poor are not merely recipients of charity or objects of concern but subjects of history and agents of their own liberation. The preferential option thus becomes a criterion of theological truthfulness, testing whether Christian faith aligns with the God who hears the cry of the oppressed and acts within history on their behalf.

Yet this chapter also argues that the option has never remained static. As global conditions have shifted, the realities of suffering to which theology must attend have multiplied and intensified. Ecological collapse increasingly shapes the lives of the poor, revealing that social injustice and ecological harm are inseparable. In response, liberation theology has undergone an ecological turn that deepens and extends its concern for the poor.

By engaging Pope Francis's *Laudato Si'* alongside Leonardo Boff's *Cry of the Earth, Cry of the Poor*, this chapter shows how the preferential option for the poor expands to include creation itself. The Earth is no longer treated as a neutral canvas for human history but as a vulnerable participant in systems of domination and exploitation.

In an age where land becomes resource, labor becomes capital, and entire communities become expendable, the inclusion of the Earth within the preferential option becomes both theologically necessary and ethically urgent.

## History of Liberation Theology

Liberation theology emerged as what Luis N. Rivera-Pagán calls an "unforeseen enfant terrible" in twentieth-century theological discourse, introducing "not only a new theme—liberation—but also a new perspective on doing theology and a novel way of referring to God's being and action in history."[2] In its reception, widely experienced as a fundamental reorientation: "Many scholars perceive in its emergence a drastic epistemological rupture, a radical change in paradigm, and a significant shift in both the ecclesial and social roles of theology."[3]

Rivera-Pagán insists that liberation theology's origins "reach beyond the realms of the theological and ecclesiastical."[4] One "important source, neglected by some accounts," was "the complex constellation of liberation struggles during the 1960s and early 1970s."[5] These decades were marked by a sense that history itself was "out of joint," and Rivera-Pagán catalogs a dense field of movements and flashpoints: "a strong antiwar movement (directed particularly against American military intervention in Vietnam and the global nuclear threat); a spread of decolonization movements. . .the feminist struggle against patriarchy and sexism; a robust challenge to racial bigotry; the Stonewall rebellion (June 1969). . . student protests in Paris, Prague, Mexico, and New York. . . and guerilla insurgencies and social unrest in many Latin American nations."[6] He highlights, too, how movements explicitly embraced the language of liberation: "Many agents of social protest adopted the title of 'liberation movement' as a means of public self-presentation, while 'fronts of national liberation' flourished in the Third World."[7] This widespread adoption of the language of "liberation" signals that liberation theology did not invent its central category ex nihilo, but arose within a historical moment already saturated with emancipatory self-understandings.

Within churches, the era's turbulence coincided with institutional and theological shifts that made new kinds of theological speech possible. Rivera-Pagán notes that "Pope John XXIII summoned the Second Vatican Council," and that Vatican II is viewed by progressive Catholic theologians as "an important turning point in the modern history of their church."[8] He frames Vatican II's objectives in ways that matter directly for liberation theology's emergence: an effort "to change the attitude of the Roman Catholic Church toward the modern post-Enlightenment intellectual world from censure and condemnation to openness and dialogue," with *aggiornamento* ("bringing up to date") as a watchword; an effort "to heal the fragmentation of Christianity" through ecumenical presence; and an effort "to face the plight of a world marked by suffering violence, oppression, and injustice with honesty and compassion."[9] In this reading, the church's public posture shifts: "The quest for peace and justice. . .was conceived as an essential dimension of the church's presence in the world."[10]

From this conciliar movement, Rivera-Pagán identifies the 1968 Latin American bishops' meeting at Medellín, Colombia, as a decisive moment. Medellín represented a stunning pastoral and political turn: "To the amazement of many observers, the Roman Catholic Church. . .now made a decisive pastoral shift. It identified solidarity with the poor and destitute as a central concern."[11] He underscores the difference in emphasis between Vatican II and Medellín: "If Vatican II was mainly concerned with the gap between the church and secular modernity, Medellín was more concerned with the scandal of social injustice in a Christian continent."[12] Medellín's own rhetoric, as Rivera-Pagán cites it, is both diagnostic and urgent: "The Latin American bishops cannot remain indifferent in the face of the tremendous social injustices existent in Latin America, which keep the majority of our peoples in dismal poverty that in many cases becomes inhuman wretchedness."[13] This is accompanied by what the text calls "A deafening cry" from "millions of men and women asking their pastors for a liberation that reaches them from nowhere else."[14]

Although Medellín was a bishops' conference ("a meeting of bishops, not theologians"), Rivera-Pagán emphasizes its catalytic effect on theologians who now perceived new possibilities: "Several Roman Catholic theologians perceived the final documents and the general tone emerging from the conference as allowing the possibility of rethinking the theological enterprise from the perspective of the liberation of the poor and downtrodden."[15] He then foregrounds Gustavo Gutiérrez as a pivotal architect. Even before Medellín concluded, "in July 1968, Gustavo Gutiérrez gave a lecture. . .titled 'Toward a Theology of Liberation,' that established a close connection between spiritual salvation and human liberation."[16] Rivera-Pagán marks this as foundational: "This lecture proved to be a pioneering text for Latin American liberation theology."[17] In 1971, Gutiérrez's landmark work appeared in Spanish: "the first edition of Gutiérrez's most famous book, A Theology of Liberation. . .remains a towering achievement of Latin American theological writing."[18] Rivera-Pagán condenses what became one of the most cited of Gutiérrez's conceptual contributions: "His triadic understanding of human liberation—liberation from social and economic oppression, history as a process of self-determined humanization, and redemption from sinfulness—quickly gained classic status."[19] By holding together material conditions, historical agency, and redemption, this framework provided an architecture capable of naming liberation as at once political, human, and soteriological, an integration that would shape liberation theology's subsequent development.

Alongside Gutiérrez, Rivera-Pagán identifies Hugo Assmann and the movement's widening circle of theologians, including Leonardo Boff, José Porfirio Miranda, Juan Luis Segundo, Jon Sobrino, Pablo Richard, Jorge Pixley, and others whose writing was "conceived as expressions of a new intellectual understanding of the faith: liberation theology."[20] Crucially, Rivera-Pagán argues that the story is too often told too narrowly. It is "a mistake to situate it solely in Latin America."[21] It is also "wrong to locate the birth of liberation theology exclusively in Roman Catholic circles."[22] He insists on Protestant antecedents in Latin America, highlighting the work of Rubem Alves, whose "first extensive monograph. . .focused on historical and social liberation as the central hermeneutical key to conceptualize the Christian faith."[23] Alves's text is important not only for chronology but for its explicit claim about the conditions of theological intelligibility: "The acts of remembering and hoping that determine the language of the community of faith. . .do not have any reality in themselves but in the engagement in the ongoing politics of liberation which is the situation and condition of theological intelligibility."[24] Theology, on this account, does not precede liberation as its interpreter but emerges from within it, with political engagement functioning as the very condition under which faith can be intelligibly spoken.

Rivera-Pagán also insists on the parallel and mutually illuminating rise of Black liberation theology in the United States. He locates its roots in the lived history of slavery and racial domination: "During the times of slavery and racial discrimination in the United States, Black churches were communities of solidarity and hope for enslaved peoples of African ancestry."[25] In this context, "the exodus story, prophetic denunciations, and the story of the crucified and resurrected Jesus were sung, preached, and hoped," sustaining communal endurance: "Bodies might have been in bondage to white masters, but hearts and minds were nourished and comforted by stories of retribution and redemption."[26] From there, Black churches became "important protagonists in the civil rights movement for the elimination of racial discrimination."[27] In this sense, the church functioned not only as a site of consolation but as a formative space of political agency, where faith generated collective action against the structures of racial domination.

Among Black liberation theologians, Rivera-Pagán identifies James Cone as "the foremost thinker."[28] Cone's claims are given in sharply programmatic form. In 1969, Cone argues that "the work of Christ is essentially a liberating work, directed toward and by the oppressed."[29] In 1970, Cone made the larger definitional move: "Christianity is essentially a religion of liberation."[30] Theology's task, in Cone's framing, is not neutral commentary but interpretation for struggle: "The function of theology is that of analyzing the meaning of that liberation for the oppressed so that they can know that their struggle for political, social, and economic justice is consistent with the gospel of Jesus Christ."[31] This names the boundary line with striking clarity: "Any theology that is indifferent to the theme of liberation is not Christian."[32] And he pushes toward an ecclesial ontology: "it seems not only appropriate but necessary to define the Christian community as the community of the oppressed which joins Jesus Christ in his fight for the liberation of humankind."[33]

Rivera-Pagán's account is especially useful for this chapter because it keeps the origins of liberation theology tethered to its formative assumptions, especially its account of history, agency, divine action, and theological knowledge.

One of the intellectual conditions that made liberation theology thinkable, he argues, was "the development of a nondogmatic Marxism" that read Marx ethically and utopically, "as an ethical critique of human oppression and as a projection of a utopian, non-oppressive future, something akin to a kingdom of freedom."[34] He notes that this heterodox Marxist reading enabled "something considered largely unthinkable until then: a constructive and affirmative dialogue between theology and Marxism," one that happened "at the margins of church and of party hierarchies, as both looked beyond rigid forms of orthodoxy."[35] That dialogue carries hermeneutical implications, because it "set forth a hermeneutic that interpreted the biblical texts as a struggle between the voices of the oppressors and those of the oppressed."[36] In framing the biblical canon as a site of struggle, this approach legitimates reading Scripture from below, granting interpretive priority to those whose lives most closely mirror the conditions of biblical oppression.

At the level of liberation theology's own stated tenets, Rivera-Pagán identifies a scriptural and historical imaginary centered on liberation as a pattern of divine action: the movement retrieves "subversive memories," gives "hermeneutical and exegetical priority to the Exodus story," and reads prophetic denunciations and Jesus's confrontations as part of a liberationist horizon.[37] The kingdom of God is construed materially and historically: "The kingdom is conceived as referring not to some otherworldly, postmortem realm, but rather to the unceasing hope of a social configuration characterized by justice, solidarity, and freedom."[38] Redemption itself is narratively and socially thickened, as Christ is named in liberative terms: certain theologians "identified Jesus as the Liberator, thereby recovering the semantic roots of the term 'redemption' (the deliverance of a captive or slave)."[39] The movement's preferential option is not merely an ethical add-on but a theological claim about God and the church: "The divine preferential option for the poor, the excluded, and the destitute of this world."[40] The ecclesial implication is direct: "The church must become the church of the poor by sharing the poor's sorrows, hopes, and struggles."[41] Rivera-Pagán observes how this option began with an emphasis that was "socioeconomic," but then broadened to "other categories of social exclusion (indigenous communities, racial and ethnic minorities, women, and sexual orientation),"[42] thus recognizing oppression as a complex, layered reality requiring theological attentiveness to race, gender, culture, and embodiment as well as economics.

The materiality of liberation theology also comes through in its account of knowledge and practice. Rivera-Pagán's fourth tenet makes praxis normative: "Theology cannot be reduced to an intellectual understanding of the faith; it must also be a practical commitment for historical transformation."[43] History is not merely "context" but a theological arena: "History, understood increasingly as the realm of the perennial struggle against oppressions and exclusions, emerged as the locus for Christian praxis."[44] Alves's line intensifies this by making liberation politics the condition of theological intelligibility: "the engagement in the ongoing politics of liberation. . .is the situation and condition of theological intelligibility."[45]

Rivera-Pagán's fifth tenet is explicitly metaphysical, where liberation theology revises classical attributes and names God in liberationist terms: "God is reconceived not as an immutable and impassible entelechy but. . .as a compassionate Eternal Spirit who hears and pays close attention to the cry of the oppressed and whose action in human history has the redemption of the downtrodden and excluded as its ultimate telos."[46] The movement's "main theoretical epistemological rupture," he argues, lies here: "a novel way of thinking about God's being and action in history."[47] The practical upshot is a naming practice: "Instead of contriving arcane scholastic definitions of the divine essence, God is named as Liberator."[48] Naming God as Liberator reframes theology as a response to divine action in history, suggesting that God is known primarily through what God does on behalf of the oppressed rather than through prior ontological definition.

Rivera-Pagán also expands the origin story by narrating how liberation theology immediately entered conflict, because its claims threatened long-standing arrangements. In Latin America, "an official linkage between the state and the Roman Catholic Church has characterized Latin American nations" since colonial beginnings.[49] This "brand of Latin American Christendom" linked "the state and the Roman Catholic Church," sometimes "juridically inscribed in several national constitutions and Vatican concordats."[50]Against this background, liberation theology's surfacing "during the somber and violent times of Latin American military dictatorships (1964–89)" shook alliances and carried mortal risk.[51] He names the most emblematic case: El Salvador, where clergy and laity were assassinated, including Archbishop Oscar Romero.[52]

Romero's words, as Rivera-Pagán quotes them, show the intertwining of martyrdom, liberation, and hope: "May my blood be the seed of liberty," and "may my death. . .be for the liberation of my people."[53] Rivera-Pagán interprets Romero's assassination as a turning point in institutional reaction: It "convinced many church authorities that liberation theology was seriously jeopardizing the social status of the Roman Catholic Church," and that "a convenient, long-standing church-state covenant was endangered."[54]The conflict, therefore, included both doctrinal and sociopolitical anxieties, culminating in official Vatican critique: Liberation theology was accused of "borrowing improperly from Marxist thought," "emphasizing historical and social liberation to the detriment of spiritual salvation," and "politicizing biblical hermeneutics, Christology, and the church."[55] The Vatican document's stated aim was "to draw attention. . .to the deviations and risks of deviation."[56]

Yet to frame liberation theology primarily as a deviation to be corrected is already to misrecognize the conditions from which it emerges. Such critiques presuppose that theology can remain insulated from the material and historical realities that give rise to its questions. What appears, from the perspective of ecclesial authority, as an unwarranted politicization of theology is, from within contexts of oppression, a necessary reckoning with the world as it is. The charge that liberation theology "borrows" from Marxism or distorts the spiritual mission of the church thus risks obscuring a more fundamental issue: whether theology can faithfully speak of God while remaining indifferent to the concrete suffering of the poor. It is precisely at this point of tension, between institutional preservation and historical accountability, that liberation theology takes shape.

## *Gutiérrez and* A Theology of Liberation: *The Grammar of Liberation Theology*

Liberation theology, as Gustavo Gutiérrez presents it, is not a political ideology seeking theological cover. It is a *reorientation of theological method and substance* that becomes necessary when theology is forced to answer to new historical realities: particularly, mass poverty, structural violence, and the church's compromised social location. From the start, Gutiérrez frames the work as a theological response to the demand that faith not be insulated from history. To refuse the novelty of these questions is to detach theology from reality; to treat them as entirely unprecedented is to sever theology from tradition. Liberation theology is born in the narrow space between these two failures, where theology must be both *historically* alert and *ecclesially* responsible.[57]

A first condition is methodological: theology is not the first act of Christian existence. Before "reflection," there is *lived faith*: prayer, discipleship, and concrete commitment shaped by the reign of God. Gutiérrez explicitly describes theology as a "second act," whose task is to read, interpret, and critically assess a complex praxis already underway in the community of faith. Thus, theology follows commitment and remains accountable to it.[58]

This second-act character is not merely pastoral advice; it changes what theology *is*. Theology becomes a disciplined labor that asks how Christian faith should understand itself when it is lived amid oppression and struggle. Consequently, theological statements are judged not only by internal coherence but also by whether they illuminate faithful action and purify it from distortion. Theology's vocation is to be a critical reflection that both clarifies and judges the church's praxis, rather than sanctifying it.[59]

Gutiérrez does not dismiss theology as wisdom or rational inquiry. Instead, he reframes them inside a new demand: theology must be "critical reflection" on praxis. Praxis here is not a generic activity. It is a historically located action aimed at transforming unjust social conditions, and it is inseparable from the experience of suffering and the struggle for liberation. Thus, a second condition arises: liberation theology assumes that *theological truth is tested in relation to practice*, and that theology must become capable of naming when ecclesial or Christian practice is complicit in oppression.[60] This is why the book's early chapters press the danger of "generalities" and "solutions without commitment." When theology evacuates concrete history, it ceases to address the real world in which discipleship occurs. Liberation theology begins as theology's refusal to remain abstract in the face of suffering.[61]

A third condition is epistemological: *theology must learn to read history truthfully*. That requires tools that classical theology did not always treat as internal to its work. Gutiérrez argues that theological reflection must take social reality seriously enough to analyze it, since oppression is not merely a personal moral defect but a structural field. This is why "development," "dependency," and "liberation" are treated not as background vocabulary but as competing interpretations of reality that theology must discern and evaluate.[62] Theology must be able to state: If a framework like "development" functions ideologically, by masking exploitation, dependency, and domination behind a rhetoric of progress and modernization, then theology cannot simply adopt it without some kind of theological loss. The conditions for liberation theology include a refusal of conceptual schemes that naturalize injustice.[63]

A fourth condition is conceptual and anthropological: "Development" is an inadequate term because it presumes a linear path of progress, often leaving the deeper structures of domination intact. "Liberation," by contrast, names a historical process that recognizes conflict, domination, and the need for structural change. While "modernization" was an in-vogue term through which U.S. State Department Latin Americanists viewed the Americas, Gutiérrez jettisons the term, making liberation the category that can accurately name what is happening in Latin America and what must happen if human dignity is to be honored.[64] This shift carries theological weight because it redefines what "human flourishing" means. It does not mean merely more goods or increased efficiency. It means the breaking of relationships of domination and the recovery of human agency. Liberation theology, therefore, requires a theological anthropology that treats persons and peoples as historical agents, not objects of charity or targets of paternalistic improvement.[65]

A fifth condition is ecclesiological: The older settlement in which the church handles "religion" and the world handles "politics" collapses in the face of oppression. Even when that model was meant to protect the autonomy of temporal realities, it became pastorally and theologically untenable in contexts where oppression is decisive, and silence functions as legitimation.[66] The crisis becomes explicit when the church's "nonintervention" is exposed as impossible. If the church maintains "friendly relationships" with oppressive regimes or remains silent, as it did with several Latin American dictatorships, it participates in the moral economy of domination. The theological condition here is severe: the church cannot claim purity by abstaining from politics when abstention sustains injustice. Liberation theology arises when theology must name ecclesial neutrality as a theological problem rather than merely a strategic one.[67]

A sixth condition is a theological interpretation of modernity. Gutiérrez treats secularization as a historical process in which human beings increasingly understand themselves as responsible for history rather than governed by "metaphysical tutelage." This does not mean God is absent; it means the human vocation in history becomes newly visible and urgent. Liberation theology depends on the claim that Christian faith can affirm historical responsibility without surrendering transcendence.[68] In other words, liberation theology requires a theology that does not panic at an "entirely worldly world," but can interpret it within the horizon of God's reign and human responsibility. This becomes one of the conditions for refusing both religious escapism and naive sacralization of political projects.[69]

A seventh condition is soteriological: Salvation cannot be treated as a separate "religious" track running alongside "real" history. Gutiérrez insists that conventional theological dualisms (nature/grace split into separate planes; "religious" salvation detached from social life) must be overcome.[70] A pivotal formulation here is that there are not "two histories," one sacred and one profane. Instead, there is one history in which God's salvific work and human historical life are inseparably related. This does not collapse salvation into politics. It asserts that salvation is *integral*: It concerns the totality of human life, including social existence, because God's saving work is not indifferent to oppression and suffering. Liberation theology becomes possible only when salvation is conceived in a way that can speak meaningfully to history.[71]

An eighth condition is eschatological: Christian hope must be able to sustain political struggle without turning it into an idol. Gutiérrez insists that commitment to a just society presupposes confidence in the future and a hope open to what is coming. The question is not whether faith has political implications but how these implications are understood, considering eschatology. Liberation theology requires an account of the Kingdom of God in which historical liberation is genuinely significant, yet never the final horizon.[72] This becomes crucial for avoiding two errors at once: spiritualizing the gospel so it becomes socially harmless, and absolutizing political projects so they become messianic.[73]

A ninth condition is spiritual and moral: the encounter with God is not primarily a flight from history but an engagement within it. Gutiérrez develops this insight through his claim that human history itself is God's dwelling. Because God's salvific activity embraces the entirety of creation and history, there is no genuinely "profane" realm existing outside the temple (*pro fanum*). Political, economic, and social life are therefore not secular spaces detached from God's presence but the very arenas in which communion with God and neighbor is enacted. From this follows one of Gutiérrez's most decisive theological claims: Christian spirituality necessarily takes the form of a "conversion to the neighbor." Because God has chosen to dwell within the concrete realities of human history, faithful communion with God cannot be separated from concrete solidarity with those whom history has rendered vulnerable. The forms of God's presence, therefore, determine the forms of Christian discipleship.[74] This yields a spirituality of liberation that contests both privatized piety and ecclesial self-enclosure. To meet God is inseparable from turning toward the neighbor, and thus inseparable from the demand for justice in concrete situations. Liberation theology requires spirituality to be re-formed by the suffering neighbor as a locus of divine encounter.[75]

A tenth condition is that "poverty" cannot remain a marginal ethical concern or a mere object of charitable sympathy. Poverty becomes a theological theme because it forces theologians to ask what witness really means in a church seeking authenticity. Thus, Gutiérrez frames poverty as a site of ecclesial challenge: It presses the church toward solidarity and protest, and it redefines what credibility looks like. Liberation theology requires that poverty be thought theologically, because it is one of the central historical realities that tests the truthfulness of Christian proclamation.[76]

## The Preferential Option for the Poor

For Gutiérrez, the preferential option for the poor is a central theme of liberation theology and one that has become "widely accepted in the universal church,"[77] but the option is not a slogan, nor merely an ethical add-on. It is a theological orientation that arises from (1) the biblical meaning of poverty, (2) the historical "new presence of the poor" in Latin America, and (3) a renewed account of the church's mission and salvation in history.[78]

Gutiérrez insists that poverty must be named with theological seriousness because it is a "complex human condition" whose causes require deep analysis.[79] Yet the decisive point is not methodological complexity as such, but the claim that the "meaning given to poverty in the Bible" is "a cornerstone of liberation theology."[80]

To make this concrete, he highlights Medellín's distinction among three meanings of "poverty":

1. "Real poverty as an evil—that is something that God does not want"
2. "Spiritual poverty," understood as readiness to do God's will; and
3. "Solidarity with the poor, along with protest against the conditions under which they suffer"[81]

These three meanings are critical because they prevent the option for the poor from being reduced to either romanticizing deprivation or a purely interior spirituality. Real poverty is an evil; spiritual poverty is a posture of trust and obedience; and under conditions of oppression, solidarity and protest become the social and political form that Christian fidelity must take.[82]

Gutiérrez explicitly rejects any framing in which Christians must choose between God's universal love and God's special concern for the oppressed. He describes "the great challenge" as maintaining both: "the universality of God's love and God's predilection for those on the lowest rung of the ladder of history."[83] He warns that focusing on only one is to "mutilate the Christian message."[84] This is where his reading of the word "preference" matters. He notes that Medellín spoke of giving "preference to the poorest and most needy sectors and to those segregated for any cause whatsoever."[85] The point is not to narrow the church's horizon, but to insist that authentic universality must take concrete historical shape precisely where exclusion is most severe.[86]

Gutiérrez is equally careful about the word "option." The term might sound like a voluntary emphasis that one can choose to emphasize or ignore, but he explicitly pushes back against that misunderstanding. In the context of Christian discipleship, he insists that this commitment "without exception is not 'optional.'"[87] He also rejects the idea that "option" implies the chooser is always someone outside the world of poverty. He notes that many who speak about the option do not belong to the poor, but he adds that the poor themselves also have "an obligation to make this option."[88] The point here is theological rather than moralistic. The option is not a paternalistic stance of the privileged toward the needy; it is a claim about the shape of Christian vocation, including among the poor as subjects and agents within God's history.[89]

Gutiérrez roots the preferential option within a specific ecclesial reception-history. He notes that the explicitly adopted the phrase "preferential option for the poor," building on theological usage already developing among Latin American theologians.[90] He also names a precursor to the phrase in John XXIII's statement shortly before Vatican II that the church must be "the church of all and especially the church of the poor.[91] He highlights how this line holds together the two poles already noted: "universality and preference for the poor" as "both demanding and inseparable."[92] This matters for Gutiérrez because liberation theology is not presented as a private theological invention; it is tied to ecclesial discernment in Latin America and framed as a call for the conversion of the church itself in the face of poverty.[93]

When Gutiérrez returns to the option later in his book, he defines "the poor" in a way that is explicitly structural and historical, not sentimental. By "the poor," he means those whose "social and economic condition is the result of a particular political order" and the "concrete histories" of nations and social groups.[94] This definition is pivotal: *It makes the option inherently concerned with structures of injustice, not only with individual acts of charity.* At the same time, this structural definition intensifies the theological problem: *If poverty is produced by a political order, then Christian love and ecclesial mission cannot avoid political implications.* This is why he immediately poses questions about how to live evangelical charity amid social conflict while holding together "universality of charity" and "preferential solidarity with the poor."[95] Gutiérrez frames the option as continuous with the biblical portrait of God who "intervenes in history" to "break down the structures of injustice," liberates slaves in Exodus, overturns empires, and raises prophets who call for "justice and mercy."[96] Within this biblical milieu, he describes the gospel as a "continual demand for the right of the poor to make themselves heard" and to be "considered preferentially by society," including the subordination of economic priorities to the needs of the deprived.[97] This is not an abstract moralism; it is an account of God's character and action as disclosed in Scripture. The preferential option is therefore a claim about *what faith in this God entails* when translated into historical discipleship.[98]

For Gutiérrez, solidarity entails real cost. He explicitly connects the church's fidelity to Christ with concrete solidarity with workers and with those suffering unemployment, and he notes that many Christians have paid a price for such solidarity.[99] In that context, he cites the idea that in such solidarity "our fidelity to Christ is proved."[100] The option is therefore not merely about *helping* the poor; it is about the church being converted toward a mode of presence in which its proclamation, practices, and alliances are tested by whether they embody friendship with the poor and opposition to the conditions that crush them.[101] That is why the option functions, for Gutiérrez, as a criterion of ecclesial truthfulness: the church's credibility is bound to whether it becomes a "church of the poor."[102]

Finally, Gutiérrez is explicit that the preferential option must not be collapsed into ideological identification.[103] The preferential option for the poor has unavoidable political implications because poverty is not merely an individual misfortune but the historical consequence of social, economic, and political arrangements. Yet its foundation is never primarily political. Its ground is theological: the liberating action of the God of Israel, the conviction that salvation embraces the whole of human history, and the church's vocation to bear witness to the Kingdom of God amid the conflicts and contradictions of the present age.[104] The option, therefore, demands *discernment*: it calls Christians into solidarity and structural critique while refusing to absolutize any political project as equivalent to the Kingdom.[105] Thus, in Gutiérrez's account, the preferential option for the poor means:

1. Poverty must be theologically named as evil (what God does not want), while also calling forth spiritual poverty and solidarity/protest.[106]
2. "Preferential" safeguards historical concreteness without canceling universality: Christians must hold together universal love and God's "predilection" for the oppressed.[107]
3. The option is a binding requirement of discipleship, "not 'optional,'" and not merely a stance of the non-poor toward the poor.[108]
4. "The poor" are defined structurally—as those produced by a "particular political order"—so the option necessarily addresses injustice at the level of social structures.[109]
5. The biblical God's liberating action grounds the option, including the demand that the poor be heard and considered preferentially within society.[110]
6. Solidarity with the poor becomes a test of ecclesial fidelity: in costly solidarity, "our fidelity to Christ is proved."[111]

## Creation and the Cry of the Poor

In the late twentieth and early twenty-first centuries, liberation theology increasingly turned toward creation as a locus of injustice and suffering. This development does not represent a departure from liberation theology's foundational commitments but rather a deepening of them. In *Laudato Si'*, Pope Francis articulates this extension by explicitly naming the earth itself among the poor: "the earth herself, burdened and laid waste, is among the most abandoned and maltreated of our poor."[112] In this formulation, creation is not merely the backdrop of human liberation but is drawn directly into the scope of the preferential option for the poor.

In his encyclical, Francis binds ecological degradation to the concrete suffering of marginalized communities, insisting that environmental harm must be interpreted through the experience of the oppressed. He speaks of "the tragic effects of environmental degradation on the lives of the world's poorest," refusing any separation between ecological concern and social justice.[113] This linkage echoes liberation theology's long-standing insistence that injustice is not accidental but structural. Accordingly, Francis asserts that the ecological crisis requires "profound changes in 'lifestyles, models of production and consumption, and the established structures of power which today govern societies.'"[114]

The extension of the preferential option for the poor to creation is further clarified when Francis writes that

> in the present condition of global society, where injustices abound and growing numbers of people are deprived of basic human rights and considered expendable, the principle of the common good immediately becomes. . .a summons to solidarity and a preferential option for the poorest of our brothers and sisters.[115]

In *Laudato Si'*, Pope Francis signals a momentous theological shift by placing creation at the center of Catholic moral, social, and spiritual reflection. While previous strands of Catholic social teaching addressed environmental concerns indirectly, Francis integrates care for creation into the heart of theological anthropology, soteriology, and ethics. Creation becomes a vulnerable participant in the drama of sin, injustice, and redemption.

For Francis, the ecological crisis is a theological problem rather than a technical or political one. Environmental degradation is a symptom of distorted relationships between humanity and God, among human communities, and between humanity and the rest of creation. Creation becomes a site where the consequences of sin are materially visible.

A key feature of this reorientation is Francis's insistence on the inseparability of social and ecological concerns. The ecological crisis is presented as disproportionately harming those already marginalized by global economic and political systems. In this way, Francis shifts Catholic social teaching, particularly its longstanding concern for justice and human dignity, into explicitly ecological terrain.

Francis acknowledges that the dominant scientific and technocratic paradigms of the modern era treated nature as inert matter available for unlimited manipulation. By challenging these extractive models of progress, he opens up our moral imagination to acknowledge the limits, interdependencies, and responsibilities that we face. This tilt involves a re-evaluation of concepts such as dominion, development, and human exceptionalism.

Finally, Francis situates this ecological turn within a broader spiritual and sacramental vision. Care for creation is not only an ethical obligation but a dimension of Christian discipleship and worship. By reconnecting ecological responsibility with praise, gratitude, and conversion, *Laudato Si'* reframes environmental concern as a response to God's creative and sustaining presence in the world. Creation thus becomes a privileged locus for theological reflection, moral discernment, and hope.

If *Laudato Si'* offers a broad theological and sacramental horizon for ecological concern, liberation theology presses further by asking whose lives bear the weight of ecological degradation and which social arrangements produce it. The encyclical's repeated insistence on the inseparability of environmental and social crises creates an implicit bridge to liberationist analysis, where structural sin, economic exploitation, and political marginalization are already central categories. In this sense, Francis's ecological turn does not merely invite dialogue with liberation theology; it renders such dialogue unavoidable.

It is precisely at this juncture that Leonardo Boff's work *Cry of the Earth, Cry of the Poor* establishes itself.[116] Leonardo Boff stands as one of the most important figures in the development of liberation theology and its ecological expansion. Born in Brazil in 1938, Boff entered the Franciscan order in 1959 and was ordained a priest in 1964. His Franciscan formation deeply shaped his theological imagination, especially his attention to poverty, simplicity, creatureliness, and the material world. After completing doctoral studies in philosophy and theology at the University of Munich, Boff became one of the leading Latin American theologians to articulate Christian faith from the standpoint of the poor and oppressed. Alongside Gustavo Gutiérrez, Jon Sobrino, Juan Luis Segundo, and others, Boff insisted that theology must not remain detached from historical suffering.

Boff's work brought him into conflict with ecclesial authority. His critique of hierarchical power in the church, especially in *Church: Charism and Power*, drew scrutiny from Cardinal Joseph Ratzinger, who ran the Congregation for the Doctrine of the Faith under Pope John Paul II. In 1985, Boff was silenced. This conflict revealed a deep contest over the meaning of the postconciliar church and the legitimacy of liberation theology's insistence that the poor are not merely objects of our charity. Boff eventually left the Franciscan order and priestly ministry, yet he continued to develop a theological vision rooted in liberation, justice, and care for creation.

Boff's later ecological theology is especially significant for the argument of this book. In *Cry of the Earth, Cry of the Poor*, he argues that the suffering of the poor and the suffering of the Earth must be heard together. The same logic that exploits marginalized peoples also devastates land, water, and ecosystems. Ecology, therefore, is not a departure from liberation theology but its deepening. For Boff, the preferential option for the poor expands to include creation because the poor are inseparable from the places, lands, waters, and ecological systems that sustain their lives.

Pope Francis and Leonardo Boff approach the ecological crisis from complementary perspectives: Francis highlights its theological and spiritual dimensions, while Boff situates ecology within the historical struggle for liberation. The ecological question is no longer framed only as a matter of stewardship or moral responsibility. It becomes a site where the suffering of the marginalized and the suffering of the Earth converge, demanding a theology capable of hearing both cries together.

From its opening pages, *Cry of the Earth, Cry of the Poor* insists that ecological reflection is coterminous with liberation theology. Boff states that its task is "to connect the cry of the oppressed with the cry of the Earth."[117] Thus, liberation theology's historical attentiveness to suffering must now attend to a second, inseparable wound.

Boff repeatedly emphasizes that the ecological crisis and the crisis of poverty share a single causal logic. He observes: "The Earth is also crying out. The logic that exploits classes and subjects people to the interests of a few rich and powerful countries is the same as the logic that devastates the Earth and plunders its wealth."[118]

Boff acknowledges that early liberation theology did not begin with concern for the planet as such, but with the suffering of human beings: "The most salient and challenging fact was not the threat to Earth as a whole but to the sons and daughters of Earth exploited and condemned to die prematurely, the poor and oppressed."[119] Yet this was not necessarily a limitation as it is already ecological in substance: "The relationship to ecology is direct, for the poor and the oppressed belong to nature and their situation is objectively an ecological aggression."[120] The poor are not external to the ecological crisis; their bodies, labor, land, and lives are sites where ecological violence is enacted.

He notes, "This human catastrophe is liberation theology's starting point for considering ecology."[121] Ecology clarifies the full scope of liberation theology's concern for unjust social arrangements. Boff called this "social ecology," which he defined as "the way human beings, the most complex beings in creation, relate to one another and how they organize their relationship with other beings in nature."[122]

Boff describes the systems organizing human and ecological relations as "a very exploitative and cruelly exclusionary system"[123] which produces poverty and environmental destruction. As a result, the ecological turn demands that both cries be heard together: "We are faced with the cry of the oppressed and the excluded," and at the same time, the "Earth is also crying out under the predatory and lethal machinery of our model of society and development."[124]

Boff writes: "To hear these two interconnected cries and to see the same root cause that produces them is to carry out integral liberation."[125] Liberation is no longer conceived solely as casting off economic or political oppression but as a transformation of the entire system that wounds both human communities and Earth's life systems. Care for the poor thus becomes constitutive of ecological concern, because ecological devastation cannot be addressed without dismantling the social structures that generate poverty.

Justice cannot be divided into separate domains. Boff writes: ". . .social justice—the right relationship between persons, roles, and institutions—implies some achievement of ecological justice, which is the right relationship with nature."[126] A society that violates the dignity of the poor will necessarily violate the integrity of the Earth. Conversely, ecological degradation reveals the failure of social justice.

Strikingly, Boff declares: "It is not whales or panda bears that suffer the greatest injustice in creation, but rather the poor of the world."[127] This is not to deny the value of nonhuman life. Instead, it is to insist that ecological concern must be ordered by justice. The preferential option is not weakened by ecological concern; it is intensified and given planetary scope.

Ultimately, liberation theology and ecological discourse cannot proceed independently. "They must be an indispensable mediation in the safeguarding of everything created and in rescuing the dignity of the poor majorities of the world."[128] These discourses are mutually dependent.[129] Care for the poor is thus not one application of ecological theology among others; it is the criterion by which ecological discourse remains faithful to liberation's theological core.

## The Preferential Option for the Poor Against Neoliberalism

Liberation theology has always insisted that the poor are not accidental victims of history but are produced by specific political and economic arrangements. In an age of neoliberal globalization, this insight must be widened to include ecological devastation as a structurally generated injustice. Environmental destruction is not a tragic side effect of economic growth; it is a predictable consequence of an economic logic that externalizes costs onto the vulnerable. The same mechanisms that displace communities through austerity, privatization, and deregulation also degrade land, water, and climate systems.

Neoliberal ideology often treats environmental concern as a luxury of the affluent or as a technocratic issue best managed by market solutions. In contrast, an ecological preferential option insists that environmental degradation is fundamentally a justice issue. When soil is depleted, water is poisoned, or the climate is destabilized, it is the poor who lose livelihoods, homes, and futures. To opt for the poor, therefore, is already to opt for the Earth upon which their lives depend.

Theologically, the inclusion of the Earth within the preferential option challenges neoliberalism's reduction of creation to property. An ecological preferential option affirms creation as a shared, finite, and vulnerable good entrusted to human care. This shift reorients ethics away from mastery and toward responsibility and relationality, reclaiming the moral imagination from fateful neoliberal narratives of inevitability, growth, and efficiency.

Decision-making authority in our neoliberal world rests in transnational markets and corporate institutions that are largely unaccountable to the communities and ecosystems they affect. Ecological destruction thus becomes a form of domination exercised at a distance, obscured by both the jargon and reality of financial instruments and global supply chains. To propose an ecological preferential option involves re-centering moral judgment on those who suffer the consequences of these arrangements, both human and nonhuman. It demands that theology attend not only to who benefits from economic systems but to who and what are rendered expendable.

To extend the preferential option to the Earth is vital for sustaining hope and moral agency in the face of neoliberal predestination. The ideologues of neoliberalism echo Prime Minister Margaret

Thatcher's insistence that "There is No Alternative," framing ecological collapse and social inequality as regrettable but unavoidable. An ecological liberation theology resists this resignation by naming both the Earth and the poor as subjects of God's concern and as sites of divine promise. By refusing to separate care for creation from care for the marginalized, this expanded preferential option affirms that ecological and social futures remain open to transformation. In doing so, it preserves liberation theology's core conviction: that God's justice is disclosed not in the triumph of markets or the logic of efficiency, but in solidarity with the vulnerable and in the defense of life in all its forms.

## Excursus: The Poor Are Never Poor in the Abstract

If the preferential option for the poor is to avoid becoming another abstraction, it must attend to the concrete lives of those whom it seeks to name. Poverty is never experienced in isolation from the bodies, histories, and social locations through which human beings inhabit the world. Poverty is lived through the intersecting realities of race, gender, disability, migration, colonial dispossession, environmental vulnerability, and political exclusion. To speak theologically of the poor, therefore, is not to identify an abstract economic class but to attend to particular persons whose lives bear the cumulative weight of multiple forms of marginalization.

Womanist, feminist, and mujerista theologians have consistently reminded the church that liberation cannot proceed by universalizing experiences drawn primarily from male or economically reductionist accounts of oppression. In one of the pioneering works of womanist theology, Delores Williams argues that the survival strategies of Black women reveal dimensions of oppression often obscured within traditional liberation theologies, demonstrating that redemption must attend not only to economic exploitation but also to histories of racial violence, gendered domination, and bodily vulnerability.[130] Likewise, Ada María Isasi-Díaz insists that theology must arise from *lo cotidiano*—the everyday practices through which marginalized communities negotiate survival, resistance, and hope.[131] Liberation is therefore not merely the transformation of structures but the affirmation of concrete lives whose theological significance emerges precisely within the ordinary rhythms of daily existence.

M. Shawn Copeland argues that Christian theology must recover the irreducible significance of embodied existence. The human body is never merely an object of economic production or political regulation but the very site where divine communion is encountered and where the wounds of injustice become visible. Consequently, the Eucharist cannot remain detached from the violated bodies of those excluded by racial hierarchy, economic inequality, or social marginalization.[132]

These voices deepen rather than revise the preferential option for the poor. They remind us that God's preferential concern is never directed toward an abstract category but toward particular persons whose suffering is mediated through complex histories of exclusion. The poor are not merely economically disadvantaged; they are frequently those whose bodies have been rendered invisible, whose voices have been silenced, whose lands have been taken, whose labor has been exploited, and whose humanity has been denied. Christian solidarity, therefore, begins not with generalized compassion but with careful attention to the concrete conditions through which persons experience vulnerability.

Disability theology offers a similar corrective to neoliberal accounts of creation. Nancy Eiesland's groundbreaking vision of the "disabled God" challenges the church's tendency to identify liberation with the elimination of weakness or dependency. Instead, the resurrected Christ remains visibly wounded, revealing that disability is not an obstacle to communion but a site through which God's presence is disclosed.[133] John Swinton likewise argues that vulnerability and dependence are not deviations from authentic humanity but constitutive features of creaturely existence. Human flourishing is discovered not through autonomy but through belonging within communities that receive one another as gifts rather than burdens.[134] Amos Yong further insists that disability exposes the poverty of anthropologies that define human dignity according to productivity, rational capacity, or economic usefulness. Every human life possesses irreducible worth because every person is created for communion with God and neighbor.[135]

These theological developments also require a fuller account of complicity. Systems of exploitation are sustained not merely by distant institutions but through the recursive and quotidian practices by which communities participate in economies of consumption, exclusion, and privilege. Few Christians stand entirely outside the structures they seek to criticize. The preferential option for the poor, therefore, demands not only structural transformation but continual repentance as individuals and communities discern the subtle ways their own lives remain implicated in patterns of domination. Liberation begins not by imagining ourselves outside unjust systems but by confessing our participation within them while opening ourselves to the reconciling work of Christ.

This distinction also clarifies the relationship between charity, justice, and solidarity. Charity responds generously to immediate need and remains an indispensable expression of Christian love. Justice asks why such a need persists and seeks the transformation of the structures that perpetuate it. Solidarity moves still further. It refuses the distance that often separates giver from recipient by recognizing that the flourishing of one is inseparable from the flourishing of all. The preferential option for the poor, therefore, culminates not simply in acts of benevolence nor only in political reform, but in communities whose common life embodies the reconciled relationships inaugurated in Jesus Christ. Such solidarity does not erase difference but receives difference as the very place where the body of Christ becomes visible.

## Fear of Beggars and the Preferential Option for the Poor

The preferential option for the poor is often described as a moral commitment—a call to prioritize those who suffer deprivation and exclusion. Yet such a description risks flattening the depth of the claim. The option is not merely a distributive principle nor an ethical addendum to otherwise intact social arrangements. It is a theological reorientation. It asserts that the poor are not simply recipients of Christian care but the privileged site of divine disclosure. To choose the poor is not first to perform charity but to inhabit a different vantage point from which the world itself appears differently.

If this is true, then the preferential option, as suggested in the previous section, cannot remain abstract. It must interrupt the structures that produce poverty and the imagination that sustains them. Neoliberalism presents a profound obstacle here. It collapses sociality into capital, reduces value to productivity, and renders relationships legible primarily through exchange. Within this order, even solidarity risks becoming strategy, and even compassion risks becoming leverage. The poor are "included" through development schemes, "empowered" through access to networks, or "assisted" through managed benevolence. Yet inclusion often occurs without displacement of the logic that made them vulnerable in the first place.

What disappears in this arrangement is not simply justice but *place*. Neoliberalism not only commodifies goods and labor; as noted earlier, it transforms the spatial conditions under which moral life unfolds. It abstracts lived and messy places into functional spaces optimized for circulation and exchange. In such an abstract space, relationships become scalable and monetizable.

If the poor are to disclose divine truth, then the church must encounter them not as data points or beneficiaries within abstract systems, but as neighbors in concrete places. The option requires proximity and requires a transformation of space back into place: a recovery of environments where bodies cannot be reduced to units of capital and where claims cannot be indefinitely deferred.

Such a recovery also demands the reconsideration of practices that modern economic rationality often dismisses as irrational, inefficient, or socially unproductive. One such practice is voluntary begging, particularly as it appears within older Christian traditions of mendicancy. To modern neoliberal sensibilities, begging frequently appears only as failure, dependency, or economic dysfunction. Yet within certain theological traditions, voluntary poverty and mendicant life functioned not merely as acts of renunciation but as disruptions of economic assumptions surrounding value, autonomy, productivity, and exchange.

It is precisely here that Kelly Johnson's retrieval of voluntary begging becomes theologically disruptive. Rather than asking whether one should give to a beggar—a question easily absorbed into neoliberal moral reasoning and progressive moral aggrandizing—Johnson asks what begging itself reveals about wealth, power, and the good life. In the Christian tradition, voluntary begging is not a tactic for accumulating social capital. A classic example of voluntary begging utilized by Johnson is the early Order of Friars Minor, founded by Francis of Assisi. Francis and his companions intentionally renounced ownership of property and material wealth, traveled among towns and villages, and depended upon alms and hospitality for daily sustenance. Their begging was not understood as economic failure but as a spiritual discipline meant to imitate Christ's poverty, cultivate dependence upon others and God, and resist social systems built upon wealth, status, and accumulation.

Voluntary begging was also significant because it disrupted ordinary social hierarchies. Medieval society often tied dignity, honor, and authority to property, status, and economic control. Mendicants intentionally placed themselves in positions of vulnerability and dependence, thereby identifying with the poor rather than ruling over them from positions of privilege. In doing so, they exposed how wealth frequently creates forms of insulation from both suffering and genuine human mutuality. The beggar could not maintain the illusion of total independence because survival depended upon relationships, hospitality, and communal responsibility.

The practice also carried a profound critique of possessiveness. Christian traditions have long warned that wealth can distort desire by encouraging self-sufficiency, domination, and anxiety over control. Voluntary poverty and begging functioned as ascetic disciplines meant to free persons from attachment to possession and status. In this sense, begging was not glorification of misery but resistance to the idea that security, value, or salvation could be secured through accumulation.

Interestingly, voluntary begging revealed something deeply theological about Christian understandings of grace. The mendicant receives life as gift rather than as entitlement or achievement. Dependence upon alms becomes a lived acknowledgment that existence itself is received rather than mastered. This is one reason the practice remains so disruptive to modern economic rationality, especially under neoliberalism. The voluntary beggar stands as a visible contradiction to a world organized around optimization and market value. Thus, voluntary begging is a renunciation of the right to command wealth. It is a refusal to secure identity through possession. It is a choice to embrace dependence in a world ordered by autonomy.

Begging, therefore, does more than align the church with the poor; it destabilizes the economic and spatial grammar that produces poverty. The beggar interrupts abstract space by forcing encounter. It reasserts place by binding giver and receiver in a moment that cannot be fully controlled, optimized, or monetized. It exposes the fiction that one can circulate freely without being claimed. In this sense, begging is not simply ethical; it is spatially transformative.

To be clear, *voluntary* begging should be clearly distinguished from *involuntary* begging. Voluntary begging exposes the fiction that one can circulate freely without being claimed. The mendicant chooses dependence as a theological and ascetic practice, whereas involuntary begging often reflects conditions of social exclusion and material desperation imposed upon the poor. Yet the existence of voluntary begging nevertheless unsettles modern assumptions about autonomy and self-sufficiency precisely because it transforms dependence from a mark of failure into a visible acknowledgment of creaturely need and mutual obligation. In this sense, begging is not simply ethical; it is spatially transformative.

And this transformation is sacramental. For the sacrament is not an escape from the material world but its intensification. It is the act by which ordinary space becomes charged with divine presence. Bread, wine, water, bodies gathered in locations. These are not generic elements but *placed* realities. The sacramental act reveals that grace does not circulate abstractly; it takes place. It gathers a community in which dependence is normalized and gift precedes exchange.

To retrieve begging, then, is to anticipate a sacramental politics of place. It is to perform, within neoliberal abstraction, a gesture that reconfigures space into a morally binding place. The beggar does not seek to be integrated into networks of advantage but to inhabit a world where it might become easier to be good, a world where dependence is neither shame nor deficit, but the condition of communion.

The preferential option for the poor thus demands more than redistribution. It demands transformation, of imagination, of space, and of power itself. It calls the church not merely to stand with the poor within neoliberal space, but to participate in the conversion of that space into a place, where grace is not managed but received, and where human life is not capitalized but consecrated.

The central idea that enables this is the idea of pilgrimage by way of blasphemy. What does this mean? The church that follows the God who grasps at nothing on pilgrimage continually disrupts the place of neoliberalism in society. Thus, if begging promotes a world where it is easier to do good, then it must challenge the central place of neoliberalism. It does not create a new economy but meets neoliberalism in ever-new ways as it seeks the good of each neighbor it meets. Thus, pilgrimage "does not rest," as cultural theorist Alexander Weheliye helpfully states, "on the mirage of Western Man as the mirror image of human life as such."[136] The figure of Western man operates as a proxy for the neoliberal subject, representing both the normative social subject and the epistemic limits of what can be conceived as human in the present. Admittedly, a sociality not predicated on capital is almost impossible to imagine, but it is precisely in this direction that the church journeys on pilgrimage.

## Space Versus Place: A Neoliberal Reduction

Neoliberalism's most enduring achievement may not be its reshaping of markets or its reconfiguration of states, but its quiet transformation of the spatial conditions under which moral life unfolds. While neoliberalism is typically analyzed in terms of privatization, deregulation, and market expansion, its success depends upon a deeper and more subtle reordering of the world: the systematic conversion of place into abstract space. This conversion is not merely economic. It is moral, anthropological, and theological. Neoliberalism does not simply monetize what occurs within space; it produces spatial forms that make monetization possible, desirable, and seemingly inevitable.

At stake in the distinction between space and place is not semantic nuance but the question of how obligation appears, or fails to appear, within social life. Place gathers memory, bodies, and claims; space disperses them. Neoliberalism thrives not by eliminating moral concern, but by relocating it into abstract spaces where responsibility can be managed, deferred, or individualized.

Phenomenological accounts of place insist that place is not an optional overlay atop an otherwise neutral spatial grid. As Edward S. Casey argues, place is ontologically prior to space insofar as existence itself is always emplaced; one does not first exist and then enter a location but rather comes to selfhood *through* emplacement.[137] Place is eventful. It gathers bodies, histories, affects, and meanings into a lived horizon. Yi-Fu Tuan similarly emphasizes that place emerges through experience, duration, and attachment. Place is "space made meaningful," but that meaning is not imposed arbitrarily; it accrues through dwelling, repetition, and vulnerability.[138]

Place, therefore, resists abstraction. It is thick with memory and saturated with moral significance. A home is not merely a shelter. A parish is not merely a venue. A neighborhood is not merely a zone.

Each is a site is a place of belonging where identities are formed, obligations are learned, and claims are made without being chosen.

Of course, neoliberalism finds this density intolerable. Drawing on Henri Lefebvre's claim that space is socially produced, we can see neoliberalism as a regime that actively produces abstract space—space emptied of particularity, rendered homogeneous, and organized according to function rather than meaning.[139] Abstract space is *useful* space. It is space that can be mapped, priced, optimized, securitized, and exchanged. In abstract space, everything becomes potentially fungible. Neighborhoods become "markets." Hospitals become "delivery systems." Universities become "campuses" governed by metrics and outputs. Even churches increasingly imagine themselves as "spaces for programming" rather than as places of shared life. In each case, what is lost is not merely tradition or intimacy, but the capacity of place to generate non-optional moral claims.

David Harvey's analysis of neoliberalism as a project that privileges the mobility of capital while externalizing social cost clarifies the stakes of this transformation.[140] What appears as freedom of movement is often the freedom of institutions and capital to detach from responsibility. Corporations relocate. Supply chains shift. Platforms expand and contract. Meanwhile, embodied persons, whether workers, patients, or our neighbors, remain exposed to the consequences. Individuals are exhorted to be flexible and adaptable, while communities are rendered unstable and disposable. The result is a world in which people are highly mobile yet profoundly placeless: connected everywhere yet accountable nowhere.[141]

Neoliberal space functions as a technology of moral distancing. It allows suffering to remain elsewhere, out of sight, and therefore out of claim. Charity fits comfortably within abstract space because it preserves control and maintains distance. Donations can be routed through institutions, platforms, or campaigns without requiring proximity or transformation. Justice, by contrast, resists abstraction. Justice demands redistribution, structural change, and shared vulnerability. Justice requires place.

This is why the fear of beggars is inseparable from a fear of place itself. Beggars threaten not simply economic order but moral insulation. As M. Therese Lysaught's engagement with Paul Farmer demonstrates, abstract ethical frameworks often remain sincere yet complicit precisely because they refuse this exposure.[142] Abstract space allows the fortunate to remain morally concerned while structurally untouched.

Neoliberalism does not merely reorganize environments; it forms subjects. Abstract space trains moral perception. It habituates persons to think in terms of choice rather than obligation, access rather than belonging, efficiency rather than care. It renders dependence shameful and proximity risky. Over time, this spatial formation reshapes ethical intuition. Responsibility appears excessive. Claims feel intrusive. Beggars become threats rather than neighbors.

This is why the fear of beggars is not reducible to prejudice or ignorance. It is a learned moral affect produced by spatial arrangements that reward distance and penalize proximity. Neoliberal space teaches that well-being is a private achievement and that claims made by others are potential violations of autonomy. Place, by contrast, teaches that life is shared, that dependence is ordinary, and that obligation precedes choice. When persons are rooted in place, the suffering of others cannot easily be displaced or ignored. The beggar is no longer an anonymous disruption in a field of abstract movement but a neighbor whose need emerges from the same shared terrain of life.

For theological ethics, the neoliberal production of abstract space therefore poses a fundamental challenge. Christian moral traditions are irreducibly *placial*. The incarnation is not an abstraction but a taking-place, God dwelling in a particular body within a particular land among a particular people. Eucharist gathers bodies in specific locations where bread and wine bind persons into concrete forms of shared life. Parish, pilgrimage, hospitality, and neighbor-love all presume a world where responsibility emerges through proximity and cannot be indefinitely deferred. To erode place is therefore not only to weaken social solidarity but to undermine the grammar of Christian ethics itself.

The abstraction of land is never merely an economic phenomenon. As Willie James Jennings argues, modern Christianity became deeply implicated in the colonial project through a distorted social imagination that severed peoples from place while simultaneously teaching Christians to imagine land as an object available for possession, extraction, and control rather than as God's gift to be received in communion.[143] Colonialism did not simply produce racial hierarchy or territorial expansion; it reshaped Christian identity itself by disconnecting belonging from creaturely participation and embedding theology within habits of ownership, mastery, and displacement.[144] Rather than inhabiting creation as a shared gift, Western Christianity increasingly learned to inhabit the world through the grammar of possession.

Jennings, therefore, complicates any straightforward theological appeal to place. Place is indeed a locus of communion, memory, and creaturely dependence, yet Christian history demonstrates that appeals to place have also served to justify conquest, exclusion, and racial domination. Colonial Christianity repeatedly transformed belonging into possession and hospitality into ownership. The problem, therefore, is not attachment to place itself but the corruption of place through possessive desire. Land ceases to be received as gift and instead becomes property through which identity, power, and exclusion are secured.[145]

This insight significantly deepens the preferential option for the poor. Poverty is not simply the absence of material resources but is frequently the consequence of systematic displacement from the places in which communities have historically belonged. The poor are often those rendered landless, uprooted, environmentally vulnerable, or geographically expendable through the intersecting histories of colonialism, racialization, and economic exploitation. Land theft, forced migration, environmental racism, and extractive economies are therefore not secondary concerns but constitutive dimensions of contemporary poverty. A preferential option that neglects these histories risks treating poverty merely as economic deprivation while leaving unexamined the deeper patterns of dispossession that continually produce it.[146]

Jennings also offers an important theological caution for the constructive proposal advanced in this chapter. The recovery of place cannot become another romantic appeal to locality or rootedness, for belonging itself can become exclusion when detached from the reconciling work of Christ. Christian belonging is never grounded in possession but in participation within God's reconciled creation. It receives land as gift rather than property and neighbors as fellow creatures rather than competitors or intruders. The sacramental imagination developed throughout this study, therefore, seeks not merely a return to place but the healing of place through practices of hospitality, mutual dependence, and creaturely communion that resist both the colonial logic of possession and the neoliberal logic of commodification.[147]

Recovering place also clarifies the meaning of the church's preferential option for the poor. The poor are not abstract categories within global systems, but persons located within specific communities, neighborhoods, and ecologies. A placial ethics refuses the neoliberal tendency to treat poverty as a distant problem managed through technocratic solutions. Instead, it insists that the suffering of the poor confronts us within shared life. The beggar at the corner, the worker displaced from land, the family living near toxic waste or degraded soil; each reveals how poverty is inseparable from the places people inhabit.

For this reason, emphasizing place does more than recover the preferential option for the poor; it expands it. When theology begins with place rather than abstract space, the option for the poor necessarily becomes an option for the environments in which the poor live. Neoliberal abstraction treats land, water, and ecosystems as interchangeable resources, detachable from the communities that depend upon them. But the poor most often suffer first and most severely from environmental degradation, whether it's from polluted rivers, exhausted soil, collapsing fisheries, toxic air, or displaced habitats. To defend the poor while ignoring the destruction of the places that sustain their lives would be incoherent. A placial ethics, therefore, recognizes that care for the poor cannot be separated from care for the land, waters, and ecosystems that make life possible.

The sacramental life of the church deepens this insight. The Eucharist is not merely a symbolic act but a material gathering of bodies around elements drawn from the earth: grain and vine, soil and sun, labor and cultivation. These elements testify that human life is always embedded within ecological systems. The sacrament, therefore, refuses the neoliberal illusion that space is empty and infinitely exploitable. Instead, it reveals creation itself as a network of places where life is received rather than extracted. In this way, the Eucharist becomes not only a sign of solidarity with the poor but also a reminder that the flourishing of the poor depends upon the flourishing of the earth.

To resist neoliberalism, then, is not only to critique unjust policies or redistribute resources but to reclaim place as a moral and theological category. This requires renewed attention to where lives are lived, where suffering is borne, and where responsibility takes concrete form. It requires resisting the fantasy that ethical concern can be abstracted from location, embodiment, and material conditions. It also requires recognizing that the defense of human dignity and the defense of creation belong to the same moral horizon.

## The Meaning of the Preferential Option

Before concluding, it is important to clarify what is meant by the church's preferential option for the poor. Throughout this chapter, the option has been presented not as a sociological slogan or political strategy but as a theological orientation that shapes how Christians perceive God, neighbor, and the common life of the church. Yet this orientation encompasses several distinct, though inseparable, dimensions.

First, the preferential option possesses an *epistemic* significance. Those who experience poverty, exclusion, and displacement frequently perceive the distortions of social life with a clarity unavailable to those whose privilege insulates them from its consequences. This is not because suffering itself confers infallible knowledge or because the poor possess a privileged revelation inaccessible to others. Rather, social location discloses realities that dominant communities often fail to perceive. The cries of Israel in Egypt, the lament of the prophets, Mary's Magnificat, and the ministry of Jesus all testify that God repeatedly exposes the truth of unjust social orders through those who bear their burdens. The church, therefore, learns to see more truthfully when it learns to see from alongside those whose lives have been rendered vulnerable.

Second, the preferential option possesses *moral* significance. Christian love requires more than equal concern for all persons in the abstract; it demands particular attention to those whose lives are most threatened by violence, deprivation, or exclusion. Just as a physician devotes greater care to the gravely wounded without thereby valuing other patients less, so the church directs particular concern toward those whose flourishing has been most profoundly denied. The option for the poor is therefore not partiality against the wealthy but fidelity to the demands of justice.

Third, the preferential option possesses a *theological* significance. Scripture consistently reveals that God identifies with those whom the world disregards. This does not mean that God is absent from the lives of the wealthy or that poverty itself possesses redemptive value. Poverty is an evil to be overcome, not a condition to be romanticized. Rather, God freely chooses to reveal the divine solidarity through the vulnerable, the oppressed, and the forgotten because such revelation exposes both the depth of human sin and the character of divine mercy. The incarnation itself discloses this pattern. In Jesus Christ, God does not merely act *for* the poor but enters fully into the conditions of human vulnerability, receiving creaturely dependence and exposing the false securities upon which human societies so often rely.

Finally, the preferential option possesses an *ecclesial* significance. The poor are not simply recipients of the church's ministry but indispensable members of Christ's body whose gifts, witness, and participation are necessary for the church's own faithfulness. A church that ministers to the poor without receiving from them has misunderstood both charity and communion. The preferential option, therefore, culminates not in philanthropy but in solidarity—in communities where distinctions between benefactor and beneficiary are overcome through shared participation in the life of Christ.

Taken together, these dimensions reveal that the preferential option for the poor is neither merely epistemic, nor simply moral, nor exclusively theological. It is a Christological orientation that orders the church's perception, moral life, worship, and common existence. The poor do not replace Christ as the source of revelation; rather, because Christ has freely identified himself with "the least of these," the church encounters its Lord precisely where it learns to receivethe lives of the poor not as objects of ministry but as members of the communion into which all are graciously called. The option for the poor is therefore not ultimately an option at all. It is the concrete form that participation in the life of Jesus Christ necessarily assumes within a world fractured by sin, exclusion, and inequality.

## Conclusion

The trajectory traced in this chapter reveals that the preferential option for the poor cannot remain confined to social analysis or charitable intention alone. As liberation theology has increasingly recognized, the structures that produce poverty also devastate the Earth, binding human suffering and ecological destruction together within a single logic of domination. To extend the preferential option to creation is therefore not to shift attention away from the poor but to name more truthfully the conditions under which their lives are threatened. The ecological turn clarifies that care for the poor and care for the Earth are not competing priorities but mutually implicating demands.

In an age of neoliberalism, this expanded option takes on heightened significance. Neoliberal rationality fragments reality, isolates crises, and treats both people and ecosystems as expendable when they fail to serve market efficiency. Against this backdrop, an ecological preferential option functions as a theological refusal of abstraction. It insists that justice must be measured not by growth or profitability but by the flourishing of the most vulnerable, human and nonhuman alike.

By naming the Earth as among "the most abandoned and maltreated of the poor," liberation theology exposes the moral cost of economic systems that externalize suffering and displace responsibility.

Yet the force of this claim cannot remain at the level of theory alone. If the inclusion of the Earth within the preferential option for the poor is to shape Christian life meaningfully, it must be sustained by concrete practices. What is required are ecclesial, economic, and sacramental practices that make visible the interdependence of human life and creation. Without such practices, the expanded option risks remaining an aspiration rather than a lived orientation.

These practices must resist neoliberal patterns of consumption, extraction, and disposability while cultivating varying modes of solidarity. They must shape communities that learn to hear both cries, the cry of the poor *and* the cry of the Earth. In this sense, the future of the preferential option depends not only on its conceptual expansion but on its embodiment within forms of life that witness to another way of inhabiting the world.

The task that remains is therefore constructive, as well as critical. Having traced how liberation theology arrives at the inclusion of creation within its core commitments, the question now becomes: how might Christian communities practice this truth? The option for the poor, extended to the Earth, calls for disciplines, liturgies, economies, and patterns of common life that render justice tangible and hope credible. Only through such practices can the theological insight articulated here become a durable form of Christian witness in a wounded world.

## Notes

1. See Philip Shenon, *Jesus Wept: Seven Popes and the Battle for the Soul of the Catholic Church* (Knopf, 2025).

2. Luis N. Rivera-Pagán, "Karl Barth and the Origins of Liberation Theology," in *Karl Barth and Liberation Theology*, ed. Kaitlyn Dugan and Paul Dafydd Jones (T&T Clark, 2022), 16.

3. Rivera-Pagán, "Karl Barth and the Origins of Liberation Theology," 16.

4. Rivera-Pagán, "Karl Barth and the Origins of Liberation Theology," 16.

5. Rivera-Pagán, "Karl Barth and the Origins of Liberation Theology," 16.

6. Rivera-Pagán, "Karl Barth and the Origins of Liberation Theology," 16.

7. Rivera-Pagán, "Karl Barth and the Origins of Liberation Theology," 16.

8. Rivera-Pagán, "Karl Barth and the Origins of Liberation Theology," 17.

9. Rivera-Pagán, "Karl Barth and the Origins of Liberation Theology," 17.

10. Rivera-Pagán, "Karl Barth and the Origins of Liberation Theology," 17.

11. Rivera-Pagán, "Karl Barth and the Origins of Liberation Theology," 18.

12. Rivera-Pagán, "Karl Barth and the Origins of Liberation Theology," 18.

13. Rivera-Pagán, "Karl Barth and the Origins of Liberation Theology," 18.

14. Rivera-Pagán, "Karl Barth and the Origins of Liberation Theology," 18.

15. Rivera-Pagán, "Karl Barth and the Origins of Liberation Theology," 19.

16. Rivera-Pagán, "Karl Barth and the Origins of Liberation Theology," 19.

17. Rivera-Pagán, "Karl Barth and the Origins of Liberation Theology," 19.

18. Rivera-Pagán, "Karl Barth and the Origins of Liberation Theology," 19.

19. Rivera-Pagán, "Karl Barth and the Origins of Liberation Theology," 19.

20. Rivera-Pagán, "Karl Barth and the Origins of Liberation Theology," 19.

21. Rivera-Pagán, "Karl Barth and the Origins of Liberation Theology," 24.

22. Rivera-Pagán, "Karl Barth and the Origins of Liberation Theology," 24.

23. Rivera-Pagán, "Karl Barth and the Origins of Liberation Theology," 23.

24. Rivera-Pagán, "Karl Barth and the Origins of Liberation Theology," 24.

25. Rivera-Pagán, "Karl Barth and the Origins of Liberation Theology," 24.

26. Rivera-Pagán, "Karl Barth and the Origins of Liberation Theology," 24.

27. Rivera-Pagán, "Karl Barth and the Origins of Liberation Theology," 24.

28. Rivera-Pagán, "Karl Barth and the Origins of Liberation Theology," 25.

29. Rivera-Pagán, "Karl Barth and the Origins of Liberation Theology," 25.

30. Rivera-Pagán, "Karl Barth and the Origins of Liberation Theology," 25.

31. Rivera-Pagán, "Karl Barth and the Origins of Liberation Theology," 25.

32. Rivera-Pagán, "Karl Barth and the Origins of Liberation Theology," 25.

33. Rivera-Pagán, "Karl Barth and the Origins of Liberation Theology," 25.

34. Rivera-Pagán, "Karl Barth and the Origins of Liberation Theology," 16.

35. Rivera-Pagán, "Karl Barth and the Origins of Liberation Theology," 16.

36. Rivera-Pagán, "Karl Barth and the Origins of Liberation Theology," 16.

37. Rivera-Pagán, "Karl Barth and the Origins of Liberation Theology," 19–20.

38. Rivera-Pagán, "Karl Barth and the Origins of Liberation Theology," 20.

39. Rivera-Pagán, "Karl Barth and the Origins of Liberation Theology," 20.

40. Rivera-Pagán, "Karl Barth and the Origins of Liberation Theology," 20.

41. Rivera-Pagán, "Karl Barth and the Origins of Liberation Theology," 20.

42. Rivera-Pagán, "Karl Barth and the Origins of Liberation Theology," 20.

43. Rivera-Pagán, "Karl Barth and the Origins of Liberation Theology," 20.

44. Rivera-Pagán, "Karl Barth and the Origins of Liberation Theology," 20.

45. Rivera-Pagán, "Karl Barth and the Origins of Liberation Theology," 24.

46. Rivera-Pagán, "Karl Barth and the Origins of Liberation Theology," 21.

47. Rivera-Pagán, "Karl Barth and the Origins of Liberation Theology," 21.

48. Rivera-Pagán, "Karl Barth and the Origins of Liberation Theology," 21.

49. Rivera-Pagán, "Karl Barth and the Origins of Liberation Theology," 21.

50. Rivera-Pagán, "Karl Barth and the Origins of Liberation Theology," 22.

51. Rivera-Pagán, "Karl Barth and the Origins of Liberation Theology," 22.

52. Rivera-Pagán, "Karl Barth and the Origins of Liberation Theology," 22.

53. Rivera-Pagán, "Karl Barth and the Origins of Liberation Theology," 22.

54. Rivera-Pagán, "Karl Barth and the Origins of Liberation Theology," 21.

55. Rivera-Pagán, "Karl Barth and the Origins of Liberation Theology," 22.

56. Rivera-Pagán, "Karl Barth and the Origins of Liberation Theology," 22.

57. Gustavo Gutiérrez, *A Theology of Liberation: History, Politics, and Salvation*, rev. ed., trans. Sister Caridad Inda and John Eagleson (Orbis Books, 1988), 45–49.

58. Gutiérrez, *A Theology of Liberation*, 28.

59. Gutiérrez, *A Theology of Liberation*, 49–52.

60. Gutiérrez, *A Theology of Liberation*, 49–56.

61. Gutiérrez, *A Theology of Liberation*, 45–47.

62. Gutiérrez, *A Theology of Liberation*, 55–66, 123–145.

63. Gutiérrez, *A Theology of Liberation*, 55–62; 64–66.
64. Gutiérrez, *A Theology of Liberation*, 55–66; 123–145.
65. Gutiérrez, *A Theology of Liberation*, 55–63.
66. Gutiérrez, *A Theology of Liberation*, 77–88.
67. Gutiérrez, *A Theology of Liberation*, 77–84.
68. Gutiérrez, *A Theology of Liberation*, 81–83.
69. Gutiérrez, *A Theology of Liberation*, 81–86.
70. Gutiérrez, *A Theology of Liberation*, 121.
71. Gutiérrez, *A Theology of Liberation*, 120–123.
72. Gutiérrez, *A Theology of Liberation*, 156–160.
73. Gutiérrez, *A Theology of Liberation*, 156–163.
74. Gutiérrez, *A Theology of Liberation*, 145.
75. Gutiérrez, *A Theology of Liberation*, 145–147.
76. Gutiérrez, *A Theology of Liberation*, 197.
77. Gutiérrez, *A Theology of Liberation*, 19.
78. Gutiérrez, *A Theology of Liberation*, 19–20.
79. Gutiérrez, *A Theology of Liberation*, 19.
80. Gutiérrez, *A Theology of Liberation*, 19.
81. Gutiérrez, *A Theology of Liberation*, 19.
82. Gutiérrez, *A Theology of Liberation*, 19.
83. Gutiérrez, *A Theology of Liberation*, 19.
84. Gutiérrez, *A Theology of Liberation*, 20.
85. Gutiérrez, *A Theology of Liberation*, 20.
86. Gutiérrez, *A Theology of Liberation*, 19–20.
87. Gutiérrez, *A Theology of Liberation*, 20.
88. Gutiérrez, *A Theology of Liberation*, 20.
89. Gutiérrez, *A Theology of Liberation*, 20.
90. Gutiérrez, *A Theology of Liberation*, 20.
91. Gutiérrez, *A Theology of Liberation*, 20.
92. Gutiérrez, *A Theology of Liberation*, 20.

93. Gutiérrez, *A Theology of Liberation*, 39.
94. Gutiérrez, *A Theology of Liberation*, 191.
95. Gutiérrez, *A Theology of Liberation*, 191.
96. Gutiérrez, *A Theology of Liberation*, 106.
97. Gutiérrez, *A Theology of Liberation*, 106.
98. Gutiérrez, *A Theology of Liberation*, 106.
99. Gutiérrez, *A Theology of Liberation*, 195.
100. Gutiérrez, *A Theology of Liberation*, 195.
101. Gutiérrez, *A Theology of Liberation*, 19–20; 195.
102. Gutiérrez, *A Theology of Liberation*, 195. Cf. 20.
103. Gutiérrez, *A Theology of Liberation*, 195.
104. Gutiérrez, *A Theology of Liberation*, 19–20; 191; 195.
105. Gutiérrez, *A Theology of Liberation*, 191; 195.
106. Gutiérrez, *A Theology of Liberation*, 19.
107. Gutiérrez, *A Theology of Liberation*, 20.
108. Gutiérrez, *A Theology of Liberation*, 20.
109. Gutiérrez, *A Theology of Liberation*, 191.
110. Gutiérrez, *A Theology of Liberation*, 161.
111. Gutiérrez, *A Theology of Liberation*, 195.
112. Francis, *Laudato Si': On Care for Our Common Home* (Libreria Editrice Vaticana, 2015), §2.
113. Francis, *Laudato Si'*, §13.
114. Francis, *Laudato Si'*, §5.
115. Francis, *Laudato Si'*, §158.
116. Leonardo Boff, *Cry of the Earth, Cry of the Poor* (Orbis Books, 1997).
117. Boff, *Cry of the Earth, Cry of the Poor, 11.*
118. Boff, *Cry of the Earth, Cry of the Poor,* 11.
119. Boff, *Cry of the Earth, Cry of the Poor,* 136.
120. Boff, *Cry of the Earth, Cry of the Poor,* 136.

121. Boff, *Cry of the Earth, Cry of the Poor*, 142.
122. Boff, *Cry of the Earth, Cry of the Poor*, 142.
123. Boff, *Cry of the Earth, Cry of the Poor*, 142.
124. Boff, *Cry of the Earth, Cry of the Poor*, 142.
125. Boff, *Cry of the Earth, Cry of the Poor*, 142.
126. Boff, *Cry of the Earth, Cry of the Poor*, 134.
127. Boff, *Cry of the Earth, Cry of the Poor*, 166.
128. Boff, *Cry of the Earth, Cry of the Poor*, 144.
129. Boff, *Cry of the Earth, Cry of the Poor*, 144.
130. Delores S. Williams, *Sisters in the Wilderness: The Challenge of Womanist God-Talk* (Orbis Books, 1993), 19–36, 161–67.
131. Ada María Isasi-Díaz, *Mujerista Theology: A Theology for the Twenty-First Century* (Orbis Books, 1996), 67–92.
132. M. Shawn Copeland, *Enfleshing Freedom: Body, Race, and Being* (Fortress Press, 2010), 87–115.
133. Nancy L. Eiesland, *The Disabled God: Toward a Liberatory Theology of Disability* (Abingdon Press, 1994), 89–103.
134. John Swinton, *Becoming Friends of Time: Disability, Timefulness, and Gentle Discipleship* (Baylor University Press, 2016), 93–122.
135. Amos Yong, *The Bible, Disability, and the Church: A New Vision of the People of God* (Eerdmans, 2011), 27–54.
136. Alexander Weheliye, *Habeas Viscus: Racializing Assemblages, Biopolitics and Black Feminist Theories of the Human.* (Duke University Press, 2014), 43.
137. Edward S. Casey, *Getting Back into Place: Toward a Renewed Understanding of the Place-World* (Indiana University Press, 1993), 9–15.
138. Yi-Fu Tuan, *Space and Place: The Perspective of Experience* (University of Minnesota Press, 1977), 6–12, 136–148.
139. Henri Lefebvre, *The Production of Space*, trans. Donald Nicholson-Smith (Oxford: Blackwell, 1991), 49–53, 285–291.

140. Harvey, *A Brief History of Neoliberalism*, 65–98.

141. This critique should not be read as rejecting abstraction, mobility, or markets as such. Each has generated genuine goods, including scientific cooperation, legal universality, innovation, migration, and economic opportunity. The concern throughout this chapter is with their absolutization into anthropological and theological norms that subordinate creaturely relationships to the logic of efficiency, exchange, and accumulation. Likewise, although this chapter foregrounds neoliberalism, this emphasis is intended to complement rather than displace the histories of settler colonialism, racial capitalism, and nationalist expansion that also shaped modern economic life.

142. M. Therese Lysaught, "Liberating Theological Ethics from the Invisible Hand: Paul Farmer, the World's Poor, and the Quandaries of the Fortunate," *Journal of Moral Theology* 4, (2023): 3–28, https://doi.org/10.55476/001c.71376.

143. Willie James Jennings, *The Christian Imagination: Theology and the Origins of Race* (Yale University Press, 2010), 6–11, 15–22.

144. Jennings, *The Christian Imagination*, 7–10, 15–22.

145. Jennings, *The Christian Imagination*, 250–67.

146. Jennings, *The Christian Imagination*, 250–67. See also George E. Tinker, *Missionary Conquest: The Gospel and Native American Cultural Genocide* (Fortress Press, 1993), 3–27; Randy S. Woodley, *Shalom and the Community of Creation: An Indigenous Vision* (Eerdmans, 2012), 17–46.

147. Jennings, *The Christian Imagination*, 289–94.

## CHAPTER 3

# Sacrament as Currency: A Genealogy of Eucharistic Exchange

Christian theology has long insisted that salvation is a gift, as grace is given freely and not earned. Yet across the history of Christian thought and practice, this insistence has repeatedly coexisted with, and at times quietly depended upon, abstract systems of exchange that translate divine life into measurable forms of value. These systems rarely announce themselves as economic. Rather, they emerge through theological concepts meant to safeguard mystery: *oikonomia*, incarnation, sacrifice, honor, election, and purity. Over time, these concepts generate logics of circulation, profit, and comparison that shape not only how Christians imagine God, but how they organize bodies, labor, sexuality, and social belonging. At the center of these logics stands the Eucharist, ostensibly the sacrament of gift, which is repeatedly burdened with the work of underwriting value, identity, and communal legitimacy.

This chapter traces a genealogy of Christian theology's participation in exchange logics by following how *oikonomia* evolves from a term of household management into a governing theological rationality. What begins as an attempt to hold together divine transcendence and immanence gradually becomes a framework for imagining what this book calls *durable networks*: forms of relationship and mutual belonging that endure through shared commitments rather than contractual exchange. The concept first emerges in the life of the Triune God, extends into the church as a community of covenantal fellowship, and ultimately provides a way of envisioning political and economic life ordered toward solidarity rather than disposability. As this genealogy unfolds, Christ himself comes to function as a form of currency: first as divine capital whose incarnation sets value in motion, then as blood whose circulation binds communities and marks their borders, and later as moral proof whose benefits must be demonstrated through productivity, discipline, or purity.

The Eucharist repeatedly emerges as the privileged site where these abstract systems of exchange are ritualized. Whether through coin, blood, honor, or moral capital, the sacrament becomes a mechanism for translating divine life into socially legible value. Participation promises access to the "durable network" of salvation, while exclusion marks bodies as impure, unprofitable, or disposable. In this way, the Eucharist does not merely symbolize unity; it often functions as the hinge upon which belonging, hierarchy, and violence turn.

By following these logics from early trinitarian theology through medieval blood economies, Reformation moral accounting, and contemporary evangelical purity culture, this chapter does not argue that Christianity simply *caused* neoliberalism. Rather, it shows how theological attempts to secure order, meaning, and mediation repeatedly generate abstractions that lend themselves to economic capture. The result is not a single origin story but a recurring pattern: theology, in seeking to render divine life governable, produces systems of exchange that render human life comparable, profitable, and expendable. The Eucharist, meant to interrupt such systems, is instead enlisted to sanctify them.

Before considering the relationship between sacramentality and commodification, an important conceptual clarification is necessary. Throughout this chapter, I argue that the Eucharist resists the commodifying logic of neoliberalism because it forms persons through gift rather than exchange. Such a claim, however, should not be understood as opposing every form of reciprocity, obligation, gratitude, or mutuality. Christian theology has rarely understood these realities as corruptions of gift. On the contrary, they are often the very means by which gift achieves its proper end.

The distinction developed throughout this chapter is therefore not between gift and response, but between *gift ordered toward communion* and *exchange ordered toward equivalence*. Every genuine gift calls forth a response. The Eucharist itself is named from *eucharistia*—thanksgiving—because God's gracious self-giving necessarily evokes praise, gratitude, and participation. The problem is not reciprocity as such but reciprocity governed by calculation. Exchange becomes commodifying when gifts are evaluated according to equivalence, utility, debt, or accumulation. In such economies, the recipient remains obligated to restore balance through repayment, thereby transforming the relationship into a transaction.

Christian gift operates according to a fundamentally different grammar. Divine grace can never be repaid because it is not given in order to create indebted consumers but to form participants in God's own life. Gratitude, therefore, is not repayment. Thanksgiving does not complete the gift by restoring equivalence; it receives the gift by participating more deeply within the communion that the gift itself establishes. Likewise, mutual obligation is not inherently opposed to grace. Christians genuinely owe one another love, forgiveness, hospitality, and service, yet these obligations arise not from contractual exchange but from participation in Christ's reconciling life. The language of covenant, sacrifice, and ecclesial communion, therefore, belongs not to an economy of scarcity but to an economy of superabundant gift.

This distinction also clarifies the use of economic language throughout this chapter. Christian theology has long employed metaphors drawn from debt, redemption, sacrifice, purchase, and exchange in order to articulate aspects of salvation. Such language is neither discarded nor rejected here. Rather, this study argues that these metaphors function analogically rather than literally. They illuminate particular dimensions of God's saving work without determining its deepest logic. The governing grammar of Christian existence is not economic exchange but participation. Economic language remains theologically fruitful insofar as it serves this deeper sacramental reality. It becomes problematic only when market rationality ceases to function as an analogy and instead becomes the organizing principle through which grace itself is imagined.

## Early Christian *Oikonomia*: A Genealogy of the Trinity and Economic

Wealth and the desire for it have existed in every age of human history, but recent studies uncover the Christian metaphysics of wealth embedded in our theology from the beginning and extending to the present day. Furthermore, the language of wealth bequeathed to the West relied heavily on the codification of profit discovered in the account of neoliberalism in chapter 1. However, the execution of neoliberal power through monetary capital in the praxis of governmentality. In short, the theological origin of neoliberalism creates a never-ending desire for profit amid a coordinate desire for the divine.

Though I will narrate much more of this account below, I want to briefly acknowledge how genealogy works through the term *oikonomia*. Recalling Aristotle, the ancient Greeks recognized that the well-ordered home contributed to the well-ordered state and vice versa. Foucault, Kotsko, and others all recognize that the great emphasis placed on the structures of the *oikonomia* (i.e., the economic), not only in and for themselves but also to construct a broader discourse on politics, causes immense historical distress.

Agamben, through a genealogy of the economic, recognizes the importance of *oikonomia* as a chief concept that helps early Christians organize their thoughts about God as Trinity. However, this concept also energizes early Christian economic thinking. As Agamben recognizes, early Christian depictions of the Trinity include a God who is transcendent but who nonetheless becomes immanent. This is paradoxical and must be overcome to fit early Christian witness. According to Agamben, *oikonomia* is a crucial term for describing the incarnation and God's ability to be both transcendent and immanent, synthesized into a single *oikonomia*.[1] Thus, *oikonomia* became an inherently political theo-logic that not only harmonizes the creation in the oneness of the Godhead, but also harmonizes a diverse community into one *oikonomia* of people.[2]

The unity of diverse people won through the Father and Son exists, according to Agamben, as an activity of the Son on behalf of the Father to establish the Father's rule in the world. This distinction and union of the work of the Father and Son signal a larger point for Agamben. He presents the work of the Son in the absence of the Father as the impotence of the Father. To be clear, this is a perception that Agamben draws through interpreting 1 Corinthians 15:24 and other texts that emphasize the Son's presence in creation through the incarnation. The Son is the only person of the Godhead to become incarnate and, therefore, seemingly present in creation. The conception of rule as structured through presence and absence possesses a long intellectual and theological history. Drawing an analogy from Arthurian studies, Agamben discusses the impotence of the Fisher King, who, being so badly mutilated and injured, cannot directly participate in the governance of his kingdom.[3] Much like the Fisher King, the Father, according to Agamben, must rely on the ministry of Christ to carry out his will in the kingdom.

In this framework, durable networks of relation are understood through a logic of exchange rooted in the trinitarian *oikonomia* and materialized through practices of currency, circulation, and reciprocal obligation. The perfect triune community enters creation by incarnation. The use of *oikonomia,* as with Gregory of Nazianzus, signals a means of relation. However, Devin Singh has noted that historically, *oikonomia* "is tied to the management of material resources in the household and money outside the *oikos*."[4] To conceive of the Godhead through the category of *oikonomia* is to introduce a logic of ordered administration that governs both the internal relations of the Trinity and God's external activity toward creation.

Singh specifies that the transition from the triune *oikonomia* to the worldly *oikonomia* occurs through the redemption offered by the former.[5] In salvation, creation gains access to the inner trinitarian life (i.e., durable network). In various ways, many early church salvation narratives rely on a payment of some kind made on God's behalf to redeem humanity. In response, there is an expectation of a return upon this payment through salvation of the world, namely a profit.[6] Once welcomed into the durable network, humanity must participate in the means of exchange by embodying the network through almsgiving, care for the poor, and even the structure of government and the economy.[7] Therefore, *oikonomia* fully embodies the durable network itself while also providing a means to participate in it. As Singh writes, "the heavenly Logos and administrator, associated with precious material resources, the image of God and the redemption of the material world, will become the stuff of economy itself as its chief currency."[8]

In short, through Christ's redemptive exchange with humanity, creation is drawn into the work of salvation. By participating in this triune, durable communion, human beings receive redemption from sin and are invited to embody in their own material and economic practices the self-giving pattern of divine generosity. Christ is currency and the highest virtue toward which human currency strives. Thus, Singh argues that articulating the doctrine of the Trinity and redemption leads to a "sacralization" of a particular economic order.[9]

The Eucharist stands at the center of this order. In one reading, shaped by the genealogical arc traced above, the Eucharist can appear as a site of sacred transaction. Christ's body is offered; believers receive; a return is expected in obedience, piety, and moral performance. The altar becomes a place where divine capital is distributed, and the faithful participate in the durable network of salvation through ritualized exchange. Even when not articulated crudely, a subtle logic persists that grace is received in order that something might be generated—growth, virtue, expansion, return. But sacramental theology, at its deepest, resists precisely this logic.

The Eucharist is not a transaction. It is not an exchange of equivalents. It is not the circulation of divine currency that expects profit. It is a sheer, unmerited, non-reciprocal gift. The body of Christ is not a divine capital placed into motion to generate measurable return. It is broken bread given "for you." It is not a management of resources but a self-giving that refuses calculation. If neoliberalism sacralizes exchange, the Eucharist desacralizes it.

David Graeber's *Debt: The First 5,000 Years* sharpens this concern by showing how deeply the language of debt penetrates moral, religious, and political life. Graeber's central claim is that debt is more than an economic instrument but a moral grammar through which human beings come to understand obligation itself. When economic exchange becomes the dominant framework for understanding social relations, Graeber argues that it inevitably shapes religious imagination as well. If human life is interpreted through the lens of commercial calculation, then humanity will begin to interpret its relationship with the divine in the same way. As Graeber observes, once people assume that "buying and selling are the basis of human society," they will also begin "to think about our relationship with the cosmos in similar terms." In such a world, one will "necessarily conceive of it in terms of debt."[10] This insight is crucial for theological reflection on sacramentality within neoliberal conditions. If exchange becomes the dominant grammar of social life, then divine–human relations risk being interpreted according to the same logic. Grace becomes credit, salvation becomes repayment, and worship becomes the ritual management of an obligation that cannot be discharged. The danger Graeber exposes is that economic language does not remain metaphorical. Instead, it gradually becomes the governing imagination of moral life. When this occurs, religious practices themselves may begin to function as mechanisms that reproduce the logic of debt rather than interrupt it.

Graeber presses this concern most clearly in his discussion of Christian language surrounding redemption. He notes how striking it is that "the very core of the Christian message, salvation itself, the sacrifice of God's own son to rescue humanity from eternal damnation, should be framed in the language of a financial transaction."[11] Graeber does not claim that Christianity is reducible to financial thinking; rather, he argues that religious traditions emerged in historical contexts where disputes about money, obligation, and justice were pervasive. Consequently, economic language often provided the conceptual framework through which religious communities articulated the meaning of sin and redemption. Yet here lies the theological risk. Once redemption is habitually imagined as payment, salvation itself may be received less as a divine gift than as the settlement of an account. The logic of the market threatens to become the interpretive key of divine action.

Long before contemporary critiques of neoliberalism and economic abstraction, Friedrich Nietzsche recognized the extent to which morality itself had become entangled with the logic of debt, exchange, and punishment. In *On the Genealogy of Morals*, Nietzsche argues that moral categories do not emerge from timeless rational principles or transcendent truths, but from historical relations of power shaped by domination, resentment, and economic obligation.[12] Morality, particularly in its modern form, emerges through the transformation of material indebtedness into spiritual and psychological guilt. The German word *schuld*, Nietzsche famously notes, means both "debt" and "guilt," revealing the extent to which moral consciousness is genealogically bound to economic relations.[13]

For Nietzsche, the creditor-debtor relationship becomes one of the foundational structures through which human beings learn memory, obligation, and punishment. The debtor who cannot repay becomes subject to violence, humiliation, and symbolic extraction. Punishment originally functions not as moral correction but as compensation and pleasure for the injured party.[14] In this sense, morality is not initially concerned with justice in an abstract or universal sense, but with systems of equivalence, repayment, and retribution. What later becomes internalized as conscience or guilt begins as a relation of calculability and exchange.

Nietzsche's insight is significant because it exposes the extent to which modern moral systems remain structured by economic imaginaries even when they appear secularized or universalized. The moral subject becomes one who perpetually owes, one whose existence is interpreted through the lens of deficiency and repayment. This dynamic intensifies with the rise of Christianity as Nietzsche understands it, where guilt becomes infinite before an infinite God. Humanity becomes incapable of repaying the debt incurred by sin, producing what Nietzsche describes as the "bad conscience," an inward turn of violence against the self.[15] The result is a moral psychology rooted in ressentiment, self-surveillance, and perpetual indebtedness.

While Nietzsche's critique of Christianity is often crude and reductionistic and fails to account for the radical interruption of grace within the Christian tradition, his genealogy nevertheless remains illuminating for understanding the hidden metaphysics of modern economic life. The moralization of debt does not disappear with secularization. Rather, it becomes intensified within capitalist modernity. Economic relations increasingly shape not only markets but the very structure of personhood. Human beings come to understand themselves through productivity, optimization, utility, and measurable worth. The indebted self becomes the normative self.

Nietzsche thus anticipates later critiques of capitalism by revealing how systems of exchange colonize moral consciousness itself. The neoliberal subject is not merely economically indebted but existentially indebted, constantly seeking self-justification through labor, efficiency, and self-management. In this way, morality becomes inseparable from administration. The self is transformed into a project of endless repayment. Even virtue becomes intelligible through economic metaphors of investment, accumulation, and return.

At this point, David Graeber's analysis becomes particularly illuminating. Where Nietzsche traces the psychological and moral genealogy of guilt and indebtedness, Graeber demonstrates how debt functions historically and anthropologically as a mechanism of social organization and domination. Together, they reveal that debt is never merely economic. It is theological, moral, political, and deeply formative of human identity.

Graeber further illuminates this dynamic through his engagement with Nietzsche's genealogy of guilt and debt. Graeber explains that when early human communities imagined themselves indebted to their ancestors or to divine powers, sacrifice became the primary means through which they attempted to repay this obligation. Yet because the debt to the divine is infinite, no sacrifice can ever finally suffice. As Graeber notes, in this account "no sacrifice (not even the sacrifice of our first-born) will ever truly redeem us."[16] Christianity, in Nietzsche's reading, radicalizes this logic by presenting God as the one who ultimately pays the debt owed to God. Graeber writes that "a sense of debt is transformed into an abiding sense of guilt, and guilt to self-loathing, and self-loathing to self-torture."[17] Such an account bears directly on sacramental theology. If redemption is governed by the imagination of debt, then eucharistic practice can easily be drawn into a cycle not of thanksgiving but of managed guilt. The eucharistic table becomes the site where the believer repeatedly returns, still owing. Participation in the sacrament is then understood as reception of a benefit made possible by an infinite payment that one could never provide. The communicant receives grace precisely because another has satisfied the obligation on their behalf.

Graeber's treatment of biblical redemption further clarifies this dynamic. He notes that the language of redemption in the Hebrew Scriptures originally referred to concrete social practices in which persons or property were liberated from debt bondage.[18] In this context, redemption meant release from obligation, not merely the payment of a debt. Indeed, Graeber observes that the biblical vision of final redemption imagines a moment when "all slates are wiped clean, and all debts finally lifted."[19] This insight leads him to a striking conclusion: if redemption is understood in its deepest biblical sense, then "'redemption' is no longer about buying something back. It's more a matter of destroying the entire system of accounting."[20]

For sacramental theology, this observation is crucial. If redemption ultimately abolishes the ledger rather than balancing it, then the Eucharist ought to function as a sign of the end of calculation rather than its continuation. Yet under the pressure of an economic imagination, the opposite can occur. The Eucharist can become the liturgical preservation of divine accounting: the place where the cost of redemption is continually remembered and where the believer is reminded of the debt that Christ has paid.

Graeber's reading of the parable of the unforgiving servant illustrates the impossibility of imagining divine–human relations as reciprocal exchange. In the parable, the servant owes the king an impossibly large sum, so vast that it represents "a sum no human being could ever, conceivably, repay."[21] Graeber observes that the story reveals a deeper truth about sovereignty and obligation: "Kings, like gods, can't really enter into relations of exchange with their subjects, since no parity is possible."[22] If no parity exists between God and humanity, then any sacramental practice that imagines communion as a reciprocal settlement is already theologically distorted. Yet this distortion becomes increasingly plausible in a social world governed by the logic of neoliberal exchange. The Eucharist risks becoming the ritual acknowledgment of humanity's permanent indebtedness before the divine sovereign.

When placed alongside the genealogies of Agamben and Singh, Graeber's analysis becomes even more illuminating. If the trinitarian *oikonomia* can be interpreted as a structure of managed relations and if the Son can be imagined as the currency through which divine value circulates, then the Eucharist becomes one of the primary sites where such a logic is enacted. Bread and wine may come to function not merely as signs of divine generosity but as tokens within a sacred economy. The sacrament thus trains desire according to the logic of debt. One approaches the table not only in gratitude but in recognition of what has been paid and what remains owed. Thanksgiving becomes intertwined with obligation, and the sacrament subtly reinforces the idea that humanity exists in a permanent state of indebtedness to God.

Yet Graeber also gestures toward a theological alternative. If redemption ultimately entails the destruction of the ledger rather than its maintenance, then sacramental life cannot finally be grounded in the logic of repayment. As Graeber writes, "paying one's debts is not the essence of morality."[23] The Eucharist, therefore, stands at a crossroads. It can be interpreted as the ritualization of divine–human debt, confirming the believer as one who lives from borrowed grace. Or it can be received as the sacramental sign of jubilee, the moment in which the accounting system itself is abolished, and divine gift replaces the logic of exchange.

## Blood: A Medieval Capital

There has been a debate between Singh and Heather Ohaneson over the significance of blood in church history. Singh provides a necessary critique of the early Christian economy that must temper all uncritical readings of the early trinitarian dogma. However, one can find Singh's divine currency beyond the realm of coin and in other periods of Christian history. If genealogy uncovers hidden power relations without final concern for origins, it is possible to locate these relations elsewhere.

One such place is in the medieval emphasis on blood currency. As Heather Ohaneson recognizes, coin is not the only image of redemption offered in the Christian tradition. Quoting 1 Peter 1:18–19, Ohaneson argues that Singh emphasizes to his detriment the economy of coin, when the economy of blood was far more ubiquitous in theology. She writes, "the contrast between Christ's blood and the perishability of profane metal implies that the value of Christ's blood is linked to its eternal power, which far outlasts and outstrips the most durable earthly substance."[24] This possibility is not outside Singh's view. He responds to this criticism by clarifying that currency, and for that matter capital, exists in many forms, and that one of the most ancient forms of currency is blood.[25] Sacrifice is the life exchanged in order to cleanse sinners from inequity. Though both Singh and Ohaneson highlight a few early church resources on blood, the medieval church is the best place to explore the blood currency that informs a non-coin form of capital.

The medieval church exists at its zenith of church power, an extra-territorial entity that the pope operates as a political power and wields the ability to mobilize armies toward the defense of Christendom. Blood, thus, plays a crucial metaphor in the medieval church as it emerges as a metaphor that binds together the burgeoning nation-states in Europe and the logic that undergirds the life of the crusader. The reason blood serves as such a crucial currency, according to scholar of religion Gil Anidjar, is that it energizes capital through one crucial living metaphor, namely circulation. This metaphor at once draws the imagination into the place of blood through the circulatory system and how value moves through an economic system. In Anidjar's description, circulation involves an entire process of movement independent of the individual.[26] In short, circulation prefigures meaning before humans come to recognize it.

Circulation resembles the module of liquidation. Briefly, liquidation is the convertibility of assets into currency. The blood of an individual already exists in the bloodstream as a liquid asset more precious than any commodity. It is life itself. However, blood plays a far more influential role in signifying social roles, a fact that becomes more evident in the early modern period. As Thomas Hobbes established, blood is a communal commodity that serves as the background and basis of political and economic communities.[27] Blood, therefore, is more of a cultural metaphor that divides communities according to belonging to kinship (Anidjar's term for nation). Though all cultures traded and exchanged across kinship lines, blood is a means to bracket, as Anidjar writes, "blood [that] counts – and. . .bloods that count less."[28] In short, blood is the first liquid asset that creates durable networks.

Circulation, then, emerges not merely as a signifier of blood's movement through the body or commodities through an economic system, but rather as capital as social value that enables profit creation. Therefore, admittance into the body of Christ through Christ's blood was the new measure of blood that counts and blood that does not. The blood of Christ provides a "value in motion" (i.e., capital) as it extends from the veins of the incarnate God into the practice of the Eucharist. As Anidjar writes,

> the identification of each and every Christian individual with Jesus' flesh and blood and the incorporation of those individuals with that flesh and blood; an active and collective participation in the novel community that emerged through the Eucharist; the particularly charged status of blood, which, in eucharistic practice, was quickly deemed so vulnerable that it could no longer be tasted by the community of laymen and laywomen. . .All of this points to a refiguration of the Christian community (that is to say, of the community *as* Christian) and the Christian individual ("flesh and blood") as determined by blood and, more strikingly, as vulnerable community of pure blood.[29]

The connection between the incarnation as the liquification of the divine and the circulation of value in the Eucharist creates a community of value centered on a common identity found in the Eucharist itself. Anidjar draws connections between the blood of Christ and the purity of blood that binds communal identity. He writes, "blood functions dominantly to unify that community around it, regardless of leadership or government."[30] Blood, then, serves to invite the individual into a circulation of value in which they could participate. The result was, however frail, an entire durable network centered on partaking the Eucharist. This was the first nation of "distinct blood" united around a common identity.[31] The matrix of ethnic and theological blood falls heavily on Jewish and Islamic blood: in the former, the narrative of blood libel, and in the latter, the narrative of crusade. Violent policing of the Christian border arises from a narrative logic in Christ's blood perfected in the practice of the Eucharist. Anidjar provides two points to illustrate this.

First, the "blood libel" critique of the Jewish community occurs inside the supersessionist desire in early Christian theology to separate from the Jewish community. This led, furthermore, to an overt rejection of Jewish believers as those responsible for the death of Christ. However, the blood libel originated as a virulent slander against Jewish believers in the twelfth century in England, claiming Jews would capture and consume Christian youth for ritual purposes.[32] This came to a head in the years leading up to the Fourth Lateran Council of 1215 CE, where European Christians accused Jews of desecrating the host and mixing gentile blood with matzo.[33] The intensity of the offense increased as the council affirmed and defined the real presence of Christ's blood in the sacrament, which, naturally, only intensified the perceived crime. Though the church issued numerous papal bulls to reject the blood libel, stating clearly and unequivocally that Jews did not engage in Host desecration, this did nothing to lessen its appeal in the popular imagination.[34] As Robert Weinberg recognizes, any "disappearance of a child was often sufficient to raise the cry of ritual murder, and if the child's body turned up bruised or mutilated, Jews would be arrested, tortured, and even executed by local authorities."[35] Therefore, blood libel funded a popular imagination of hematology that created a strict and observable border tied to the Christian community's blood ties as practiced in the Eucharist. Even the condemnation by papal bull is not as strong as a theological durable community tied to blood. Certain blood (i.e., Christian) was profitable, and other blood (i.e., Jewish) was not. In short, blood was value in motion that yielded durable networks.

Second, in addition to the rejection of the Jewish people, the killing of the Islamic infidel by the crusader becomes a means to honor the blood of the Eucharist. In the early ritualizing of the crusade, a manumission of sin was a centerpiece of its theology. As Pope Urban II writes, anyone who "goes on the journey to free the church of God in Jerusalem. . .can substitute the journey for all penance for sin."[36] The reason for such a stark promise comes as a result of the crusaders' defense of Christian blood.[37] It is not the worship of another God, but rather the threat to blood communities that most singles out the Islamic threat for Urban. This blood is Christian blood redeemed by the blood of Christ.[38] One should note the hostility between Christian blood during this period, evident in the rift of 1054 CE. As Rita Brock and Rebecca Parker argue, Urban sought to improve relations between Eastern and Western Christianity.[39] Even though the blood communion had been broken between East and West through excommunication, a theological severing from Christ's blood, the blood of Christians redeemed through *Christ's* blood nevertheless means more than the blood of the invader.

This being said, the piety of the crusader finds its highest expression in the Eucharist and the Eucharist in it. According to the medieval theologian Anselm of Canterbury (1033–1109), best known for articulating the satisfaction theory of atonement in *Cur Deus Homo*, as Brock and Parker suggest, receiving the Eucharist creates a disposition of empathy for Christ's suffering.[40] Through the liturgy, the believer must mourn Christ's suffering in order to approach the Eucharist. This affective posture is not incidental but emerges from a particular theological imagination shaped in the medieval West. Anselm placed a profound emphasis on the necessity and gravity of Christ's suffering as the means of reconciling humanity to God. Within this framework, devotion to Christ's passion becomes central to Christian piety and moral formation. As Brock and Parker write,

> Anselm's theology and piety crystallized the religious foundation of the Crusades. "Peace by the blood of the cross" would become the path to unity among those who shared in Christ's blood, released for human consumption through his crucifixion. Those who shared in the bread and cup incurred obligations either to convert or to kill those who did not eat and drink with them. No one who stood outside the ritual circle of Communion was safe. This consuming vision of peace permeated Christ spiritual practices of the eleventh century. Killing and being killed imitated the gift of Christ's death, the anguish of his self-sacrifice, and the terror of his judgment.[41]

This peace, by the blood of the cross practiced in the Eucharist, reconciled a host of peoples together. This was only because those who took up the task of the crusade violently guarded and policed the borders of this blood communion. Only those inside the ritual understood the value and, thus, the need to maintain the boundary. Blood counts, but Christ's blood counts meritoriously more than that of the infidel.

In summary, blood is value in motion, which marks the borders of a durable network. Much like the symbolic representation of Christ as coin, Christ's blood creates an identity for the community capable of great violence. Christ's blood divides between pure and impure, which calls the Christian community to fiercely guard its border. The blood creates a *habitus* of devotion that at once encourages mourning and permits killing in its defense. Possibly much more than coin, but not without coin, blood encourages the durable networks so prevalent in neoliberalism. Though tied to life in the blood of Christ, the blood cults of medieval Christianity nevertheless signaled death for those who did not eat or drink from its communion.

## Excursus: Blood as Life, not Capital

Blood is a powerful metaphor for death, as illustrated by Anidjar, Brock, and Parker, but it is also a metaphor for life. As Eugene Rogers argues, blood imagery pervades Christian theology, but not all fits the description of blood capital just offered in medieval Christianity.[42] Rather, blood takes on a different meaning, as Rogers argues, in the scholarship of women in Christian theology. This is not a denial of the issues created by medieval blood theology, but rather an engagement with a rival tradition that must be a conversation partner with the medieval tradition just described. Taking women scholars as a point of departure in theology, I turn to the blood theology in Julian of Norwich's work to express this tradition.

Julian of Norwich was a medieval theologian and, thus, serves as an interesting tangent in the trajectory of medieval blood theology. Julian's blood theology emerges amid her own illness and visions of Christ's flowing blood amid a century of war and plague. Julian, in the grips of an unknown illness, prays for a vision of Christ's passion.[43] God grants this vision, and Julian sees Christ's blood flowing like a river.[44] The blood of Christ abundantly flows and washes away the sin of humanity.[45] This binds humanity together into new kin, in which each individual can recognize their belovedness in their particularity. As Amy Laura Hall argues based on Julian's understanding of blood, body, and Eucharist,

> God endlessly delights in us, you and me—and us—kinned in a manner that challenges how God's people in England, in Julian's time, received the body of Jesus Christ. If you and I are together part of God's crown, then God's spectacle of profligate abundance often appears backwards, or at least mixed up. The Lord's Supper is a mixed-up blessing of kinning, so that we see one another as siblings and as each, incalculably, part of God's beautiful, exquisitely unique crown.[46]

Julian refuses to see the "kinning" of blood as an opportunity for division between class, race, or nation. It is a gift that also confuses systems of economic calculation. As Hall continues, "Julian's visions swirl the feudal system together into a funnel that mixes everyone up so that no one can distinguish lord from lady from farmer from king from prince from priest from orphan left at the monastery from monk to nun."[47] Julian's blood invites an interpretation of the world where people are neither divided according to valuable blood or a mass of humanness. Rather humans "are kinned in a way that has us seeing one another as people with particularity instead of as groups of people with carefully calculated qualifications or lack of power."[48] In sum, Julian's vision of the flowing blood of Jesus is not death, but new life and new community that finds value in all kin, all people, in the abiding love of God.

Like Anidjar's account, Julian argues that Christ's blood establishes kinship among people. However, rather than supporting and reifying structures of power, Julian envisions the kinship created by blood as a deconstruction of feudal kinship lines. A failure to listen to Julian's account of blood is to miss a crucial trajectory of blood theology that must be considered alongside and in contradiction to the blood theology that births such atrocities as blood libel and crusading. The central shift that Julian permits in a blood theology is the shift from death to life. One should not surmise from this shift that Julian was naïve about this reality and thus grants her readers, at best, the permission to minimize or dismiss it, thereby reifying harmful structures. Rather, Julian was aware of the reality of suffering and the Christian involvement in suffering.

Julian understands that the suffering of Christ's blood (i.e., the cross) is a profound solidarity with humanity, while critiquing the power structures that cause such suffering. Julian compares Christ's wounds and blood to signify Christ's motherhood for creatures. The suffering of Christ is an avenue to heal our humanity and serves as a balm to suffering, not an impetus for it. She writes, Christ's "task is to save us, and it is his glory to do so, and it is his wish that we know of it; for he wants us to love him tenderly, and trust him humbly and strongly."[49] Christ does not desire suffering but the cross. According to Julian, by Christ's flowing blood and suffering through the cross, he draws the suffering of his kin closely to himself. However, by no means does this mean that suffering is a prerequisite for participation in God's life. Christ's suffering is far more reckless than that. As Hall summarizes,

> The cross of Jesus Christ is the source of human one-ing in such a way that it is non-necessary and definitive. . .The cross did not *have* to be. God made everything from nothing, and so creation did not *have* to be. The cross is also the definition of everything that is, so that you and I. . .and anyone suffering under any system that renders us nothing know ourselves saved.[50]

The ones who suffer under unjust systems are Christ's kin. Therefore, the kinning envisioned by Julian is not to reify structures of power, but rather to undermine them through Christ's solidarity with those who suffer.

The cross is Christ's solidarity and salvation, even with those cut down by Christian attempts to defend the blood. In fact, the cross stands in contradiction to such enactments of the cross. The blood of Christ, as Julian presents, does not need to be offended. Those who police an imaginary border of Christ's blood do so embarrassingly in Julian's thought. Blood is not the offering for a debt, nor is it a commodity upon which one can gain interest. As Hall writes, "Jesus's blood is not part of an economic calculation at all. It is recklessly given and constantly flowing."[51] To store up the blood is foolish because it flows in abundance and escapes human capacity to own. God, as Julian states, "does not only concern himself with great and noble things, but also with small, humble, and simple things, with both one and the other; and this is what he means when he says, 'All manner of things shall be well': for he wants us to know that the smallest things shall not be forgotten."[52] As is stated in Ecclesiastes, "God seeks out what has gone by" (3:15b).

Thus, Julian presents a stunning vision of Christ's ever-flowing blood in the Passion. The blood flowing from the cross is not the basis of economic profit, nor does it need to be defended to the point of killing another in its name. This blood, unlike the blood of the crusaders, of the blood libel, or even neoliberalism, resists the tidy categories of profit and commodity by which value is preserved for some at the expense of others. This world of scarcity finds no expression in the glorious abundance of Julian's vision of Christ's blood. It is a vision that affirms the least and the oppressed, is given to those who have nothing, and, as Mary praises, sends those with means away empty-handed. (Luke 1:53) Like the desecrating, blaspheming work of the cross that typifies the core of the present book, Christ's blood challenges the economic common sense of neoliberalism (i.e., the code of profit) by calling it nonsense. The goal, in Julian's vision, is not profit, but, as Hall states, to recognize that if "everything that is is God's loving extravagance, held like a hazelnut, this can free me from succumbing to the tactics of fear and division."[53]

## Conclusion

The genealogy traced in this chapter reveals a sobering continuity: Christian theology has repeatedly translated the mystery of divine life into systems of exchange that mirror economic rationalities of profit, circulation, and governance. From the trinitarian *oikonomia* to the monetization of Christ, the medieval valorization of sacrificial blood, and later developments such as the Protestant work ethic and modern evangelical emphases on moral productivity, theology has often reinforced the very logics it seeks to resist.

At each juncture, the Eucharist is pulled into this economy. Rather than disrupting systems of exchange, it is often made to stabilize them. It functions as a site where divine gift is rendered measurable, participation promises return, and exclusion carries real and terrible consequences. The church's sacramental practice thus became entangled in broader histories of violence, from the Crusades and colonial conquest to chattel slavery and contemporary regimes that measure human worth according to productivity, exchange, and economic value. This genealogy does not deny the genuinely liberative strands within Christian tradition. It does, however, expose a persistent danger: when theology seeks stability through abstraction and measurable outcomes, it becomes vulnerable to capture by logics of profit. The desire for God is subtly redirected toward accumulation.

What is required, then, is not the abandonment of theology or sacrament, but their reconfiguration. The Eucharist must be recovered as a gift rather than an exchange—an interruption of profit rather than its sanctification. Only such a reorientation can begin to disentangle Christian practice from the economies it has too often mirrored and sustain forms of life no longer governed by calculation, comparison, or exclusion.

## Notes

1. Giorgio Agamben, *The Kingdom and the Glory: For a Theological Genealogy of Economy and Government*, trans. Lorenzo Chiesa and Matteo Mandarini (Stanford University Press, 2011), 1, 39, 208.
2. Agamben, *The Kingdom and the Glory,* 39.
3. Agamben, *The Kingdom and the Glory,* 69.
4. Devin Singh, *Divine Currency: The Theological Power of Money in the West* (Stanford University Press, 2018), 32.
5. See Singh, *Divine Currency,* 57–82.
6. Singh, *Divine Currency,* 36.
7. Singh, *Divine Currency,* 39–46; 66–68.
8. Singh, *Divine Currency,* 103.
9. Singh, *Divine Currency,* 36.
10. David Graeber, *Debt: The First 5,000 Years* (Melville House, 2011), 79–80.
11. Graeber, *Debt,* 80.
12. Friedrich Nietzsche, *On the Genealogy of Morals*, trans. Walter Kaufmann and R. J. Hollingdale (Vintage Books, 1989), 25–26.
13. Nietzsche, *On the Genealogy of Morals*, 50.
14. Nietzsche, *On the Genealogy of Morals*, 45–49.
15. Nietzsche, *On the Genealogy of Morals*, 57–60.
16. Graeber, *Debt,* 78.
17. Graeber, *Debt,* 80.
18. Graeber, *Debt,* 81–82.
19. Graeber, *Debt,* 82.
20. Graeber, *Debt,* 82.

21. Graeber, *Debt,* 83.

22. Graeber, *Debt,* 83.

23. Graeber, *Debt,* 390.

24. Heather Ohaneson, "Warp and Woof," *Syndicate* https://syndicate.network/symposia/theology/divine-currency/

25. Devin Singh, "A Reply" *Syndicate* https://syndicate.network/symposia/theology/divine-currency/

26. Gil Anidjar, *Blood: A Critique of Christianity.* (Columbia University Press, 2014), 17.

27. Anidjar, *Blood,* 126.

28. Anidjar, *Blood,* 19.

29. Anidjar, *Blood*, 69.

30. Anidjar, *Blood*, 68.

31. Anidjar, *Blood*, 75.

32. Robert Weinberg, "The Blood Libel in Eastern Europe," *Jewish History.* (2012) Vol 26, 275.

33. Weinberg, "The Blood Libel in Eastern Europe," 275.

34. Weinberg, "The Blood Libel in Eastern Europe," 275.

35. Weinberg, "The Blood Libel in Eastern Europe," 276.

36. Pope Urban II, "The Privilege of Urban to the Pilgrims," quoted in Rita Nakashima Brock and Rebecca Ann Parker, *Saving Paradise: How Christianity traded Love of This World for Crucifixion and Empire* (Beacon Press, 2008), 264.

37. Brock and Parker, *Saving Paradise,* 262–263.

38. Brock and Parker, *Saving Paradise,* 263.

39. Brock and Parker, *Saving Paradise,* 263.

40. Brock and Parker, *Saving Paradise,* 270.

41. Brock and Parker, *Saving Paradise,* 270.

42. Eugene Rogers Jr., "The Genre of this Book," *Syndicate: Blood.* Feb. 2, 2015. Accessed Feb. 3, 2021. https://syndicate.network/symposia/theology/blood/

43. Julian of Norwich, *Revelations of Divine Love,* trans. Elizabeth Spearing Penguin, 1998), 3 (Short Text §1).

44. Julian of Norwich, *Revelations of Divine Love,* 20 (Short Text §13).

45. Julian of Norwich, *Revelations of Divine Love,* 13 (Short Text §8).

46. Amy Laura Hall, *Laughing at the Devil: Seeing the World with Julian of Norwich.* (Duke University Press, 2018), 88.

47. Hall, *Laughing at the Devil,* 63.

48. Hall, *Laughing at the Devil,* 63.

49. Julian of Norwich, *Revelations of Divine Love,* 144 (Long Text §6).

50. Hall, *Laughing at the Devil,* 83. Italics original.

51. Hall, *Laughing at the Devil,* 88.

52. Julian of Norwich, *Revelations of Divine Love,* 85 (Long Text §32).

53. Hall, *Laughing at the Devil,* 79.

## CHAPTER 4

# Sacraments in the Order of Creation

Christian faith is not a flight from creatureliness but a schooling in it. Scripture consistently depicts human life as irreducibly embodied. We breathe air, drink water, eat bread, inhabit land, and keep time. It is precisely within these ordinary material conditions that God addresses, judges, heals, and gathers a people. This chapter argues, therefore, that sacramental theology cannot be treated as a specialized appendix to "spiritual" doctrine; it belongs within the order of creation itself. Baptismal water and eucharistic bread and wine are not religious props added onto an otherwise neutral world. They are elements of the created order that, by divine generosity, become sites where creaturely desire is reoriented toward God's redemptive purposes. As the chapter puts it, the sacraments are "fundamental to our bodily participation in God's purposes for humanity in the order of creation," and they press Christian practice toward a "non-dualistic, embodied" life rather than an abstracted piety that forgets the body. To develop this claim, the chapter begins by establishing a theological grammar for material goodness and for the meaning of space as "room" made by the Creator, space that is blessed, bounded, and meant to be filled by creaturely flourishing.

Against this creational horizon, the chapter then traces four biblical stories: Naaman and manna, Christ's baptism, and the apostolic formation of table fellowship, as witnesses to how God meets human beings at the site of their bodily needs (washing, hunger, eating, thirst) and trains those needs toward communion rather than domination. Throughout, the thread is consistent: sin is not merely "moral failure" but the misdirection of desire, where creation is seized and transformed into a resource, managed as a commodity, and used to enthrone the self over God and neighbor. The sacraments, by contrast, are God's concrete interruption of such distorted economies, returning embodied life to the posture of gift, gratitude, and shared life. In short, participation is the fundamental grammar of creation.[1]

## Created, Material Things

God desires that humanity live embodied lives, namely, lives within the created order. Humans live among other human and non-human creatures, breathe the air, drink the water, and eat food that is God's creation. Therefore, it is not accidental that creation is essential to what it means to be human. Creation places a limit on our being. It also expresses the way that humanity is intended to flourish as creations of the triune Lord. As such, any understanding of the sacraments must exist within this creational framework. This is because the sacraments are created, finite things that assist our participation and enjoyment of the triune Lord. When a believer celebrates the Lord's Supper or is submerged in Baptismal waters, these are elements of the created order. As such, the creation has the potential to communicate divine grace and purpose.

To this end, it is worth noting the way in which created material things function in the order of salvation and how sacraments function in the Christian imagination. To do so, a careful comparison between the sacramental elements and the material element of our condemnation, namely the fruit in the garden as narrated in Genesis, is in order. The fruit serves as an antithesis to the sacraments, namely by showing how a material, created thing becomes a means by which humanity places itself over God. If a sacrament is an outward sign of an inward grace, the fruit anticipates this function of the sacrament by being its reverse. Therefore, the sacraments work to undo the damage that the fruit does. This is an extension of the division of creation, where God divides and blesses created things, naming them as good.

In Genesis, the Creator fashions a variety of spaces and materials for the flourishing of created beings. God, as theologian Robert Jenson writes, "makes. . .room" for created spaces such as a space for light to exist out of the dark (1:3), separating land, sky, and water (1:6–10), and seasons of the year (1:14–17).[2] These spaces are filled by forms of life such as vegetation (1:11–13), swarms of living creatures in the waters (1:20–23), creatures on the land (1:24–25), and even human beings (1:26–27). There is a mutual need for each other for each to flourish according to their purpose. Each place has a mutually supportive role in the order of God's creative activity. In this way, they worship God by being their own local embodiment of the creaturely reality that God intends for all of creation. The cadence of "good" that follows the ordering and marshaling of creation is one that expresses divine purpose and creaturely goodness in a mutual need of space and material for all members to thrive and flourish.

Flourishing within the space and the flourishing for the space is simultaneously a command to grow. This is a command to human and non-human creation alike, namely that the life on earth is purposefully created to fill space, to occupy it. The purpose of space is the goodness of material space, but it also names certain limits for human and non-human creation. So, for example, humanity must not transcend or abuse this space. Humanity needs this space to understand itself as a part of this creation, as its own creatures, and as, ultimately, good.

Despite this life of flourishing, the center of creation is God, not humanity. To say that creation exists and operates within bounds is to worship God. The ancient Jews, whether planting seed in the soil of the earth or drinking cool water from a stream, would thank the Creator who provided such material blessings. Therefore, the goodness toward which creation always moves is within the goodness of God. As Paul states in Acts 17, God is the one in whom "we live and move and have our being" (Acts 17:28). Therefore, one does not choose one over and against the other in living a created life. Creation worships God by existing within its divinely created boundaries, and God, thus, blesses creation through material reality. Material reality, then, is not a barrier to worship of God. Rather, creation is an embodied existence, intentionally brought about by God's creative activity.

Embodied existence is challenged in the Fall of humanity. Again, the narrative is fascinating in what it reveals about embodied existence. Humanity is given a particular role within creation. As it is written, "God said to them, 'Be fruitful and multiply, and fill the earth and subdue it; and have dominion over the fish of the sea and over the birds of the air and over every living thing that moves upon the earth'" (Genesis 1:28). This command, historically misread, has often led to the violent subjection of creation to the will of humanity. How contrary this runs to the material goodness of creation!

Therefore, the command must be read within the created material goodness of creation. In the second creation narrative (Genesis 2–3), humanity is confronted with another understanding of material existence, namely one outside the bounds and limits of creaturehood already established by God. Rather than existing within these limits, humanity, embodied in Adam and Eve, is confronted with a different possibility, namely to be "like God."[3] In this second account, God provides a vast amount of material, created goods in which Adam, and later by extension Eve, may experience the goodness of creation. However, the tree of the knowledge of good and evil is off limits to humanity (Genesis 2:15–17). The rationale for this prohibition is not provided within the command; it is only depicted as a threat to the life of the humans who have the potential to eat of it.

This, then, provides an opportunity for the serpent. He confronts Adam and Eve with a rationale that is more persuasive than the threat posed by the tree. The rationale is that if Adam and Eve eat of the tree, they will become "like God." Early twentieth-century German theologian Dietrich Bonhoeffer argues that this rationale was very convincing. The alluring potentiality of the serpent's promise, namely, to be like God, strikes at two anxieties in humanity. First, it strikes at the anxiety that humanity itself is not God, yet is asked to be in relationship to God. Humans, seemingly, must carry the burden of relating to that which is infinitely better than themselves. The allure of the serpent's promise, "you will be like God," must be understood within this anxiety. What must have finally outweighed God's command was the potentially more equitable relationship that the human creatures and God could have. No longer would humanity relate to God as a creature to God, but as one who is "like God" to God. Thus, it is a better relationship that appeals to humans.

Second, the serpent appeals to humanity as a hungering creature. The command to be fruitful and multiply comes with the command to eat and partake of every fruit and food in the garden, as desired by God. The serpent presents the fruit, almost liturgically, to Adam and Eve so that it might appear as "good for food, and that it was a delight to the eyes, and that the tree was to be desired to make one wise" (Genesis 3:6). Humanity hungers for food, but also for wisdom. And as desiring creatures, humans desire certain things rather than others. This underscores humanity's dependency on the physical world and God. By hungering for food, humanity needs the world. But the world is not an object merely at the disposal of humanity. Rather, creation is a partner with God in sustaining life. By hungering for wisdom, humanity needs God because God is the source of all things from which humanity should draw. Therefore, by humanity's own hunger, they are driven from God because they seek sources of life outside of created life.[4] This is truly the death of humanity as created, material beings.

The precise meaning of this death needs to be briefly described. As Orthodox theologian Alexander Schmemann writes, as humanity distances itself from created goodness, "everything becomes itself a value and consequently loses all value, because only in God is found the meaning (value) of everything and the world is meaningful only when it is the 'sacrament' of God's presence."[5] This is the point where humanity commodifies and manipulates creation to serve humanity. The command to "have dominion" as a violent marshaling of creation to humanity's desires is only possible *after* the Fall. Consequently, only when creation is cut off from the sacramental presence of God does it lose its intrinsic worth. Exploiting nature for human pleasure, without a reciprocal and life-sustaining partnership, is fundamentally errant. Nature becomes a human dominion. Creation no longer participates in the sacramental presence of God.

This is what must be restored, then: humanity as a creature in the order of creation and creation itself as the sacramental presence of God. The salvation offered by God, in this restoration, is an attempt to realize what God intended for humanity in the beginning. This salvation, though brought about by Christ, does not discourage human participation. In fact, the means by which humanity embodies the salvation of Christ is precisely a liturgical one. It is *material* and shifts our desires away from purely individualistic responses toward the desires of God. In what follows, I describe a few key pictures of how God does this with material things as understood by the canonical witness of the Old and New Testaments.[6]

## Created Material Life

### *Old Testament: Mammon and Naaman*

The Old Testament witness, though existing before the incarnation, still offers several crucial and important examples of God's material reorientation of humanity back towards the desire of God and a sacramental understanding of creation. The faithful life is an embodied life, so God naturally uses material things to express it. Therefore, a careful analysis of two Old Testament passages reveals the consistency of God's material reorientation of creation back to God through humanity's desires. (Admittedly, I am selective in these two witnesses, but I am selective of the elements of bread and water as they ultimately serve the sacraments of Eucharist and Baptism.)

The first witness is the Israelites' receiving bread from heaven in the Exodus. The bread prefigures a eucharistic meal. In the preceding chapters of Exodus, the Israelites are delivered from Egypt and slavery to Pharaoh. However, despite this deliverance, the Israelites forget God's saving activity that leads them out of bondage. In slavery, they were taught to desire the good of Egypt. Despite the harsh work conditions and bondage, as the Israelites wander through the desert, they still desire that good. It is written, "The Israelites said to [Moses and Aaron], 'If only we had died by the hand of the Lord in the land of Egypt, when we sat by the flesh pots and ate our fill of bread; for you have brought us out into this wilderness to kill this whole assembly with hunger'" (Exodus 16:3).

This passage is pregnant with insight about the material means and purpose for our creaturely lives. First, Egypt represents a former way of life, namely one under bondage. This is not God's desire for the Israelites, and as God looks down on their groanings (Exodus 2:24–5) it is a new desire that God wishes for God's people.

Second, the actual bondage of the Israelites arises from the original sin of Adam and Eve. This is the groaning of the people in Egypt amid their oppression. (Exodus 2:24) In the curse of the Fall, there is a resulting disordered relationship between Adam and Eve, which is symptomatic of all human interactions that lead to one desiring lordship over another. As Gregory of Nyssa understands, this is the issue at the heart of slavery. He writes, "But once you have freed yourself from servitude and bondage, you desire to have others serve you."[7] Sin is a form of bondage, but the freedom of salvation is muted by our desire to subject others to our will. This is not God's desire for human embodied existence and the material means through which this embodiment is expressed. Therefore, it is not God's desire that humans be in bondage, oppression, or under the lordship of another.

Third, despite their groaning and oppression, the people desire their bondage. The Israelite hunger for their "fill of bread" (Exodus 16:3) is coupled with a desire for the stability of Egypt. I want to be clear: this is not an indictment of the oppressed. Rather, the desire for oppression is an indictment of the oppressors and the logic of sin, namely, a counter-liturgical act in the lives of the Israelites. To construct a world, as ones who attempt to be like God, is to try and make others serve your will. Oppression is sinful, and sin is oppressive. The two go hand in hand. Therefore, we see in the Israelites that the logic and desires created by sin and oppression are operating against their ability to flourish.

These insights help the reader understand the bread from heaven. The Exodus generally concerns the Israelites learning a new life outside the logic of sin previously known in Egypt. The bread represents a new type of embodied life outside the logic of slavery, namely, a new hunger. Confronted with the ease of their former life in Egypt, despite its deforming characteristics, the Israelites are fed by God, who now asks them to "hunger and thirst for righteousness"

(Matthew 5:6). This is clear because not only do the Israelites need to be filled, but they might "know that I am the Lord your God" (Exodus 16:12). Therefore, this bread does not just fill a need for basic sustenance to maintain the metabolic processes of human life, but also a new life based on prayer and reliance on God for their very being. As such, the bread is a sacramental gift that enables a new way of being.

To summarize, Israel's wandering in the desert is a wandering in the middle path between an alien structure of oppression which constantly reappears in explicitly embodied ways, here illustrated in their desire for Egypt, and the saving activity of God for Israel. By providing bread from heaven, God gives them a new desire centered on God's own activity. It is expressed through the material means of bread and thus provides an entry into an entirely new way of embodied life with God as the source. If Egypt represented a source of stability and food, then God was to be a new way. The logic of the passage is clear in its deployment of various types of embodied liturgies. Two rival ways of life stand in opposition. The first is the continual reenactment of Egypt's logic—a world ordered by domination, slavery, and the power of sin that claims Israel for itself. The second is God's liberating act, which frees Israel into an entirely new way of being in the world, ordered by covenant, communion, and life.

The second witness is the story of Naaman. In 2 Kings 5, there is written an account of a great commander of Aram named Naaman. He suffered from leprosy, but through the circumstances of an Israelite slave who served Naaman's wife, a potential cure to his leprosy appears in the prophet Elisha. However, when Naaman appears before Elisha's home, Elisha sends out a messenger to greet him. It is written, "So Naaman came with his horses and chariots, and halted at the entrance of Elisha's house. Elisha sent a messenger to him, saying, 'Go, wash in the Jordan seven times, and your flesh shall be restored, and you shall be clean'"

(2 Kings 5:9–10). The curious point is that this news, owing to its lack of complexity, does not please Naaman. Naaman, justifiably, believed that a complicated disease such as leprosy must require a complicated treatment. Therefore, he believes his request was not treated with the utmost seriousness and leaves. However, in a seemingly "what have you got to lose" moment, Naaman's servant beseeches Naaman to wash in the Jordan, which he does.

Naaman's commitment is evident in the dilemma he immediately raises with Elisha. Although he now confesses that there is no God except the God of Israel, Naaman remains a military commander in the service of the king of Aram. As part of his official duties, he must accompany the king into the temple of Rimmon, where the king leans on his arm and bows in worship. Naaman knows that his own posture will necessarily mirror the king's, creating the appearance that he, too, is participating in the worship of a foreign god. He therefore asks Elisha in advance for the Lord's pardon in those unavoidable moments of political service (2 Kgs. 5:18). What had once been an ordinary civic responsibility has now become a matter of conscience because Naaman's body has been claimed by a new allegiance. The soil he carries back from Israel therefore becomes more than a memorial. It is a material means of grace, a tangible sign through which Naaman may rehearse an embodied life reordered toward the worship of the God of Israel.

Before departing from Naaman's story, two more elements of the narrative must be examined, namely his request for soil and the greed of Gehazi, Elisha's servant. First, the soil further entrenches the understanding that what is at stake in this scene of cleansing and baptism is creation. The connection between the dirt of creation and Naaman becomes pressing. Humans praise God by living *as* creatures *within* creation. The mule loads of soil will serve as a new material means to offer praise to God for Naaman. It will be through this soil that Naaman, through offerings to God, will envision his new life in the God of Israel. Without this soil, without the very elements of creation of soil and water, Naaman's creaturely imagination is limited.

Second, the greed of Gehazi mirrors Naaman's by providing the inverse response to God's gracious means of being a creature. The proper response to God's saving activity, here embodied in Naaman's cleansing, is a new embodied life that gives back to God. For Naaman, this is evident in his gathering of creation for the sake of giving back to God through offerings and sacrifices. However, Gehazi's response is quite the opposite. The issue that sets the context for Gehazi's sin is Elisha's refusal to take an offering from Naaman. As it is written, after being cleansed, Naaman beseeches Elisha to "a present from your servant" (2 Kings 5:15). Elisha recognizes that the proper response to the saving activity of God is not a gift for himself, but for God. Elisha, rather than accepting Naaman's gift, enables Naaman to give gifts back to God. This is the proper response.

On the other hand, Gehazi saw Naaman's gratitude as a chance to profit personally. The comparison is evident in both Elisha and Gehazi calling upon the name of God as a buttress for their actions. Both say, "As the Lord lives," as a necessary emphasis to proclaim their activity. Both are supplicating God in their action, but one precedes as an activity of gift and the other is for personal gain. Gehazi says, "As the Lord lives, I will run after him and get something out of him" (2 Kings 5:20b). This posture inverts the life established in God's saving act by getting from rather than giving to. This is a crucial difference. For Gehazi, who not only commits this act but then lies about it to Elisha, the difference results in Elisha afflicting him with Naaman's former leprosy. In short, the failure to live according to the logic of gift leaves one captive to a way of life alien to the saving activity of God.

### *Jesus and Sacraments: Sanctification of Material Things*

The new connection between sacraments and material life established in the Old Testament is that God provides material means through which human beings learn to live faithfully as creatures before God. When transitioning to the New Testament, the physical manifestation of God's presence is found within the specific life of one person, Jesus Christ. By establishing the sacraments, Jesus gives us a material, embodied means of living that participates in his life and sets up new patterns of habituation. The sacraments not only provide this new framework but also have the additional bonus of transformation. In short, God in Christ not only gives humanity the pattern but also the means to achieve it. Therefore, Christ will provide a necessary re-narration of the sacraments, grounding them in his own bodily life.

The baptism of Jesus is an example of this re-narration. Jesus's baptism is not a rejection of the Old Testament position on the use of water in ritual cleansing, such as with Naaman. Rather, it enhances and clarifies it, considering Jesus's own body. It is written in the Gospel according to Matthew,

> Then Jesus came from Galilee to John at the Jordan, to be baptized by him. John would have prevented him, saying, "I need to be baptized by you, and do you come to me?" But Jesus answered him, "Let it be so now; for it is proper for us in this way to fulfill all righteousness." Then he consented. And when Jesus had been baptized, just as he came up from the water, suddenly the heavens were opened to him and he saw the Spirit of God descending like a dove and alighting on him. And a voice from heaven said, "This is my Son, the Beloved, with whom I am well pleased." (Matt. 3:13–17)

Two questions are raised in this passage: what does it mean that Jesus must be baptized to "fulfill all righteousness," and what do we do with this seemingly Trinitarian appearance?

First, the mandate to fulfill all righteousness can be read to suggest that Jesus must become God, and the baptism is the means for that becoming. However, this is a misreading. Rather, his baptism must point to a new means of material life made possible by the life of this one identified as the Son.

This second interpretation is not only more plausible, but theologically richer. In Year B of the Revised Common Lectionary, the Baptism of our Lord pairs the Gospel of Mark's account of the Baptism of Jesus and the creation account in Genesis 1:1–5. The pairing in the lectionary cycle, no less than during Epiphany, reveals God's solidarity with created material things. In the creation account, the text indicates that God hovers over the face of the deep to tame the chaos. However, the hovering of God's Spirit is coupled with God's speech. As it is written, "Then God said, 'Let there be light'; and there was light. And God saw that the light was good; and God separated the light from the darkness. God called the light Day, and the darkness he called Night. And there was evening, and there was morning, the first day" (Genesis 1:3–5). God's Word and God's hovering presence over the formless void are acts of gracious ordering, shaping creation for the sake of its own goodness. God creates to affirm good, material life. This goodness is an embodied promise, but it is precisely that which humans have always struggled to embody. This failure signals the opportunity for God's solidarity with creation and embodied existence.

The creation account pairs well with the scene of Christ's baptism. Christ's descent into the water mirrors God's descent into the formless void through speech and Spirit. Christ is the indwelling of the divine

Word (John 1:1), and the Spirit's own presence reclaims the material world to order, namely, for God's order. As such, a new type of embodiment is made known and real. This embodiment is a particular type of material living in the world, which forms the Christian disposition that Baptism creates.

The disposition enabled by Jesus's baptism requires a brief examination of Paul's Christ hymn in Philippians. Paul writes,

> Let the same mind be in you that was in Christ Jesus,
>
> who, though he was in the form of God,
> did not regard equality with God
> as something to be exploited,
> but emptied himself,
> taking the form of a slave,
> being born in human likeness.
> And being found in human form,
> he humbled himself
> and became obedient to the point of death—
> even death on a cross.
>
> Therefore God also highly exalted him
> and gave him the name
> that is above every name,
> so that at the name of Jesus
> every knee should bend,
> in heaven and on earth and under the earth,
> and every tongue should confess
> that Jesus Christ is Lord,
> to the glory of God the Father. (Philippians 2:5–11)

Philippians provides an interpretive key to understanding why Jesus, in submitting to John the Baptist's ministry, might fulfill all righteousness. The Greek word utilized by Matthew means both righteousness and justice. The new righteous, just way of being in the world is born of this baptism. Though Christ could have come on a cloud of fire or with a triumphant army, Christ comes in humility. Living a human life, though as also one who is God, Christ's baptism invites an understanding of him and his ministry in the context of humility. The pattern for the followers of Christ will be established here. In Paul's words, we should be imitators and have this same mind, namely that righteousness requires emptying of oneself. Furthermore, the followers of Christ do not "exploit" their power but use it for the common good. In short, Christ's life, and indeed the life of the Christian, is not marked by power, exploitation, or advantage, but by obedience to the one true God who calls Christians to a new way of being in the world. Jesus Christ's refusal to exploit his own equality with God is evident in his submission, not only to God, but to John. Therefore, the resituating of baptism in this context is an invitation for followers of Christ to submit themselves to God and thus to be open to the ways in which they must be humble in their own lives.

In addition to the mandate to fulfill all righteousness, there is the Trinitarian element apparent in Jesus's baptism. As Paul writes of Christ, God reconciles the world to God's own self (1 Corinthians 5:19). Christ is drawing humanity deeply inside the triune life here through Christ, upon whom the Spirit descends, and the Father calls the Son. The Trinity dances before our eyes here as Christ brings humanity, through his own body, into the dance. But what is being reconciled? The reconciliation that Christ offers here is a material reconciliation when one considers his baptism as the culmination of John's ministry of repentance. John's calling for repentance is realized in Christ's reconciliation here, which makes repentance possible.

This realization begs the question: How is reconciliation apparent in the Baptism of Christ? As theologian Stanley Hauerwas writes,

Christ "is the beloved Son who must undergo the terror produced by our presumption that we are our own creators. He submits to John's baptism just as he will submit to the crucifixion so that we might know how God would rule the world."[8] God in Christ reconciling the world back into God means that God is reconciling humanity back to its original place as creatures. Hauerwas helps connect Christ's baptism with original sin and the disordered material life humanity attempts to build for itself in the garden. Here we witness God submitting to a new material means to be human so that we might repent of our desire to be like God.

Finally, the most glorious revelation of the baptism scene is God's place with sinners. Imagining this scene, Lauren Winner writes, Christ stands

> with Sam, the notorious adulterer; Jack, who's known for swindling old ladies out of their last bits of income; Lila, who's rumored to have committed infanticide; and also Mina, who's just not very nice; and Michael, the prideful prig; and Gary, who made a fortune using shady business tactics. . .before the voice from heaven and the celestial dove, it is also Jesus' standing in line by the river that tells us who he is. . .He is the One who stands with humanity in this line that is all about our sinning, our shame.[9]

Christ stands in the line as God with us, offering a new way. This way is of humility rather than abuse, a way of love rather than defrauding, and God's own life made possible through God's Son. As it is written in 1 Peter 3:21, "And baptism. . .now saves you—not as a removal of dirt from the body, but as an appeal to God for a good conscience, through the resurrection of Jesus Christ." The resurrected life of Jesus is made operative in the believer's life through baptism. Like in the

Old Testament narrative, this reorders material sensibilities and priorities toward that which is found in the triune life.

### *The Lord's Supper: Acts 10, Paul, and the Desire for New Community*

Christ's baptism is coupled with his institution of the Lord's Supper. As philosopher Ludwig Feuerbach writes, "Man is what he eats."[10] This is nowhere more evident than in the Lord's Supper. Without reading something alien into the text, there is a connection between these material elements and Christ's own body. In each of the four gospels, a similar pattern emerges with the institution of the Lord's Supper. In each Synoptic Gospel account of the Last Supper (Matt 26:26–29; Mark 14:22–25; Luke 22:15–20) and even the Gospel of John's own allusion to this meal (John 6:51–58), the body, which is meant for consumption through bread, brings life. Furthermore, it is through this eating that the embodiment of divine mission appears. Much like Abraham, whose covenant is expressed through circumcision, the New Covenant is expressed through this body and blood (Matthew 26:28), and Christians must drink of it until the Lord's return (1 Corinthians 11:26)

Though these connections are evident in Christ's own prescription for the meal, Peter and Paul help establish the meal's meaning in its context for Christian embodied, material life. Both these figures interact with Christ's own prescription of the Lord's Supper at the site of their own eating. In both cases, eating reorients participants' physical activities toward the mission of God in the world. Much like the manna in the desert, it is this new bread from heaven that will give life beyond sinful divisions. I will begin with Peter's own vision of unclean meat and then proceed to Paul's moral exhortations concerning meat offered to idols and the Lord's Supper.

Acts 10:1–8 sets up the narrative necessary to understand Peter's vision. In it, Cornelius, a Gentile and Roman centurion, hears a message from an angel of God. The message was for Cornelius to send for Simon Peter, who resided in Joppa at the time. This peculiar divine message to a non-Jewish figure is characteristic of the Acts narrative, which can be characterized as the opening of the Jewish story to the Gentile world.

Peter's vision in Acts 10:9–16 comes from a "heaven opened," *ton ouranon aneogmenon* (Acts 10:11). As New Testament scholar Carl Holiday explains, this is not an accidental or minor detail, but "signals access to God's space."[11] Hence, an open heaven is closely tied to apocalyptic events and visions.[12] An open heaven both here to Peter and implied in the earlier message to Cornelius signifies the state that humanity finds themselves in relation to God. Due to Christ's apocalyptic invasion of the world, creatures have greater access to God. This is what precipitates the mission to the Gentile world that Peter and the apostles must engage. Thus, openness to God is directed also at the fellow human, as evidenced in this vision's purpose to prepare Peter for ministry to the Gentiles.

Peter's vision is amid a twofold desire that he experiences in hunger and prayer. As theologian Willie Jennings writes of this moment where God enters the scene,

> Now God comes. Peter will be the site of the inbreaking. . .the new order drops from the sky. God comes to Peter inside of Israel's first and deepest gesture—in the moment of prayer. God comes to Peter inside the creature's deepest truth—in the moment of his hunger. Prayer and hunger, hunger and prayer – these will be the pillars on which God will build the future of the creature.[13]

Jennings is interpreting this passage theologically with an eye toward the apocalyptic work Christ had done and is now available through the Spirit after Pentecost, namely that God meets the *creature* at the site of his/her own desires. First, the desire for God in prayer: it is the first and most important desire of the creature to desire its creator. Second, the creature's hunger, namely that desire which names Peter as a creature. In short, God enters Peter at the site of that which he desires.

God's appearance to Peter at the site of his desires reorients him to the divine mission to the Gentiles. In Acts 10: 11–12, Peter is presented with all kinds of creatures. Peter is instructed to "kill and eat" (13), but he refuses due to the cleanliness of the creatures in question (14b). It is here that God calls Peter to reorient his desires. Not only must he eat, but he must call good what God calls good. As he will see with Cornelius (Acts 10: 17–23a), this classification is not just extended to animals, but also to all people. As a creature who hungers, he is called to desire God and that which he formerly called unclean. In the form of this command to eat is a radical intimacy with all of creation that harkens back to Genesis 1:24.[14] This is a disruptive continuity for Peter that joins him back to creation and to those human and non-human creatures around him. This invitation signals two important truths for the Lucan narrative.

First, it signals the act of eating practiced in the Eucharist. In short, "Get up, Peter; kill and eat" (Acts 10: 13) corresponds to "This is my body, which is given for you." (Luke 22:19) Jennings takes this further in that Christ's offering of his body not only corresponds but rather Peter's command to kill and eat "grows out of. . .[Christ's] invitation to eat."[15] This prefigures Paul's moral exhortation toward unity in the body through eating, offered in the moral act of memory. By eating, Peter enters a new world of intimacy and unity made possible by Christ, who takes on created flesh and recalls it to goodness.

Second, the invitation of the Spirit here is realized in Peter and Cornelius. As Jennings writes, "The Spirit of God is on both sides, outside the door with the seekers and inside the door with the perplexed Peter."[16] Cornelius and Peter both receive messages from God, and it is the Spirit that speaks and brings them together (Acts 10:19). God is changing the relational structures by which Cornelius and especially Peter come to define the world. God is placing them within the Spirit's logic, which gathers many nations and tongues into a single people (Acts 2). As Jennings writes, "God is simply, beautifully interrupting conventional and normal structures of relating by mapping God's own relational logic across their bodies."[17] By eating in a way that recalls Christ's invitation to take and eat and the Spirit's drawing together of scattered individuals, a Trinitarian dynamic surfaces at the center of this sacramental reordering of desire. The inner-trinitarian dynamic of relationality draws damaged social bonds into Godself, establishing a new center of intimacy around God's life. Only when Peter recognizes that God has declared the Gentiles clean can he enter the new communion God has created in Christ. Through the Son and by the power of the Spirit, those once divided by hostility are drawn into the Father's household as fellow heirs and children of God.

Acts 10 shows us a God who draws humanity into Godself. This properly sets the context for Paul's views on whether Christians should eat meat sacrificed to idols. We can assume the relevance of Acts to Paul's discourses in 1 Corinthians 8 and Romans 14 for two distinct reasons, in addition to its role in naming the intimate center of the community formed by God's new relational network. To begin with, Paul seems to make clear reference to this in Romans 14: 14–20, "I know and am persuaded in the Lord Jesus that nothing is unclean in itself"[18] (14a). In discussing the nature or appropriateness of consuming idol meat, though not the central issue in Paul's passage, it appears that Peter's vision at least plays a role in showing that nothing is unclean.

Second, Paul rebukes Peter for, seemingly, failing to adhere to the message of his vision. In Galatians 2:11, Paul opposes Peter face-to-face because, as it is written, "he stood self-condemned" (κατεγνωσμένος). Peter's condemnation is self-imposed if one considers the testimony of Acts a credible witness. The central issue is that Peter still treats some as unclean (Gentiles) and others clean (Jews). Peter, at the behest of Paul, is reminded of the movement of the Spirit that is bringing these two groups together into one body. The purpose of the vision was precisely to discourage this type of behavior.

It is for these reasons that I began with Acts 10. It is clear that after the resurrection and ascension of Christ, his disciples engaged in a missionary effort among the Gentiles to participate in the new order God is creating on earth. Peter's call to the mission of God to the Gentiles arises from a sacramental experience of creation where all are called "good" by God. Thus, mission is a sacramental activity arising from old, sinful means of dividing the world. Therefore, the themes and central convictions of Acts are essential to the discourse on idol meat in Romans and 1 Corinthians, for in here Paul sets up the moral/political task of attention as central to the practices of the church. In his exhortations, we see Paul's intentional formation of a Christian community centered around intimacy with God and neighbor.

Paul's theology of the Lord's Supper is most explicit in his exhortation over abuses. This suggests, as has been the argument of this chapter, that the meal unmasks a unique sacramental embodiment made possible through the meal. In the Corinthian community, there have arisen abuses of the Lord's Supper. The Lord's Supper serves as a communal meal for the Corinthians. During the practice of this meal, we are told that some in the community abuse this meal by overindulging while others go hungry (1 Corinthians 11:21). Paul's issue is the personal indulgence and arrogance displayed by this clique, over and against their neighbor. The gravity of this abuse is established when it is contrasted to the unity described by the Supper in 1 Corinthians 10:16–17. This unity is compared to the unity of the Israelites, who, similarly, in the wilderness with Moses, "ate the same spiritual food, and all drank the same spiritual drink" (1 Corinthians 10:4). There is no correspondence to the problem of individual overindulgence in 1 Corinthians 11. Rather, the unity forged in the early Israelite communities is one where worship binds the community together over and against other deities and demons. It is Christ whom the Corinthians worship, and it is his body and blood they partake. This is how they, too, are the body of Christ.

The practice and theology of the meal is given by means of remembrance. This remembrance in Paul's exhortation is twofold. First, the Supper is performed "in remembrance" of Christ (1 Corinthians 11: 24–5) as a command of Christ. Second, Paul's recounting and passing on this practice as a reenactment of Christ's life, specifically of his betrayal and death. Working from the logic of betrayal is the "blood of the new covenant" (1 Corinthians 11:25). This statement of new covenant signals two things in Paul. The new covenant, as commentator Hans Conzelmann argues, is apocalyptic.[19] The new covenant is juxtaposed with Paul's description of the old covenant (2 Corinthians 3:14). As Conzelmann states, Paul's use of new covenant here corresponds to Jeremiah 31:31. This new covenant disrupts the old covenant. The community was formerly, like in baptism, separated by divisions of Jew/Greek, Slave/Free, etc. (1 Corinthians 12:13) However, through the partaking of this meal they/we become "one body" (1 Corinthians 10:17; 12:13). Therefore, in remembering Christ we unlearn a way of division and learn a unity that is a continuation of table fellowship with the exalted Lord.

Second, the practice gives life to a trinitarian disruption of community. The practice is not done for its own sake but finds its meaning in God. As Ernst Käsemann understands, there is a parallel between Christ and the Spirit in the sacraments in its function of unifying the body of Christ.[20] In the sacrament, "the exalted Lord conveys, along with his gift, participation in himself as the Giver, therefore the gift of the sacrament must also be *Pneuma*."[21] The sacraments are the site of a cosmic battle where Christ, through the Spirit, is given to the believer, and a transformation occurs. Käsemann continues, "[humanity] finds redemption when the *pneuma* invades his earthly nature and recaptures him for the heavenly world."[22] This mirrors Paul's words to the Galatians,

> But when the fullness of time had come, God sent his Son, born of a woman, born under the law, in order to redeem those who were under the law, so that we might receive adoption as children. And because you are children, God has sent the Spirit of his Son into our hearts, crying, "Abba! Father!" (Gal. 4:4–6)

However, this cosmic disruption, where the believer is returned to the Father, or, as Käsemann terms it, the heavenly realm, has a material expression. In short, Paul does not envision the Spirit of Christ as a "disembodied force."[23] Rather, it manifests itself in the sacramental event, which is for Paul "the substance of resurrection corporeality and the dimension in which the Risen One exists."[24] Therefore, Paul calls the Corinthians to the remembrance of this embodied reality as the possibility to obeying Christ.[25]

Paul presents the story of the Eucharist by way of a reminder of the Gospel. Paul's goal is simply to remember Jesus, namely the reality of freedom and unity with other believers. As Verhey writes, Paul tells the story of Christ's death and institution of the Lord's Supper to "remedy. . .forgetfulness."[26] The story of the Lord's Supper is *their* story. This story and its continual practice in the community is a constant retelling and practicing of something that demands a particular type of obedience.

William Cavanaugh helps tease out the implications of remembering in the Eucharist. As he writes,

> The word *anamnesis* (remembering) had the effect not so much of a memorial, as one would say kind words about the dead, but rather of performance. The emphasis is thus on the entire rite of the Eucharist as action, and not simply on the consecration of the elements. . .since the consecration turns the bread and wine into the body and blood of Christ, what the church does in the Eucharist must be what Christ did with his body and blood – offer them in sacrifice. . .since we are Christ's body performing His will, what we offered must be what he offered in the events on Calvary, His own body and blood.[27]

While Cavanaugh is not speaking of Paul and 1 Corinthians 10–12 directly in this quote, what he summarizes is the essence of Paul's thought. In 1 Corinthians 10 and 12, Paul recalls the unity of the body of Christ for those who partake of the body of Christ. This unity is created for those freed from the powers of sin and death carved out from the world. Here sin is not understood merely as the accumulation of individual immoral acts, but as a dominion that conditions human existence within what Paul calls "this present evil age" (Gal. 1:4). Sin appears not simply as personal transgression but as an enslaving power that manifests through the principalities and powers, through systems of domination, patterns of desire, and structures of death that hold humanity captive. In this apocalyptic sense, humanity does not merely commit sins but exists under Sin as a tyrannical reality from which it cannot liberate itself. The unity of the community therefore emerges not through voluntary association or shared moral achievement, but through Christ's deliverance of a people from the reign of Sin, Death, and the powers that deform creaturely life.

However, there is a threat to this unity in the "factions" that create "divisions" among believers. Into this problem, Paul inserts the story of Christ's betrayal and sacrificial death. If the Corinthians are the body of Christ, then they must, as Cavanaugh stipulates, live sacrificially and sacramentally. What is against both, as is clear by Paul, is each individual going ahead with their meal where some become intoxicated and others go hungry (1 Corinthians 11:21). The current state of the Corinthian congregation lies in selfishness, the opposite of sacrifice and sacrament. The community is answerable to the body and blood (1 Corinthians 12:27). It is unworthy of the body and blood of Christ to treat members of the body in this way. In short, the Eucharist makes visible the members of the body of Christ. In so doing, it condemns the maltreatment taking place in Corinth.

In Paul's work, the Eucharist serves to form an imagination of a truly corporate polity that resists the present position of the Corinthian congregation. Therefore, the practice of the Eucharist locates the neighbor inside of the body of Christ against any private interest, such as hunger. As Cavanaugh writes, "The emphasis [in the practice of Eucharist] is on the *externality* of the liturgy to individual bodies, the way it incorporates individuals into the body of Christ."[28] The Eucharist provides a tangible rehearsal that resists all forms of "fragmenting discipline."[29] The Eucharist is a counter-discipline, where

> Christ's true body is enacted. . .by the incarnation of the church in the bodies of the poor. The true body of Christ is the suffering body, the destitute body, the body which is tortured

> and sacrificed. The church is the body of Christ because it performs an *anamnesis* of Christ's sacrifice, suffering in its own flesh the affliction taken on by Christ. In the church's communities of solidarity, the poor are fed by Christ but, insofar as they become Christ's body, they also become food for others.[30]

Therefore, the affluent Corinthians must be for those in the midst of the congregation who have nothing. Attention on the Eucharist, through its simple practice, focuses the congregation on the suffering death of Christ's poverty, and thus, to remember Christ appropriately, they too must become poor. The affluent learn to love Christ by surrendering their privilege and becoming poor.

In sum, only by remembering Christ's poverty as their own can they see the poor in their midst with a just and loving gaze. There is a connection between the gift received in the Eucharist through the Spirit, meditation on the gift, and the vision it creates. Therefore, the church practices and remembers to learn how private interests can impact other members in the body of Christ and the world.

## Incarnation: the Sacramental Theology of the Early Church[31]

The Apostolic Fathers and early church theologians emphasized the profound mystery of the Incarnation, God's ability to become flesh in Jesus Christ. They taught that this mystery extended into the sacraments of the church, particularly baptism and the Eucharist. These theologians saw a direct connection between the Word becoming flesh (John 1:14) and God's sanctification of creation through material elements such as water, bread, and wine. This theological emphasis defended the reality of Christ's incarnation against heresies like Docetism and laid a sacramental foundation for the Christian life. Ignatius of Antioch, Polycarp of Smyrna, Irenaeus of Lyons, and Cyril of Jerusalem each contributed to this sacramental understanding, affirming that God's incarnation in Christ makes possible His presence in the eucharistic elements.

Before turning to the patristic tradition, an important methodological clarification is necessary. The argument that follows does not suggest that the church Fathers anticipated modern liberation theology or that their theological projects can be straightforwardly enlisted in support of contemporary political concerns. Such an approach would flatten significant historical, ecclesial, and doctrinal differences. Ignatius of Antioch's reflections on ecclesial unity, for example, cannot be separated from his robust defense of episcopal authority and the ordered life of the church. Athanasius's theological vision was forged in the crucible of the trinitarian controversy, where questions of poverty and social life were inseparable from the defense of the incarnation against Arianism. Likewise, Maximus the Confessor's account of creation, participation, and deification belongs within a comprehensive ascetical and liturgical vision in which liberation from disordered desire occurs through spiritual discipline, prayer, and conformity to Christ. Even where the Fathers speak forcefully about wealth, almsgiving, or the obligations owed to those experiencing poverty, these concerns remain embedded within broader theological accounts of salvation, virtue, ecclesial communion, and the transformation of human desire.

Accordingly, this chapter does not retrieve the patristic tradition as a collection of isolated quotations supporting contemporary liberationist claims. Rather, it approaches these theologians as conversation partners whose distinct theological grammars continue to illuminate questions of poverty, embodiment, and social life, even when their historical concerns differ substantially from our own. Their writings require careful interpretation precisely because they emerge from contexts shaped by martyrdom, doctrinal controversy, imperial transformation, and ascetical practice rather than by modern capitalism or neoliberal globalization. The constructive task undertaken here is therefore one of theological retrieval rather than historical identification: allowing the Fathers to challenge contemporary assumptions while also discerning how their visions of creation, communion, and participation may fruitfully inform the church's witness within radically different historical conditions.

Ignatius of Antioch (c. 35–107 AD) stands out for his robust defense of the Incarnation and its sacramental implications. Writing to combat Docetism, which denied the reality of Christ's flesh, Ignatius underscores the tangible and real nature of Christ's humanity. In his *Letter to the Smyrnaeans*, he declares, "They [the Docetists] abstain from the Eucharist and from prayer, because they do not confess that the Eucharist is the flesh of our Savior Jesus Christ, the flesh which suffered for our sins and which the Father, in His kindness, raised again" (*Smyrnaeans* 7). Here, Ignatius links the Eucharist directly to the Incarnation, asserting that the bread and wine of the Eucharist become the very body and blood of the crucified and risen Christ.

For Ignatius, the sacramental elements of bread and wine embody Christ's real presence, affirming God's ability to work through creation. This incarnational theology reflects a deeply sacramental worldview, where the physical world becomes a vessel for divine grace. The Eucharist, for Ignatius, is not a symbol, but a true participation in the flesh and blood of Christ, emphasizing the continuity between the Incarnation and the sacramental life of the church.

Polycarp of Smyrna (c. 69–155 AD), a disciple of the Apostle John and a close contemporary of Ignatius, also affirmed the reality of Christ's incarnation and its sacramental implications. While Polycarp's surviving writings are limited, his martyrdom and legacy reflect a deep commitment to the Eucharist as the locus of Christ's real presence. The *Martyrdom of Polycarp*, a document commemorating his death, describes his sacrifice as being akin to Christ's own. During his martyrdom, the imagery of bread and wine permeates the narrative, suggesting a sacramental understanding of his life and death in imitation of Christ. Although Polycarp does not expound in detail on the Eucharist, his faith in the God-man, Jesus Christ, aligns with the sacramental theology of Ignatius. His reverence for the Eucharist and willingness to suffer martyrdom underscore his belief in the transformative power of Christ's incarnation, which extends into the sacraments of the church.

Athanasius of Alexandria (c. 296–373 AD), one of the most influential theologians of the early church, developed a theology of the Incarnation that is deeply integrated with his understanding of creation. For Athanasius, the Incarnation is not an isolated event but the culmination of God's creative and redemptive work, uniting the doctrines of creation and salvation. In his seminal work, *On the Incarnation*, Athanasius argues that through the Word (Logos), God both creates and redeems the world, emphasizing that the Incarnation is how humanity and creation are restored to their intended purpose. The life, death, resurrection, and ascension of Jesus Christ reveal the fullness of God's saving plan, which is rooted in the original goodness of creation and directed toward its ultimate renewal.

Athanasius begins his theology of the Incarnation with the doctrine of creation, highlighting the Word's role as the agent through whom all things were made. He writes, "For it will appear not at all contradictory if the Father works its salvation in the same one by whom he created it."[32] For Athanasius, creation is inherently good, and humanity is uniquely created in the image of God (Genesis 1:26–27), endowed with reason and the capacity for communion with the Creator. This connection between creation and the Creator underscores the dignity and purpose of human life, which is to live in harmony with God.

However, Athanasius also emphasizes the fragility of creation, particularly humanity's vulnerability to corruption due to sin. He explains that through the Fall, humanity turned away from God, introducing death and decay into the created order. Sin is not merely a moral failing but a cosmic disruption, leading to humanity's alienation from God and the disintegration of creation. Athanasius describes this as a descent into non-being, as sin distances humanity from the source of life. In this context, the Incarnation is necessary not only to redeem humanity but also to restore the integrity of creation itself.

For Athanasius, the Incarnation is the decisive act of God's intervention to redeem a broken creation. The Word, who is both Creator and Sustainer of the world, takes on human flesh to reunite God to humanity. Athanasius insists on the full divinity and humanity of Christ, emphasizing that only the Creator can restore the creature. He writes, "the Word of God came himself, in order that he being in the image of the Father (cf. Col 1.15), the human being 'in the image' might be recreated."[33] Athanasius views the Incarnation as a profound act of divine condescension and love. By becoming human, the Word enters the material world, sanctifying it and reversing the effects of sin. This union of divinity and humanity in the person of Christ is how God reclaims and renews creation. The Incarnation is not a contingency plan but the fulfillment of God's eternal purpose for humanity to share in divine life.

In the life of Jesus, Athanasius sees the perfect manifestation of humanity's original purpose. Jesus, as the incarnate Word, lives in perfect obedience and communion with the Father, embodying the divine image unmarred by sin. Athanasius highlights Christ's teachings, miracles, and acts of compassion as signs of the restored relationship between God and creation. By healing the sick, raising the dead, and calming the storms, Christ demonstrates his authority over creation and his power to redeem it. Furthermore, the life of Christ is an example for humanity, showing what it means to live in communion with God. Athanasius writes, "the divinity of the Word unfolded over the earth, is no longer deceived concerning God, but reveres him alone, and through him rightly knows the Father."[34] In Christ's humanity, Athanasius finds the model for human flourishing, to a life directed toward God and marked by love, humility, and holiness.

Athanasius places particular emphasis on the death of Christ as how sin and death are defeated. He argues that Christ's death on the cross is not merely an example of sacrifice but a cosmic act of redemption. Rather, it is by the divinity of Christ that all sin and death is cast from humanity, thus reuniting humanity and divinity. Athanasius explains, "He, the incorruptible Son of God, being united with all by a like nature, naturally clothed all with incorruption by the promise of the resurrection."[35] The death of Christ is also an act of divine justice, satisfying the requirements of the law while simultaneously displaying God's mercy. By dying on behalf of humanity, Christ restores the relationship between Creator and creation, defeating the forces of corruption that had enslaved the world.

Athanasius's theology of the Incarnation is deeply intertwined with his understanding of the Holy Spirit, particularly in relation to creation, redemption, and the sanctification of humanity and the material world. In addition to emphasizing the Word's role as the agent of creation and redemption, Athanasius highlights the Holy Spirit as the divine presence that completes and perfects this work. For Athanasius, the Spirit not only works in tandem with the Word in creation but also applies the redemptive benefits of the Incarnation to believers, ensuring their participation in divine life. This pneumatological dimension enriches his overarching vision of God's engagement with creation.

Athanasius sees the Holy Spirit as an integral participant in creation, working alongside the Word to bring order and life. In *Letters to Serapion*, a polemic against those who denied the divinity of the Spirit, Athanasius affirms the Spirit's co-eternity with the Father and the Son, emphasizing the unity of divine action in creation. He writes, "The Father does all things through the Word in the Holy Spirit. In this way is the unity of the Holy Trinity is preserved."[36] This collaboration ensures that creation is imbued with divine presence and purpose, with the Spirit sustaining and vivifying all that the Word has brought into being.

The Spirit's role in creation is particularly significant in Athanasius's theology because it reflects the divine commitment to the material world. Just as the Word sanctifies creation through the Incarnation, the Spirit continues to animate and renew creation, preventing it from falling into chaos. For Athanasius, the Spirit is the ongoing source of life, pointing to the ultimate renewal of creation in Christ.

Athanasius also emphasizes the Spirit's role in the Incarnation of Christ, highlighting how the Spirit prepared the way for the Word's assumption of human flesh. In his reflections on the Annunciation, Athanasius notes that Mary conceives by the power of the Holy Spirit, demonstrating the Spirit's involvement in bringing about the mystery of the Incarnation. This act not only sanctifies Mary but also reveals the Spirit's function in enabling the union of divinity and humanity in Christ.

In *On the Incarnation*, Athanasius frequently speaks of the Word assuming human flesh to restore humanity's communion with God. This restoration is mediated by the Spirit, who unites believers to

Christ and enables them to share in divinity. Athanasius writes, "But as it is, when we are said to be partakers of Christ and partakers of God, it shows that the anointing and the seal which is in us does not belong to the nature of things which have been brought into existence, but to the Son, who joins us to the Father through the Spirit that is in him."[37] Here, Athanasius emphasizes that the Spirit is the means by which humanity participates in the redemptive work of the Word, reinforcing the Incarnation's transformative impact on both individuals and creation.

The Holy Spirit's work, especially in Athanasius's telling, is not limited to individual salvation but extends to the sanctification of the material world, particularly through the sacraments. The Spirit's descent upon the elements of bread, wine, and water in the sacraments parallels the Word's descent in the Incarnation, affirming the Spirit's role in mediating divine presence through creation. This sacramental theology highlights the Spirit's role in transforming creation, making it a conduit of divine grace. As Athanasius suggests in his Sermon to the Newly Baptized,

> You shall see the Levites bringing loaves and a cup of wine, and placing them on the table. So long as the prayers of supplication and entreaties have not been made, there is only bread and wine. But after the great and wonderful prayers have been completed, then the bread is become the Body, and the wine the Blood, of our Lord Jesus Christ. "And again:" Let us approach the celebration of the mysteries. This bread and this wine, so long as the prayers and supplications have not taken place, remain simply what they are. But after the great prayers and holy supplications have been sent forth, the Word comes down into the bread and wine—and thus His Body is confected.[38]

This sermon to the newly baptized highlights the profound transformation that occurs in the Eucharist through collective prayer and the action of God's Word. The emphasis is not merely on ritual words but on the divine action that takes place through the church's liturgical prayer. The Eucharist therefore becomes a site of divine encounter where material elements are taken up into the mystery of Christ's presence and life. In this way, the sacrament reveals the broader logic of Christian salvation: God works through created realities to communicate grace and unite believers to Christ.

The same sacramental pattern appears in the church's understanding of baptism. In baptism, the Spirit works through material elements to bring about participation in Christ. In baptism, the Spirit sanctifies the water, enabling believers to die and rise with Christ, participating in the Incarnation, death, and resurrection of Jesus. This pneumatological perspective underscores the Spirit's role in making the redemptive benefits of the Incarnation accessible to believers and in renewing creation itself.

It is precisely this pneumatological framework that grounds Athanasius's doctrine of deification (*theosis*), a key area where his understanding of the Holy Spirit, the Incarnation, and creation converge most fully. He famously declares, "For he was incarnate that we might be made god."[39] This process of deification is made possible through the Incarnation of the Word and is actualized by the work of the Spirit.

Athanasius's theology integrates the Incarnation and the Holy Spirit into a unified vision of God's redemptive work in creation. The Word creates and redeems the world, while the Spirit animates, sanctifies, and perfects creation, ensuring its participation in divine life. For Athanasius, the Incarnation is not an isolated event but the culmination of God's eternal purpose to dwell with and transform creation. The Spirit's role in this process highlights the ongoing presence of

God in the world, mediating the benefits of Christ's Incarnation and ensuring the ultimate renewal of all things.

Athanasius's vision not only affirms the goodness of creation but also offers a profound hope for its transformation, as the Spirit continues to work through the church, the sacraments, and the lives of believers to bring about the new creation inaugurated by Christ.

Similarly, Irenaeus of Lyons frames this in terms of *recapitulation*: Christ retraces the steps of humanity in order to restore it. This restoration necessarily includes the material body, for it is in and through embodied existence that human life unfolds. For Irenaeus, the flesh is not an obstacle to salvation but the locus in which God's redemptive work takes place. The eucharistic theology that emerges from this tradition further reinforces the point. If Christ gives his body and blood as means of communion, then material elements (bread and wine) become vehicles of divine life. Matter is not bypassed but transfigured.

Taken together, these early theologians make a crucial theological claim: the incarnation reveals not only that God can take on flesh, but that God wills to redeem creation from within its material conditions. The body is not discarded but glorified. Salvation is therefore not an escape from materiality but its renewal. In Christ, God affirms the goodness of creation by entering into it, bearing its corruption, and restoring it to life.

## From Created Hunger to Eucharistic Participation: Maximus the Confessor

So far, this chapter has argued that sacramental life is inseparable from the order of creation itself. From the garden to the manna in the wilderness, from Naaman's washing to Christ's own baptism and table fellowship, Scripture presents material life not as a neutral substrate but as the *arena in which desire is trained.* Hunger, thirst, eating, washing, and sharing are never incidental; it is where humanity either learns to live as creatures before God or attempts to transcend creaturely limits by turning creation into an object of control, profit, or domination. The Fall, on this account, is not simply moral failure but the misdirection of desire, and creation is no longer received as gift but seized as resource.

The sacraments emerge as God's gracious reorientation of embodied life. Bread, wine, water, and table fellowship retrain desire away from exploitative economies and toward mutuality, reciprocity, and communion. Yet as earlier chapters have shown, Christian theology has not always remained faithful to this sacramental imagination. The Eucharist has often been abstracted from its creational grounding and folded into systems of exchange where Christ's body circulates as value rather than forms a community of shared life.

It is precisely at this juncture that Maximus the Confessor becomes theologically important. Born around 580 CE, likely in Constantinople, Maximus the Confessor emerged within one of the most politically and theologically volatile periods of the Byzantine world. Traditionally understood to have served as a high-ranking imperial official before entering monastic life, Maximus abandoned the prestige of imperial power for the ascetic and theological vocation of the monastery. His life unfolded amid the collapse and fragmentation of the late Roman world: Persian invasions, Arab expansion, ecclesial division, and fierce Christological controversy all pressed upon the theological imagination of the church. Yet it was precisely within this atmosphere of imperial instability and theological crisis that Maximus developed a vision of creation and redemption that refused every reduction of salvation to abstraction, legal transaction, or spiritual escape.

Maximus is most remembered for his opposition to Monothelitism, the imperial attempt to resolve Christological conflict by claiming that Christ possessed only one will. Against this, Maximus insisted that if Christ does not possess a fully human will, then humanity itself remains unhealed. Salvation requires not the negation of creaturely reality but its restoration and fulfillment in communion with God. This conviction ultimately cost him everything. Arrested, exiled, tortured, and publicly condemned, Maximus had his tongue cut out and his right hand severed so that he could no longer challenge imperial theology. He died in exile in 662, not as a protected theologian of empire, but as a confessor whose body bore witness to the very theological claims he defended. Biographical context matters because Maximus's theology cannot be separated from his resistance to every attempt to subordinate divine truth to imperial administration, abstraction, or political expediency. His theology emerges not from detached speculation but from the conviction that creation itself participates in the Logos and is destined for transfiguration rather than domination. Against every dualism that would sever spirit from matter, nature from grace, or salvation from embodied existence, Maximus articulates a profoundly sacramental vision of reality in which all creation finds its meaning and telos in Christ. The world is not raw material awaiting spiritual utilization, but a liturgical cosmos ordered toward communion.

Such a vision becomes especially significant in the face of modern technological and neoliberal imaginaries that, as we have seen, grind down creation to utility, exchange, and management. Maximus offers not merely a theology of sacramental presence but an ontology of participation in which materiality itself bears divine significance. Creation is not valuable because it can mediate some higher spiritual commodity; rather, creation is already constituted through its relation to the Logos. In this way, Maximus provides a useful theological grammar capable of resisting the shrinking of the world into consumable space. In his vision, creation is recoverable as gift, relation, and eucharistic participation.

Maximus goes beyond affirming the goodness of creation or the reality of sacramental presence. He provides a richly metaphysical and Christological grammar capable of sustaining the biblical vision developed earlier without collapsing into abstraction. Where later sacramental theologies risk turning material elements into instruments that deliver spiritual capital, Maximus insists that materiality itself is the mode of salvation, because creation is already ordered toward communion in Christ.

At the heart of Maximus's theology is a refusal to separate incarnation, creation, and sacrament. Creation, for Maximus, is never raw matter awaiting divine use. It is structured from the beginning by the *logoi*, the distinct purposes and meanings of created things. These find their unity and fulfillment in the Logos itself. This means that bread, wine, water, bodies, and communities are not arbitrary signs God happens to employ; they are creaturely realities already oriented toward participation in divine life. The Eucharist, then, does not introduce a new economy into creation but reveals what creation was always meant to be: a shared life ordered toward God.

This vision directly addresses the problem identified earlier in the chapter, the transformation of sacrament into exchange. Maximus's Christology, expressed most clearly in his defense of dyothelitism, rejects any account of salvation that overrides creaturely desire. Christ's human will is not absorbed into the divine will, nor is it used as a passive instrument. It is healed through free, obedient alignment. Salvation, therefore, is not the extraction of value from Christ's body but the *formation of creaturely freedom capable of communion.*

Applied to the Eucharist, this means that Christ is not consumed as a finite good distributed among many but shared as the one life in which many participate. Just as אָנָמ (manna) teaches Israel to depend daily on God rather than hoard resources, and just as Naaman's washing resists transactional healing in favor of obedient reception, the Eucharist in Maximus's theology resists commodification. Instead, it is pure gift that delivers the figures from consumeristic exchange, teaching the church to receive creation as gift rather than manipulate it for advantage. The Eucharist becomes the concrete rehearsal of creaturely life restored: life that eats without exploiting, receives without taking possession, and gives without calculation.

Maximus makes this explicit by situating the Eucharist within a cosmic liturgy that gathers creation into Christ. The church does not perform the sacrament to produce unity or stabilize social order; rather, the sacrament discloses the unity already accomplished in Christ's incarnation. In this sense, the Eucharist functions as a counter-discipline to the fallen logic described earlier in the chapter, the logic that turns dominion into domination and hunger into unlimited consumption. Liturgical participation retrains the body to desire rightly, drawing believers back into the creaturely humility modeled by Christ's own baptism and self-emptying.

Crucially, this also reframes embodiment. Against sacramental theologies that either spiritualize materiality or instrumentalize it, Maximus insists that bodies matter precisely because they are the place where communion occurs. Creation does not mediate grace by becoming less material, but by becoming more fully itself in Christ. The Eucharist, therefore, is not the suspension of creaturely limits but their fulfillment. Bread remains bread, wine remains wine, bodies remain bodies. Yet all are drawn into a shared life that resists exploitation and hierarchy.

Considering this emphasis on desire, Maximus's virtue ethics completes the picture. Virtue is not accumulation of moral capital but *alignment of desire with the order of creation.* The sacraments are indispensable to this formation because they retrain hunger at its most basic level. The church learns to desire God not by escaping material life but by eating, drinking, washing, and sharing differently. Here, the Eucharist is a potent interruption of all abstract economies. Christ does not circulate as value; he gathers a people.

Maximus thus provides a theological orientation capable of sustaining the biblical, creational, and sacramental vision developed in this chapter. Sacramental life becomes the site where fallen desire is healed, and creaturely existence is restored to communion. And where the logic of exchange finally gives way to the shared life of God with creation.

## Cosmic Liturgy: Sacraments as Work of the People

Maximus's cosmic vision sharpens the claim running through this book: the sacraments are not divine "services" dispensed to passive consumers, nor spiritual commodities circulating through ecclesial mechanisms of value. They are the church's *leitourgia*—the "work of the people"!—in which creation itself is taken up, offered, and returned as thanksgiving. If earlier theological economies mapped the Eucharist onto systems of exchange (sacrifice as payment, purity as access, merit as accumulation), Maximus offers a different orientation: *the sacraments are not an economy of transfer but the liturgical form of creation's vocation.*

For Maximus, the Incarnation is not a divine contingency unleashed by sin, as though God improvises a remedy when creation goes awry. The Incarnation is the telos of creation, the inner meaning toward which all things are ordered. This is why Maximus can speak as though the world is intelligible only from the event of the Word made flesh: Creation's "why" is disclosed in the union of God and creature in Christ. This Christocentric ontology is clarified through Maximus's famous account of the *logoi*. Created things are not inert; they are shaped by intelligible purposes held in God. These divine intentions are expressed in the world. The *logoi* are not "values" assigned to matter, nor spiritual meanings that float above it. As theologian Jordan Daniel Wood summarizes, "The *logoi* are at once thoughts and wills, for God knows what he wills and wills what he knows, and what he wills and knows he wills and knows to be."[40] Thus, the *logoi* are the deep grammar of created existence: each creature bears a vocation, a direction, a form of glory that is only fully understood as it is gathered into the Logos. The Incarnation, then, is not God stepping into creation from the outside. It is the unveiling of what creation has always been ordered toward: *communion without confusion, participation without absorption, unity without domination.* This matters for sacramental theology because it rescues the Eucharist and Baptism from becoming an abstract mechanism. If creation already has a Christological orientation, then bread and wine are not arbitrary instruments God happens to use; they are fitting, creational forms of communion. The elements belong to a world made for sacrament, thanksgiving, reception, and shared life. The vision of a cosmos ordered toward communion forms the foundation of Maximus's sacramental theology.

The Eucharist in Maximus's sacramental theology is not a symbolic reminder attached to a primarily spiritual salvation. It is a real participation in Christ, precisely because it is the place where creation is gathered into its intended end. Bread and wine are not merely "matter" on one side and "grace" on the other. They are creation and human labor offered to God as thanksgiving and returned as communion. This piece is crucial: *the Eucharist includes human work.*

It is not only what God does *for* us; it is what God does *with* us. The sacrament is God's gift, but it is given in a form that requires creaturely participation: planting, tending, preparing, bringing, offering, receiving, sharing. Here, "liturgy" is not a clerical performance or a sacred technology. It is the church's act as a people. It is an embodied community learning how to inhabit creation truthfully. In that sense, Eucharist is the opposite of a transactional logic. What is practiced is *creaturely dependence* and *communal life*, the retraining of desire away from possession and toward communion.

Maximus's *Mystagogia* makes the point with unusual force by refusing to separate church, Eucharist, and cosmos. The church is not a religious enclave inside the world; it is the place where the world is disclosed as destined for communion. Hear Maximus describe participation in the holy mysteries:

> Through the holy partaking of the immaculate and life-giving mysteries, grace brings about the fellowship and identity with God according to participation that is possible through our likeness with God, and through this identity man is deemed worth to become god from man. For, we believe that we have partaken of the gifts of the Holy Spirit through grace by faith here in this present life, and we believe that, after keeping the commandments to the best of our ability, we shall partake in these things in the very reality–in the age to come according to that which is ultimately true, according to the unfailing hope of our faith and the certain and infallible fulfillment of what has been promised. As we pass from the grace that is by faith to the grace according to sight, he will remake us into himself–clearly, I am speaking of 'our God and Savior Jesus Christ'–by stripping away the properties of corruption in us,

> and he will graciously give to us the archetypal mysteries that are represented there through sensible symbols.[41]

This remarkable passage draws together the full arc of Maximus's sacramental vision: the Eucharist is not merely a ritual act but the site where the eschatological transformation of the human person is already inaugurated. Participation in the mysteries is, for Maximus, a genuine ontological event—grace effects a real *methexis*, a sharing in the divine life that anticipates the age to come, when faith gives way to sight and the symbolic yields to the archetypal. Crucially, this transformation is not narrowly individualistic. The "stripping away of the properties of corruption" and the remaking of humanity "into himself" signals a cosmic reorientation, one in which Christ as the *logos* of all things draws creation back toward its original and ultimate telos. The sensible elements of the mysteries, which include bread, wine, water, and the material world received and offered, are not incidental vessels. They are participants in this movement of return. Matter itself is shown to be capable of bearing the divine, precisely because it was made for this end. Conversely, the cosmos is not secular "space" outside the church; it is creation called to become praise. The sacraments are therefore not merely the center of ecclesial piety; they are the microcosm of creation's ultimate destiny, an anticipation of the transfiguration of all things in Christ.

Here is the theological heart of Maximus's cosmic liturgy: the entire created order becomes thanksgiving. Not in the sentimental sense that nature is "spiritual," but in the liturgical sense that creation is oriented toward offering and communion. When Maximus describes the cosmos as hymn or doxology, this is not a fancy metaphor. He is describing creation's true *form*: existence as participation, creatureliness as praise. The liturgy of the church does not impose meaning on a meaningless world; it enacts the world's true meaning against the distortions of sin.

And here the phrase "work of the people" becomes more than etymology. In Maximus, cosmic liturgy names a vocation: humanity is not merely a consumer of the world but a priestly mediator within it. Human beings stand at the intersection of visible and invisible, material and spiritual. This "work" is not productivity in the neoliberal sense; it is not extraction, optimization, or accumulation. It is the labor of communion: blessing what is given, receiving without possession, offering without calculation, sharing without scarcity. Thus, the sacraments are not simply a devotional act; they are trainings in how to be human *within* creation. They teach the body to desire rightly. They teach the community to resist the habits of hoarding and competition. They teach the imagination to see the world not as raw material for self-making but as gift meant for shared life. If earlier sacramental economies made the altar mirror the market, Maximus insists that Eucharist is the market's undoing. It is a practice where value is no longer measured by profit but by participation.

Maximus's cosmic liturgy also has teeth because it is cruciform. The world becomes praise not by bypassing conflict, suffering, or death, but by being reconciled through the self-giving of Christ. The Cross is not a payment within a divine ledger; it is the act by which the *Logos* gathers fractured creation back into unity. The Eucharist, as communion in the crucified and risen Christ, forms the church into that same pattern: life given away, not life leveraged; unity as shared vulnerability, not unity as managed order. This is why later interpreters have found in Maximus such a fertile resource. Jordan Daniel Wood presses the ontological point: creation coheres in and through the Incarnation because the Logos is the archetype and end in whom all things find unity.[42] Balthasar presses the liturgical and dramatic point: the universe is not a closed system, but a doxological drama gathered into Christ the High Priest.[43] But both converge on the same insight: *The Eucharist is the sacramental form of the cosmos's reconciliation in Christ, already real, but not yet complete.*

## Sophia: the Deepening of Cosmic Liturgy

If Maximus provides the Christological and metaphysical grammar for understanding creation as participation in the Logos, Sergei Bulgakov extends this vision into a profound meditation on divine wisdom, or *Sophia*, as the inner depth and radiance of creation's relation to God. Born in 1871 in Livny, Russia, Bulgakov's intellectual journey moved from Marxism and political economy to Orthodox theology and priesthood. Initially trained in economics and deeply influenced by socialist thought, Bulgakov became increasingly dissatisfied with materialist accounts of reality and eventually returned to the Orthodox faith. Exiled from Soviet Russia in 1922 aboard the so-called "philosophers' ship," he would spend the remainder of his life in Paris, where he became one of the central figures of twentieth-century Orthodox theology and served at the St. Sergius Orthodox Theological Institute until his death in 1944.

Bulgakov's theology emerged amid the collapse of empire, revolution, secularization, and technological modernity. Like Maximus, he confronted a world increasingly organized through abstraction, administration, and economic reduction. Against this, Bulgakov developed a sophiological vision in which creation is neither autonomous matter nor merely passive substance awaiting divine intervention, but the manifestation of divine wisdom and glory. Sophia, for Bulgakov, names neither a fourth member of the Trinity nor a separate divine being, but the eternal wisdom, beauty, and ordering principle through which creation exists in relation to God. Divine Sophia refers to the fullness of God's self-revelation and self-expression, while creaturely Sophia refers to creation's participatory correspondence to this divine life.

Through this distinction, Bulgakov attempts to preserve both the transcendence of God and the genuine integrity of creation without severing the two into unrelated realms. Creation possesses its own reality and freedom precisely because it is grounded in participation rather than domination. The world is not external to God as a neutral object to be mastered, nor is it dissolved into divinity through pantheism. Rather, creation exists sacramentally, bearing within itself the traces and logoi of divine wisdom. Matter, therefore, possesses theological depth. It is capable of communion because it is already sophianically ordered toward God.

This all becomes particularly significant within the context of modern technological society. Where neoliberal and technological imaginaries reduce the world to efficiency, utility, and exchangeable resources, Bulgakov's sophiology re-enchants creation. The world is a luminous and eucharistic reality grounded in divine wisdom. In this sense, Bulgakov radicalizes the sacramental ontology already present in Maximus by insisting that all creation is internally oriented toward transfiguration and communion in Christ. In Bulgakov's terms, this is why Sophia cannot be reduced to either side of the Creator-creature divide. Creaturely Sophia identifies the divine wisdom through which God eternally knows, orders, and expresses creation, while also naming the created order insofar as it manifests that wisdom in finite form.

For Bulgakov, creaturely Sophia is that principle in creation that images the divine Sophia from before the beginning of the world. Bulgakov therefore distinguishes between divine Sophia and creaturely Sophia. Divine Sophia is the eternal fullness of God's self-revelatory life. In contrast, creaturely Sophia is the physical world that bears and participates in that divine wisdom. Creaturely Sophia, to be clear, is that structure and content of creation already anticipated inside the divine logos. The distinction safeguards the Creator–creature difference, while the unity of the two ensures that creation is not alien to God but oriented toward communion in the triune Lord. She, as Bulgakov writes, "unites God with the world as the one common principle."[44]

This sophiological framework does not displace Nicene orthodoxy; rather, it clarifies why the Nicene confession must insist on the full divinity and full humanity of Jesus Christ. If creation truly participates in the divine wisdom, then the culmination of that participation must occur where divine life and creaturely existence meet without confusion or division. Bulgakov writes, "man possesses in himself an uncreated-created principle, he pertains to the eternity of the divine world. . .Belonging to the created-animal world, he is at the same time god by grace."[45] In the Incarnation, the eternal Logos assumes creaturely Sophia in its fullest form in creation. "Only on the foundation of this co-imaging of God and man," Bulgakov continues, "can the incarnation be understood ontologically."[46] The Nicene and Chalcedonian insistence that Christ is "true God from true God" and fully human, therefore, becomes metaphysically necessary. Bulgakov writes in his magisterial work, *The Lamb of God,* that Christ's humanity was "enhypostasized" in the Second Person of the Trinity, and this act "corresponds to a primordial interrelation [between Divine and created Sophia]."[47] Furthermore, the

> real basis of the union of the two natures in Christ seems to lie in their mutual relationship as two variant forms of divine and created Wisdom [so that] the very dogma of Christology rests on sophiological foundations.[48]

Only one who is fully divine can reveal divine Sophia, and only one who is fully human can gather creaturely Sophia into communion with God. The hypostatic union in Christ is thus the personal realization of the unity Bulgakov describes between divine and creaturely wisdom.

The same logic extends to the sacramental life of the church, and especially to the Eucharist. If creation is structured according to the wisdom of God and ordered toward participation in divine life, then matter is not merely instrumental but capable of bearing the presence of God. The Eucharist reveals this most intensely. In the consecrated bread and wine, creaturely reality does not cease to be creaturely; rather, its deepest orientation toward communion with God is fulfilled. The church's insistence on the real, transubstantial presence of Christ in the Eucharist therefore corresponds to the same ontological pattern expressed in the Incarnation. Just as the humanity of Christ becomes the living bearer of divine life without ceasing to be human, so the eucharistic elements become the true Body and Blood of Christ without the annihilation of their creaturely reality.

Sophia helps illuminate why this is fitting rather than paradoxical. The created order, as creaturely Sophia, already exists in relation to the divine wisdom that grounds it. In the Eucharist, that relation becomes fully actualized: the material gifts of bread and wine become the site where divine and creaturely realities are united sacramentally in Christ. The sacrament, therefore, manifests what creation itself was always meant to be, *a participation in divine life that preserves both the transcendence of God and the integrity of the created world.* Seen in this light, the Nicene confession of Christ's full divinity and full humanity, together with the church's eucharistic realism, are not isolated doctrinal affirmations but expressions of a single theological vision. The Incarnation and the Eucharist witness to the same mystery: that the wisdom of God (Sophia) is not only the ground of creation but also its destiny, drawing the whole of creaturely existence into communion with the living God.

Divine Sophia names God's self-revelatory intelligibility and beauty the radiant form of God's own life. Created Sophia names creation as theophany: the world as meaningful, purposive, and capable of bearing God's presence without becoming God. The distinction guards against pantheism, but the relation guards against secularization, too. Together, they refuse the modern split that makes transcendence the enemy of immanence and turns the material world into an empty stage for human will and economic extraction. Sophia renders that split unintelligible because creation is *already* meaningful, *already* oriented, *already* a call to communion.

This is where Sophia presses directly into the concern with abstraction and commodification. Neoliberalism thrives on a specific metaphysic. It requires that things be detachable from ends, places, and obligations of care, so they can circulate frictionlessly as units of value. It trains us to perceive the world as an infinite warehouse of interchangeable objects and "opportunities," and to perceive ourselves as entrepreneurial subjects. Sophia interrupts this at the level of perception and desire. Bulgakov, through Sophia, insists that creation is not first a field of use but a field of wisdom, namely a structured, meaningful order that addresses us, summons us, and claims us as embodied creatures among other embodied creatures.

If Maximus teaches that the Eucharist is the church's participation in the cosmic gathering of all things in Christ, then Sophia clarifies *why* that participation is not an exchange. The Eucharist does not work by transferring spiritual goods through material tokens; it works by making the world eucharistic, by restoring the creaturely posture of thanksgiving, receptivity, and communal life. Bread and wine are not "inputs" in a religious economy; they are *the fruit of created order and human labor offered back to God.* God does not require this work as payment, just as God is not required to create. Both acts create an endless reciprocity through time, namely, gratitude begetting gratitude. In this sense, Sophia makes the Eucharist and Baptism legible as the world's true form: creation as a gift that becomes communion through offering and receiving. The sacrament is not an exit from creatureliness but the healing of creaturely life from within.

Sophia also intensifies the meaning of liturgy as *leitourgia*, the work of the people. As we have seen, in a neoliberal frame, work is primarily instrumentality: labor produces surplus; bodies become capital; time becomes a resource to optimize; community becomes a network to leverage. In contrast, cosmic liturgy is a different kind of work. It is the work of re-membering and rejoining what abstraction tears apart. It gathers creaturely life back into meaningful relations: soil to seed, seed to bread, bread to table, table to thanksgiving, thanksgiving to communion, communion to the re-formation of a people. Sophia names the wisdom of this work: the world is not saved by bypassing material processes but by reordering them into praise. The "work" at the heart of the sacraments is therefore not productivity but participation, the patient labor of becoming the kind of creatures who can receive gifts without possessing them and share life without converting it into value.

This dialectic becomes sharper when Sophia is read in explicitly Christological terms. Bulgakov's insistence that in Christ, divine Sophia and creaturely Sophia are united names the Incarnation not merely as God "entering history," but as the decisive unveiling of creation's destiny: *God's wisdom does not hover above matter; it dwells within it.* The Word made flesh is not simply a remedy for sin but the disclosure of creation's inner meaning: its capacity for communion, transfiguration, and glory. Here, Sophia complements Maximus beautifully: the *logoi* are not simply "ideas in God," but the world's sapiential structure, held in divine wisdom and destined to be gathered into Christ. The Eucharist, then, is not an isolated miracle appended to a disenchanted world; it is the concentrated enactment of the world's true vocation, whereby creation becomes communion in the incarnate Christ.[49]

As we have seen, neoliberalism not only commodifies objects, but it also commodifies space. Space becomes real estate, territory, platform, market, something to be owned, optimized, extracted, gentrified, militarized. It produces the strange modern experience of placelessness: we are everywhere connected and nowhere rooted; always circulating and rarely dwelling. Sophia offers a sacramental retrieval of space precisely because she refuses to let creation be treated as empty extension. Space is not nothing, however. Space is creaturely, and it is inscribed with meanings, histories, obligations, and limits. Sophia gives the world a theophanic density that invites reverence rather than consumption.

And this is where Sophia becomes a direct ally for a "new appreciation of space." In a eucharistic key, space is not neutral because the Eucharist is never placeless. Bread comes from somewhere. Wine comes from somewhere. Water comes from somewhere. Bodies come from somewhere. A people gather somewhere. The Eucharist, therefore, performs a quiet resistance to abstraction by forcing us back into the concreteness of creaturely life, into fields, vineyards, kitchens, tables, sanctuaries, and neighborhoods. Sophia names that concreteness as wisdom rather than accident. She teaches the church to see place not as property but as a gifted habitat, a site of creaturely dependence and mutual obligation.

Finally, Sophia re-situates humanity within creation as embodied creatures by refusing the modern conceit of disembodied autonomy. If neoliberal abstraction trains us to imagine ourselves as self-made agents who transcend the limits body, time, land, and community, Sophia returns us to a more honest anthropology. Humanity is not a sovereign will standing over the world; humanity is the creaturely site where creation becomes articulate in praise. To speak of human Sophia is to say this: that our vocation is not domination but mediation, not exploitation but thanksgiving, not conversion of life into value but participation in divine wisdom through embodied, communal, sacramental practices.

Therefore, if Maximus gives the church the vision of cosmic liturgy, Sophia gives the church its sapiential depth, the wisdom that makes liturgy not a ritual papering over of a hypercommodified world, but a meaningful alternative to it.

## Participation, Desire, and the Healing of Creation

The account of creation developed throughout this chapter should not be mistaken for an account of history. To confess that creation is ordered toward participation is not to deny the tragic reality that creaturely existence is continually distorted by sin. Creation is indeed gift, yet gifts remain susceptible to possessive desire. Participation is ordered toward communion, yet communion is repeatedly fractured through pride, fear, violence, and the relentless human impulse to transform what has been received into something owned. The goodness of creation, therefore, cannot be abstracted from the disorder of fallen desire.

Augustine's insight that sin is fundamentally a disordering of love remains indispensable at precisely this point. Human beings do not cease desiring after the Fall; rather, desire becomes curved inward upon itself, receiving creation no longer as a gift but as possession. Even the church is not immune from this distortion. The very gifts through which God intends communion can become instruments of exclusion whenever they are detached from their proper end in God. The problem, therefore, is not participation itself but participation governed by disordered desire.

This distinction also clarifies the relationship between participation and hierarchy. Christian theology has long recognized forms of order, authority, and differentiation within creation and the church that are not reducible to domination. Indeed, many of the theological voices retrieved in this chapter—including Maximus the Confessor—understand created order as expressive of God's wisdom rather than as an obstacle to communion. Hierarchy becomes destructive only when order ceases to exist for mutual participation and instead becomes a means of securing privilege, exclusion, or control. The Christian question is therefore not whether all distinctions disappear but whether every distinction is ordered toward the flourishing of the whole body.

Likewise, creation must not be confused with redemption. Creation is good because it proceeds from the generosity of God; redemption is necessary because that goodness has been wounded by sin. Participation belongs to creation's deepest vocation, but reconciliation belongs to God's redemptive work in Jesus Christ. Redemption does not replace creation with another reality but heals creation so that it may become what it was always intended to be. In Christ, creaturely participation is not abolished but restored. The church, therefore, anticipates the reconciliation of all things not because creation has already achieved its fulfillment but because the risen Christ has begun the renewal toward which creation has always been ordered.

The same distinction applies to place and belonging. Throughout this chapter, place has been presented as the ordinary context within which creaturely life is received, cultivated, and shared. Yet history reminds us that places may also become sites of exclusion, conquest, nationalism, and violence. The problem lies not in belonging itself but in the corruption of belonging through possessive desire. Whenever communities imagine themselves as owners rather than stewards, or whenever identity is secured through the exclusion of others, place ceases to function sacramentally and instead becomes a blunt instrument of domination. Christian belonging, therefore, remains fundamentally eschatological. The church receives every place as a gift while refusing to absolutize any place as the exclusive possession of any people. Creation belongs ultimately to God, and every human community inhabits it as a guest before it inhabits it as an owner.

These ambiguities do not weaken the participatory vision advanced throughout this chapter; they reveal its necessity. The goodness of creation alone cannot secure communion because creation has been wounded by sin. Nor can human desire heal itself through moral effort alone. Participation becomes genuinely reconciliatory only where Christ gathers estranged creatures into his own life through the Holy Spirit. The sacramental vision proposed here is therefore neither naïvely optimistic nor romantically nostalgic. It is a theology of hope grounded in the conviction that the God who created the world in love has also entered its disorder in order to restore every creature to the communion for which it was first made.

## Conclusion

This chapter has pressed a single conviction from multiple angles: sacramental life is inseparable from creaturely life. From Genesis's portrayal of God making "room" for creation and calling it good, to the wilderness's manna, to the waters of washing and baptism, and finally to the contested meals of the apostolic church, Scripture refuses to let us imagine that salvation happens over and above the material world. The basic textures of embodied existence, namely hunger and thirst, eating and washing, sharing and withholding, are the very sites where human desire is either distorted into domination or healed into communion. The chapter names the stakes sharply: the Fall is the misdirection of desire, where creation ceases to be received as gift and is instead grasped as an object of control, profit, and division. The sacraments are God's gracious reorientation of embodied life, retraining desire away from exploitative patterns and toward dependence, humility, and shared fellowship in God's mission.

In that light, the chapter's movement through the biblical narratives is not simply illustrative but formative. Naaman's washing and Christ's baptism render water a site of humbled receptivity rather than self-mastery. Manna and the Lord's Supper expose how God feeds creatures in ways that undermine hoarding and re-inscribe reliance. Peter's vision and Paul's admonitions show that eating can either ratify old boundaries or become the Spirit's means of remaking a community where God's "good" is spoken over those once named unclean. Put differently: sacramental practice is not an inward religious experience that happens to use outward stuff; it is God's way of reorganizing social life by reorganizing bodily life.

Maximus the Confessor then gathers these biblical themes into a sustained theological orientation capable of resisting abstraction. He clarifies how desire itself must be healed, so that virtue is not the accumulation of "moral capital" but the alignment of hunger with the order of creation. Thus, the church learns to desire God not by escaping matter, but by eating, drinking, washing, and sharing differently. Here, the Eucharist emerges as the fundamental force that destabilizes the logics of our consumer culture. Christ does not circulate as value but gathers a people. Thus, the sacraments are best named as *leitourgia*, the "work of the people," wherein creation is taken up and returned as thanksgiving.

The sacramental economy is the antipody of the modern market economy: space as gift and limit, bodies as sites of communion, and desire as ordered toward God and neighbor. In that sense, this chapter's final claim is not merely doctrinal but practical: a renewed sacramental imagination is a concrete school of freedom—freedom from the abstraction that enables commodification, and freedom for an embodied life of gratitude, mutuality, and creaturely joy within God's good world.

## Notes

1. This chapter intentionally develops its account of participation through Maximus the Confessor and Sergei Bulgakov because each offers a theological grammar capable of holding together creation, Christology, sacramentality, and cosmic reconciliation within a single constructive vision. This selective retrieval is not intended to suggest that these figures exhaust contemporary participatory theology. Significant conversation partners—including John D. Zizioulas, David Bentley Hart, Rowan Williams, and Jean-Louis Chrétien—have each emphasized complementary dimensions of participation, including ecclesial communion, divine transcendence, creaturely contingency, liturgical response, and the irreducible mystery of created existence. Their work provides important correctives against collapsing creation into redemption or diminishing the distinction between Creator and creature. While these concerns remain essential, the present chapter focuses more narrowly on the sacramental ontology of creation as the theological foundation for solidarity with the poor. The argument therefore proceeds by emphasizing those aspects of participatory theology most directly concerned with creation as divine gift while presupposing, rather than attempting to rehearse in detail, the broader theological tradition within which these insights are situated.

2. Robert Jenson, *Systematic Theology Vol. 2: The Works of God* (Oxford University Press, 1999), 34.

3. For more on this argument, see Dietrich Bonhoeffer, *Creation and Fall: A Theological Exposition of Genesis 1–3. Dietrich Bonhoeffer Works Vol. 3.*, ed. John W. De Grunchy, trans. Douglas Stephen Bax (Fortress Press, 1997), 111–114.

4. See Alexander Schmemann, *For the Life of the World* (SVS Press, 1973), 19.

5. Schmemann, *For the Life of the World,* 17.

6. Unless otherwise noted, the biblical readings developed throughout this chapter are intended as exercises in theological and figural interpretation rather than historical-critical exegesis. The argument proceeds from the conviction that Scripture may be read canonically and christologically within the church's theological tradition, while fully recognizing that the historical meaning of Israel's Scriptures must first be understood within their own literary, historical, and theological contexts. Accordingly, the sacramental significance identified here is not presented as the original intention of the biblical authors but as a theological judgment emerging through the church's long history of interpretation, worship, and doctrinal reflection. This study therefore presupposes rather than rejects the contributions of historical-critical scholarship while pursuing the distinct constructive task of Christian dogmatics. See, for example the work of: John J. Collins, James L. Kugel, Jon D. Levenson, and Walter Brueggemann.

7. Gregory of Nyssa, "The Fourth Homily," *Homilies on Ecclesiastes,* ed. John Litteral, trans. Ruichard McCambly (Litteral Christian Library Publication, 2014), 41.

8. Stanley Hauerwas, *Matthew: Brazos Theological Commentary on the Bible* (Brazos Press, 2006), 49.

9. Lauren Winner, *Still: Notes on a Mid-Faith Crisis* (HarperOne, 2012), 35–36.

10. Ludwig Feuerbach, *Sämtliche Werke.* Quoted in Alexander Schmemann, *For the Life of the World* (St. Vladimir's Seminary Press, 1997), 11.

11. Carl L Holiday, *Acts: A Commentary. The New Testament Library* (Westminster John Knox Press, 2016), 232.

12. Holiday, *Acts,* 232.

13. Willie James Jennings, *Acts*, Belief: A Theological Commentary on the Bible (Westminster John Knox Press, 2017), 105.

14. See Richard I Pervo, *Acts: A Commentary,* Hermeneia: A Critical and Historical Commentary on the Bible, ed. Harold Attridge (Fortress Press, 2009), 269.

15. Jennings, *Acts,* 107.

16. Jennings, *Acts,* 108.

17. Jennings, *Acts,* 109.

18. Pervo, *Acts,* 269.

19. Hans Conselmann, *1 Corinthians: A Commentary. Hermenia: A Critical and Historical Commentary on the Bible,* trans. James Leitch, ed. George MacRae S.J. Fortress Press, 1975), 199–200.

20. Ernst Käsemann, "The Pauline Doctrine of the Lord's Supper," *Essays on New Testament Themes,* trans. W. J. Montague (SCM Press, 1960), 113.

21. Käsemann, "The Pauline Doctrine of the Lord's Supper," 114. Emphasis original.

22. Käsemann, "The Pauline Doctrine of the Lord's Supper," 116.

23. Käsemann, "The Pauline Doctrine of the Lord's Supper," 117.

24. Käsemann, "The Pauline Doctrine of the Lord's Supper," 118.

25. Käsemann, "The Pauline Doctrine of the Lord's Supper," 119.

26. Allen Verhey, *Remembering Jesus: Christian Community, Scripture, and the Moral Life* (Eerdmans Publishing Company, 2002), 26.

27. William T. Cavanaugh, *Torture and Eucharist: Theology, Politics, and the Body of Christ* (Blackwell Publishing, 1998), 230.

28. Cavanaugh, *Torture and Eucharist,* 230.

29. Cavanaugh, *Torture and Eucharist,* 229.

30. Cavanaugh, *Torture and Eucharist*, 267.

31. This genealogy is intentionally selective and should not be read as denying the richness of alternative accounts of medieval sacramental theology. Caroline Walker Bynum has demonstrated that medieval eucharistic devotion often remained deeply embodied and materially attentive, while Henri de Lubac famously argued that the Eucharist constitutes the church through participation in Christ's body rather than merely serving as an object of devotion. Likewise, John Milbank and Catherine Pickstock have developed accounts of participation and liturgy that resist the reduction of sacramental life to modern economic rationality. This study remains deeply indebted to these retrievals. Its concern, however, is less the internal development of sacramental theology than the concrete question of how eucharistic participation is realized in solidarity with those experiencing poverty. It therefore asks not simply how the Eucharist constitutes the church, but how the church's eucharistic life becomes visible in its common life with the poor.

32. Athanasius, *On the Incarnation*, trans. John Behr, Popular Patristics Series 44 (St. Vladimir's Seminary Press, 2011), §1.

33. Athanasius, *On the Incarnation*, §13.

34. Athanasius, *On the Incarnation*, §45.

35. Athanasius, *On the Incarnation*, §54.

36. Athanasius of Alexandria, *The Works of the Spirit: Athanasius's Letters to Serapion on the Holy Spirit*, trans. Mark DelCogliano, Andrew Radde-Gallwitz, and Lewis Ayres, *Popular Patristics Series 43* (St. Vladimir's Seminary Press, 2011), §1.28.3.

37. Athanasius, *The Works of the Spirit*, §1.24.1.

38. Athanasius of Alexandria, *Sermon to the Newly Baptized*, on Orthodox.net, accessed March 5, 2026, https://orthodox.net/gleanings/holy_communion.html.

39. Athanasius, *On the Incarnation*, §54

40. Jordan Daniel Wood, "Creation Is Incarnation: The Metaphysical Peculiarity of the Logoi in Maximus Confessor," *Modern Theology* 33, no. 2 (April 2018), 34.

41. Maximus the Confessor, *On the Ecclesiastical Mystagogy*, trans. and ed. Jonathan J. Armstrong, Popular Patristics Series 59 (St. Vladimir's Seminary Press, 2019), 88. (§24)

42. Jordan Daniel Wood, "Creation Is Incarnation: The Metaphysical Peculiarity of the *Logoi* in Maximus Confessor," *Modern Theology* 34, no. 1 (2018), 98.

43. Hans Urs von Balthasar, *Cosmic Liturgy: The Universe According to Maximus the Confessor*, 2nd ed., trans. Brian E. Daley (Ignatius Press, 2003), xx.

44. Sergei Bulgakov, *Sophia: The Wisdom of God. An Outline of Sophia,* trans. Patrick Thompson (Lindisfarne Press, 1993), 74.

45. Bulgakov, *Sophia,* 57.

46. Bulgakov, *Sophia,* 57.

47. Sergei Bulgakov, *The Lamb of God,* trans. Boris Jakim (Eerdmans, 2008), 187.

48. Bulgakov, *Sophia,* 88.

49. This argument intentionally distinguishes itself from, while remaining indebted to, several important contemporary accounts of gift and sacramentality. Marcel Mauss famously demonstrated that gifts rarely exist outside networks of reciprocity, obligation, and social exchange, suggesting that gift-giving establishes enduring relationships rather than disinterested generosity. (Marcel Mauss, *The Gift: The Form and Reason for Exchange in Archaic Societies,* trans. W. D. Halls [W. W. Norton, 1990]) Jacques Derrida radicalized this insight by arguing that a "pure gift" is, strictly speaking, impossible, since the moment a gift is recognized as gift it enters economies of memory, reciprocity, gratitude, or self-consciousness. (Jacques Derrida, *Given Time I: Counterfeit Money,*

trans. Peggy Kamuf [University of Chicago Press, 1992], 7–41). Jean-Luc Marion responds by relocating the logic of gift within the phenomenology of givenness, arguing that divine donation exceeds economic calculation precisely because it is received prior to conceptual mastery or exchange. (Jean-Luc Marion, *Being Given: Toward a Phenomenology of Givenness,* trans. Jeffrey L. Kosky [Stanford University Press, 2002], 65–121.) Louis-Marie Chauvet develops perhaps the most important sacramental account for the present discussion. Rejecting both transactional understandings of sacramental grace and overly individualistic notions of gratuitous giving, Chauvet argues that Christian existence is constituted through symbolic exchange within the ecclesial body. Sacramental gifts are never commodities possessed by individuals but practices of reception, response, and mutual participation that continually form the church. (Louis-Marie Chauvet, *Symbol and Sacrament: A Sacramental Reinterpretation of Christian Existence,* trans. Patrick Madigan and Madeleine Beaumont [Liturgical Press, 1995], 95–171; Louis-Marie Chauvet, *The Sacraments: The Word of God at the Mercy of the Body* [Liturgical Press, 2001], 1–34). This study shares Chauvet's rejection of sacramental instrumentalism and his insistence that gift cannot be reduced to economic transaction. At the same time, it departs from Chauvet by locating the logic of gift more explicitly within the church's concrete solidarity with the poor. The Eucharist is not simply a symbolic economy that resists commodification; it is the sacramental participation in Christ's self-giving life that necessarily orders the church toward those whom neoliberal economies render disposable. Consequently, the question is not merely how sacramental exchange differs from market exchange, but how the Eucharistic gift forms a people whose common life refuses the abstraction of persons into commodities.

## CHAPTER 5

# A Practice for the Poor: Sacraments, Liberation, and Ecotheology

As we have seen in an earlier chapter, liberation theology has always insisted that salvation is not abstract. God's liberating action unfolds in history, in bodies, in places, and within concrete systems that either sustain or destroy life. From its earliest formulations, the preferential option for the poor named not only God's concern for the marginalized but a methodological demand: theology must begin from the underside of history, from those whose lives are rendered vulnerable by economic, political, and social arrangements. Yet the argument of the preceding chapters has revealed a growing tension within contemporary theological practice. While liberation theology has rightly centered the poor, it has too often left unexamined the material conditions—land, water, labor, climate, and space—through which poverty itself is produced and maintained.

This chapter argues that the preferential option for the poor must be extended to include creation itself: not as a replacement for concern for the poor, but as its necessary deepening. The poor are not made poor apart from land theft, extractive economies, environmental racism, climate instability, and the commodification of food and water. Creation is not a neutral backdrop to injustice but one of its primary sites. To speak of liberation while abstracting from soil, place, and ecological vulnerability is to risk repeating the very logic that renders both people and land expendable.

At the same time, extending the preferential option to creation raises a further challenge: how to do so without collapsing the distinction between human and nonhuman life, or dissolving theological responsibility into ecological sentimentality. This chapter, therefore, advances a theological reorientation around *shared creaturehood*, a way of affirming difference without domination and relation without reduction. Drawing on ecological theology, anthropology, political economy, and phenomenologies of place, it shows how creaturehood resists both anthropocentrism and commodification, grounding justice in finitude, dependence, and gift.

Central to this argument is the claim that the *sacraments are not merely symbols of liberation, but practices that train communities to inhabit the world otherwise*. Against neoliberal capitalism's abstraction of space, bodies, and land, sacramental practice re-forms perception. Baptism and Eucharist sanctify matter, place, and time, refusing to allow bread, water, bodies, or land to function as interchangeable resources. They reorient desire away from accumulation and toward communion, away from abstract space and toward inhabited place. When practiced within a theology attentive to creation, the sacraments become sites of resistance to the economic and spatial logics that produce poverty and ecological devastation.

The chapter concludes by arguing that agrarian life, understood not nostalgically but sacramentally, offers a concrete communal extension of sacramental logic. Drawing on Wendell Berry, agrarianism is presented as a disciplined way of life shaped by limits, gratitude, locality, and care. When sacramental practice and agrarian living are held together, they form communities capable of resisting neoliberal abstraction, commodification, and dispossession. Liberation, in this vision, is not escape from creatureliness but its recovery: a way of living where land is cherished, bodies are honored, and life is received as gift rather than consumed as product.

## Practicing Liberation Theology: The Preferential Option for the Poor

The preferential option for the poor is not only a moral principle within Christian ethics; it is a theological judgment about how God relates to the world. From its emergence in liberation theology in the 1960s, the option names God's concrete, historical solidarity with those made vulnerable by systems of domination. It insists that theology, ethics, and ecclesial practice must be oriented toward those whose lives are rendered expendable. Yet if the argument of the preceding chapters holds, that abstraction is the mechanism by which bodies, land, and communities are rendered exchangeable, then the logic of the preferential option presses further than it has often been allowed to go. Creation itself must be drawn inside the preferential option for the poor.

We are not bidding farewell to liberation theology but extending its territory. The biblical witness that grounds the preferential option already refuses any sharp division between social injustice and the material world. God hears the cry of enslaved Israel not in the abstract but in a land of forced labor, ecological depletion, and bodily exhaustion (Exodus 3:7–10). The prophets condemn not only economic exploitation but the desolation of land and the violent extraction of its fruits (Isaiah 5; Amos 8). Jesus's proclamation of good news to the poor (Luke 4:18–19) unfolds through healings of bodies, shared meals, restored access to land and community, and resistance to systems that concentrate wealth while stripping creation of its generative capacity. Poverty, in Scripture, is never merely economic; it is embodied, spatial, and ecological.

Gustavo Gutiérrez's articulation of the preferential option for the poor emerges precisely from this concreteness. Writing in the context of structural poverty and political violence in Latin America, he rejects theological approaches that speak about God while remaining insulated from suffering bodies and dispossessed communities. Theology, he insists, must arise from praxis, from participation in God's liberating work among the oppressed. To know God is to do justice. Yet what is increasingly clear is that the poor are made poor not only by economic systems but by ecological ones: through land theft, environmental racism, extractive industries, climate collapse, and the commodification of water, soil, and food. The poor suffer first and most intensely where creation itself is treated as expendable.

Here, the epistemological privilege of the poor becomes decisive for ecological theology. Liberation theology has long argued that the poor see realities that the powerful are structurally prevented from seeing. What must now be acknowledged is that the poor also know creation differently. They experience polluted water as sickness, degraded land as hunger, and climate instability as displacement. Their suffering exposes the fiction that economic injustice and ecological destruction are separable problems. If theology is to be accountable to the knowledge of the poor, then creation cannot remain outside the preferential option. To exclude it would be to abstract poverty itself.

An ecologically enriched perspective advances a sharpened claim: the preferential option for the poor must become a preferential option for the poor *within* creation. Not because creation replaces the poor as the subject of justice, but because the degradation of creation is one of the primary means by which the poor are produced, maintained, and sacrificed. Charity that ignores land, water, and climate merely treats symptoms. Justice that refuses to address ecological exploitation remains structurally incomplete. As Gutiérrez insists, poverty is not fate but injustice, and today that injustice is inseparable from ecological violence.

For the preferential option for the poor has never been merely a policy preference or charitable posture; it has always been a call to conversion; a confrontation with complicity in systems that privilege power. In an age of ecological crisis, that conversion must now be understood as eco-social. The question is no longer whether the church should care about the earth in addition to the poor, but whether it can meaningfully claim fidelity to the Gospel without recognizing that the poor and the earth are bound together within the same logic of sacrifice.

This chapter will therefore argue that drawing creation inside the preferential option for the poor is not an ideological move but a theological necessity. It follows from the biblical witness, from liberation theology's own epistemology, from sacramental practice, and from the concrete realities of late modern capitalism. To speak of liberation today without speaking of land, water, and climate is to abstract liberation itself. The task before the church is not to balance social justice and ecological concern, but to recognize that there is no justice for the poor apart from the healing of the earth they inhabit and no care for creation that does not begin with those whom its destruction wounds first.

## Ecologies, Ecotheologies, and the Sacrament of Embodiment

One of the most significant barriers to drawing creation within the preferential option for the poor is theology's longstanding tendency to erase the doctrine of creation in favor of narrowly construed human *need.* Even traditions deeply committed to justice for the oppressed have often assumed an anthropocentric framework in which creation functions primarily as background, instrument, or resource for human liberation. Within this paradigm, the earth matters insofar as it serves human flourishing, but rarely as a subject of theological concern. While motivated by laudable ethical aims, this approach risks reproducing the very logic of abstraction and instrumentalization that liberation theology otherwise seeks to resist.

Anthropocentrism becomes especially problematic when it treats creation as a neutral stage upon which human injustice unfolds. When land, water, climate, and nonhuman life are rendered theologically secondary, ecological devastation is easily framed as a tragic but external consequence of poverty rather than one of its primary causes. In such accounts, the poor remain the focus of God's concern, but the material conditions that produce and sustain poverty remain under-theorized. Creation is thus functionally erased, even as the suffering of the poor is named and condemned.

It is precisely this theological tendency that Sallie McFague's *The Body of God* seeks to confront. Written in response to the escalating ecological crisis, McFague's work challenges the deep assumptions of classical theism that have shaped both Christian doctrine and Christian ethics. She argues that dualistic and anthropocentric models of God, particularly those emphasizing divine transcendence as distance or separation, have contributed to a worldview in which the material world is devalued, instrumentalized, and ultimately sacrificed. When God is imagined primarily as "above" or "outside" creation, creation itself becomes disposable.

At the heart of McFague's proposal is a radical yet carefully articulated metaphor: the world as the body of God. She writes,

> were we to speak of the universe as God's body, it would not be this or that body, but *all* the bodies that have ever been or ever will be, from quarks and exploding stars to microorganisms and centipedes, rocks, mountains, and water, but not forgetting tortoises, pine trees, buttercups, giraffes, and, of course, human beings in all their various shapes, conditions, and colors.[1]

McFague's metaphor does not collapse the distinction between Creator and creation, but it resists any theology that treats the material world as theologically incidental. For McFague, metaphors are not ornamental; they are formative. The metaphors Christians use to speak about God shape how they live, what they value, and what they are willing to destroy. By reimagining creation as God's body, McFague shifts theological attention from domination to embodiment, from mastery to relationality, and from abstraction to material presence.

Creation as "the Body of God" directly challenges anthropocentric accounts of creation that privilege human needs at the expense of the wider community of life. If the world is God's body, then humanity is not its owner or manager but a member within it. Human flourishing cannot be abstracted from the flourishing of soil, water, air, and ecosystems. Ecological harm, in this vision, is not merely poor stewardship or bad policy; it is violence against the body in which all creatures, including the poor, inhabit. McFague thus exposes how anthropocentrism, even when motivated by concern for justice, risks reinscribing domination at a different scale.

McFague's theology of embodiment also provides a critical corrective to the abstraction that has often characterized both doctrinal theology and social ethics. Rather than beginning with universal principles and applying them to contexts, she insists that theology must remain embodied in material interdependence. "Embodiment gives us a commonality with everything else on the planet (including even such remote bodies from ours as trees, rocks, and mountains) with which to reconceive our place in the scheme of things."[2] This claim has profound implications for liberation theology: it suggests that liberation cannot be conceived solely in terms of human emancipation from economic or political oppression, but must include liberation from ecological systems that render both humans and nonhumans expendable.

Importantly, McFague's work also presses sacramental theology beyond anthropocentric limits. Her vision invites a reimagining of practices such as the Eucharist as a ritual deeply entangled with land, labor, grain, water, and climate. In this light, sacramental abstraction becomes ethically dangerous: when bread and wine are severed from the ecological and economic systems that produce them, the sacrament risks sanctifying the very forms of extraction that impoverish communities and devastate ecosystems. McFague's embodied theology resists this move, insisting that materiality is not a problem to be overcome but the very site of divine presence.

## Shared Creaturehood Beyond Anthropocentrism and Ecological Reduction

If anthropocentric theology risks erasing creation by subordinating it to human need, an equally serious danger emerges in ecological accounts that collapse the distinction between human and nonhuman life altogether. A renewed ecological theology must resist both errors. What is required is not a leveling of differences between creation and humanity, but a reorientation of both within a shared condition of creaturehood. Humans and forests are not identical, but neither are they ontologically opposed.

Any attempt to articulate a sacramental preferential option for the poor that includes the earth must begin with a reconsideration of the human. Much Christian theology has inherited a philosophical anthropology that subtly reinforces the same logic that animates neoliberal capitalism: the human as a self-possessing, rational subject standing over and against the world. The sacramental imagination resists this abstraction. It insists that grace meets creatures not outside material conditions but precisely through them. Consequently, an anthropology capable of sustaining a sacramental preferential option for the poor must recover the human as a materially dependent, relational, and more-than-human creature.

Recent philosophical and anthropological work provides important resources for such a recovery. Samantha Frost, Eduardo Kohn, and Elizabeth Povinelli each challenge the modern assumption that the human is an autonomous subject set apart from the world. Taken together, their work allows us to articulate a theological anthropology in which human life is constituted through relations with other humans, other creatures, and the places that sustain them. Within such an anthropology, the preferential option for the poor cannot remain limited to human social structures alone. The ecological conditions that sustain life become inseparable from the moral and theological concern for the poor.

Samantha Frost's account of humans as "biocultural creatures" offers an especially helpful starting point. Frost argues that modern political and philosophical thought has often relied upon an implicit fantasy of human independence. Against this assumption, she insists that humans must be understood as living bodies embedded within material and ecological systems. As she writes, humans "are alive and are able to stay alive because they are embedded in and draw manifold forms of sustenance from a habitat."[3] What might appear as autonomy is in fact the product of countless material relations that sustain bodily life.

To describe humans as biocultural creatures is to reject the idea that the human stands outside nature. Instead, the human emerges through ongoing exchanges with ecological systems and cultural practices. For this reason, Frost resists what she calls the "hubristic exception" that imagines humans as somehow abstracted from the conditions that sustain them.[4]

Her account immediately reframes the theological meaning of poverty. If human beings are constituted through their habitats, then environmental degradation is not an external issue adjacent to poverty. It is one of the primary ways poverty is produced. Polluted water, toxic soil, unstable climates, and extractive land use do not merely harm ecosystems; they damage the material conditions that sustain human bodies, especially those who inhabit these damaged environments, who are disproportionately poor.

Frost's account, however, also avoids collapsing the human entirely into ecological systems. Biocultural creatures are shaped by their environments but are not reducible to them. Humans possess the capacity to respond creatively to the conditions that shape them, drawing on histories of adaptation and response embedded within biological and cultural systems. As Frost notes, biocultural creatures act as "anticipatory forms whose creative responses to the provocations of habitat draw on rich histories of responses."[5] This responsiveness preserves a space for ethical agency without returning to fantasies of autonomy. Humans remain creatures formed by habitats, yet capable of reshaping those habitats through collective action.

If human life is already embedded within ecological relationships, Eduardo Kohn's anthropology pushes this insight further by challenging the assumption that thought belongs exclusively to humans. Drawing on his ethnographic work in the Amazon and the semiotic philosophy of Charles Peirce, Kohn argues that the processes of interpretation and signification that constitute thought are not confined to human language. Rather, they extend throughout living systems. As Kohn famously puts it, "Forests are good to think because they themselves think."[6] This provocative claim does not suggest that forests think in the same way humans do. Instead, Kohn argues that living beings participate in semiotic processes through which they interpret and respond to signs in their environments. Animals interpret the movements of predators and prey; plants respond to light and chemical signals; ecosystems register disturbances and reorganize themselves in response. In this sense, thought is not confined to human consciousness but emerges through networks of relational life.

Kohn's argument challenges the sharp boundary that modern thought has drawn between human subjects and a passive natural world. If nonhuman beings participate in semiotic processes, if they respond, interpret, and anticipate, then the world cannot be understood as inert matter awaiting human management. Instead, the human lives within a dynamic field of relational agencies in which other creatures also participate in processes of meaning and response. As Kohn observes, "Nonhuman living beings are constitutively semiotic. . .these nonhuman selves think."[7]

This insight has profound implications for sacramental theology. Sacraments do not merely symbolize divine realities; they mediate grace through material forms that participate in a broader ecology of meaning. Water, bread, wine, oil, and earth are *not* inert substances waiting to be assigned symbolic value by human communities. They already belong to living networks of meaning and exchange deeply embedded within God's own creation. They contain a rationality that flows from the wider ecology of signs that constitutes living worlds, where material forms already participate in a network of meaning before humans name them. The elements, then, go before and after the human as a means of grace already embedded within creation capable of divine indwelling. A sacramental worldview, therefore, resonates with Kohn's anthropology insofar as both resist the reduction of matter to passive material.

Yet this recognition of a living field of meaning also raises a political question: how have modern systems of power managed to render much of the world as inert matter available for exploitation? Elizabeth Povinelli's concept of *geontopower* adds a crucial political dimension to this rethinking of anthropology. Povinelli argues that contemporary forms of power increasingly operate not simply by regulating life and death, as Michel Foucault's concept of biopolitics suggested, but by governing the distinction between life and nonlife itself. Geontopower, she writes, is "a set of discourse, affects, and tactics used in late liberalism to maintain. . .the distinction between Life and Nonlife."[8] This distinction plays a central role in modern extractive economies. By classifying land, minerals, forests, and waters as nonliving resources, modern political systems authorize their unlimited exploitation. Such a classification simultaneously enables ecological destruction and obscures the relational systems that sustain human life.

Povinelli's critique, therefore, exposes the metaphysical assumptions that underwrite both ecological devastation and the abandonment of the poor. Both forms of abandonment rely upon the same underlying ontology: the belief that certain forms of existence can be rendered inert, disposable, or invisible within the moral imagination.

Against this background, a sacramental preferential option for the poor in creation requires an alternative anthropology that resists these divisions. Humans must be understood not as *sovereign managers* of an inert world but as *creatures* embedded within living systems that sustain and exceed them. The human person is therefore neither the master of creation nor merely one organism among others. Rather, humans occupy a distinctive place within a web of relational life: a place marked by dependence, vulnerability, and responsibility.

Such an anthropology aligns naturally with the theological logic of the preferential option for the poor. The poor reveal the truth of creaturely dependence that modern systems attempt to deny. They expose the fragile material conditions upon which human life depends. In doing so, they also reveal the ecological relations that sustain life more broadly. A sacramental preferential option for the poor, therefore, extends outward into creation itself, recognizing that the flourishing of human communities cannot be separated from the flourishing of the places that sustain them.

In this way, the sacramental imagination resists both the abstraction of neoliberal economics and the reductionism of purely ecological thought. It affirms that grace moves through material relations while insisting that these relations are not merely instrumental. They are sites of divine encounter. The earth is not simply the stage upon which salvation unfolds. It is one of the primary media through which that salvation is experienced.

To recover such an anthropology is therefore to recover the moral and theological significance of place. Human life unfolds within particular landscapes such as watersheds, forests, fields, and neighborhoods that sustain bodily existence. When these places are degraded, both the poor and the earth suffer together. Conversely, when they are restored, both human communities and ecological systems can flourish. A sacramental preferential option for the poor in creation thus calls the church to attend not only to social structures but also to the material landscapes through which God's grace is mediated.

## Sacrament, Creaturehood, and the Liberation of Place

If neoliberal capitalism depends upon abstraction, then the sacraments constitute a counter-practice that refuses abstraction at every level. They do so not merely by sanctifying human embodiment, but by re-forming how creaturehood itself is understood: as shared, placed, and materially graced.

One of the central obstacles to drawing creation inside the preferential option for the poor is theology's long habit of collapsing creation into human use, especially in moments of ethical urgency. When the poor are centered rightly, but creation is treated instrumentally, the option for the poor risks remaining anthropocentric, even as it resists economic injustice. The sacraments interrupt this tendency precisely because they do not permit matter, space, or creaturely life to function merely as means.

Here, John Chryssavgis's articulation of *creation as sacrament* is vital. For Chryssavgis, sacramentality discloses what matters already: a gifted medium of divine presence. He writes, "The divine presence is discovered in every detail, and every particle of this world; the divine Word (Logos) converses intimately with every word (logos) of creation because the divine Logos always and everywhere 'wills to effect this mystery of divine embodiment.'"[9] It is no coincidence that Chryssavgis ends his statement with a quote from Maximus the Confessor. Like Maximus, Chryssavgis knows that creation is not sacramental because it serves human salvation; rather, human salvation is sacramental because it occurs *within* creation. Thus, bread and wine have a value beyond basic human need: humans are re-educated in their creaturehood by receiving bread and wine as gifts that exceed them.

To recall Maximus the Confessor, the theological and cosmic depth of this claim. In Maximus's vision, the Eucharist does not merely gather human worshipers; it recapitulates the logoi of creation itself. Grain, vine, soil, labor, climate, and time are drawn into Christ's offering to the Father. The Eucharist is therefore not an escape from materiality but its eschatological clarification. As a cosmic liturgy, it reveals creation's vocation not as raw material for accumulation but as participant in praise. This sacramental shift relocates justice and liberation within a broader field of creaturely reconciliation. The poor are not liberated *from* creation but *with* it.

Therefore, we must return to Casey's phenomenology of place, which names the stakes spatially. Casey argues that modernity has systematically replaced place with abstract, homogenous, and easily commodified space. Abstract space is the spatial analog of neoliberal logic: memories, relationships, and real presence are erased in favor of mobility and control. Place, by contrast, is saturated with history, embodiment, and meaning; it gathers rather than disperses. Casey insists that we are not first located in space and then placed later, we are always already *implaced* beings. The sacraments enact precisely this recovery of place. Baptism happens *somewhere* in water drawn from a watershed, within a community, at a font shaped by memory. Eucharist is celebrated *here*, at an altar that gathers bodies, land, bread, and story. These are not neutral coordinates but sacred places where creaturehood is re-taught. This is why sacramental theology is inherently anti-neoliberal: It refuses the abstraction of space that makes exploitation possible.

When read alongside liberation theology, this insight becomes sharper. The preferential option for the poor has always insisted that suffering is not abstract but is materially embedded in *this* body, *this* neighborhood, *this* land. Sacramental practice reinforces this. It trains the church to see injustice not as a general problem but as a violation of place: poisoned water, stolen land, displaced communities, exhausted soil. Extending the preferential option to creation, then, is not an add-on but a deepening of its logic.

Here, sacramental practice functions as a pedagogy of resistance. By sanctifying places, it resists the neoliberal fiction that all space is equally available for use. By blessing matter, it refuses the reduction of creation to commodity. By gathering bodies without price, it interrupts the logic of exchange. The Eucharist does not circulate value; it halts circulation long enough for gift to be recognized as gift.

Seen this way, the sacraments are not merely symbols of liberation; they are counter-formations that reshape desire, retrain perception, and relocate human life within a shared creaturely world. They form a people capable of imagining justice beyond growth, abundance beyond accumulation, and salvation beyond escape.

This is why the extension of the preferential option for the poor to creation is not a dilution of liberation theology but its fulfillment. It names what neoliberalism cannot: that creaturehood itself is the site of grace, that place is holy before it is profitable, and that liberation begins not with mastery but with reverent participation in a world already addressed by God.

## Excursus: A Shift From Ecclesial Being

Zizioulas's influential claim that "being is communion" seeks to overturn the individualism that has dominated modern metaphysics by locating personhood within relational existence. In his account, the eucharistic community becomes the primary site where this ontology is realized, for "the person is an identity constituted by relationships" rather than by autonomous substance.[10] The church gathered in eucharistic communion thus reveals the deepest truth of being: existence emerges through relational participation rather than isolated individuality. This insight remains one of the most powerful theological responses to modern liberal anthropology. Yet the relational ontology Zizioulas develops remains strikingly confined to the sphere of human and ecclesial communion. The material world appears primarily as the setting in which eucharistic relationships unfold rather than as an active participant in the relational life he describes. Creation mediates communion but rarely appears as a subject within it.

John Chryssavgis's ecological sacramental theology presses precisely at this point. For Chryssavgis, the sacramental principle cannot be restricted to ecclesial rites because "the entire world is a sacrament of communion with God."[11] If sacramentality is intrinsic to creation itself, then the Eucharist cannot be understood apart from the material processes that sustain it. Bread and wine are not generic substances but the fruits of particular soils, climates, and agricultural practices. Chryssavgis insists that sacramental vision demands attentiveness to the ecological conditions that make these elements possible, arguing that "no place is without its sacredness, and no part of creation is devoid of divine presence."[12] When sacramental theology limits communion to the liturgical assembly without attending to the environments that sustain it, the Eucharist risks becoming detached from the very creation through which divine life is mediated.

The anthropological assumptions underlying Zizioulas's account become even more fragile when read alongside Eduardo Kohn's challenge to human exceptionalism. Kohn argues that the capacity for interpretation and meaning is not uniquely human but characteristic of living systems themselves. "Life is constitutively semiotic," he writes, meaning that organisms continuously interpret and respond to signs within their environments.[13] Forests, animals, and ecosystems therefore participate in forms of relational meaning that exceed human language and intention. If relationality already permeates the living world, then the eucharistic community cannot be the exclusive origin of communion. Instead, the sacrament intensifies and reveals relational processes already embedded within the more-than-human world. Zizioulas's ontology of communion thus risks reproducing a subtle anthropocentrism: relational being may define human personhood, but the relational life of nonhuman creation remains largely invisible.

Elizabeth Povinelli's analysis of geontopower exposes a further limitation by highlighting the political consequences of treating land as inert matter rather than a living environment. Povinelli argues that late liberal societies govern through a distinction between Life and Nonlife that legitimizes extractive economies. These regimes "regulate the relations between Life and Nonlife in order to sustain forms of accumulation and extraction."[14] When land is treated as passive substance, it becomes available for exploitation without moral consequence. Zizioulas's sacramental ontology does little to challenge this logic because it does not explicitly confront the economic systems that degrade the environments *in which* sacramental life occurs. Bread and wine may symbolize communion, but they are produced within agricultural systems shaped by industrial farming, land dispossession, and ecological degradation. Without attending to these material realities, a theology of communion risks celebrating relational harmony within the church while ignoring the destruction of the places that sustain it.

Recent work in biocultural anthropology reinforces this critique by emphasizing that human beings are not simply rational agents who inhabit neutral space but organisms whose identities are formed through ecological relationships. As one account of biocultural life notes, "humans are biocultural creatures whose existence is inseparable from the habitats that sustain them."[15] This insight reveals the limitations of sacramental theologies that treat bread, wine, and water as interchangeable materials. Each element carries the history of a particular place, its soil, rainfall, climate, labor, and ecological conditions. When sacramental theology abstracts these materials from their environments, it inadvertently mirrors the spatial abstraction characteristic of modern capitalism.

Taken together, these philosophical perspectives suggest that Zizioulas's ontology of communion, while profoundly important, remains insufficiently attentive to the ecological and political dimensions of relational life. Communion cannot remain confined to the eucharistic gathering if the environments that sustain that gathering are simultaneously degraded through extractive economic systems. A sacramental theology adequate to the present ecological crisis must extend communion beyond the human assembly to include the living world itself. The Eucharist then becomes not merely the gathering of persons around sacred elements but the intersection of divine grace, human community, and the ecological systems that sustain life.

Zizioulas's argument ultimately rests on a particular understanding of ontology itself. For him, the fundamental question of theology is not simply how individuals relate to one another but what it means to exist at all. Against the classical metaphysical assumption that being is grounded in substance, Zizioulas argues that being must instead be understood in terms of relational personhood. Drawing on the Cappadocian Fathers, he insists that "being is communion" and that existence itself is constituted through relationality rather than self-contained essence.[16] The doctrine of the Trinity, therefore, becomes the ontological foundation for all reality: just as the divine persons exist through mutual relation, so too human existence becomes authentic only through participation in communion. This leads Zizioulas to a striking claim that the church, and particularly the eucharistic assembly, is the place where true being is realized. As he writes, "the being of God could be known only through personal communion and love," and this mode of existence becomes the pattern for human ontology.[17]

Yet this move subtly shifts the center of ontology away from creation itself and toward ecclesial communion. In classical creational ontology, the being of creatures is grounded in their existence as created realities sustained by God. The world possesses its own ontological integrity as the good creation of God, and human beings participate in this order alongside other creatures. Zizioulas, by contrast, emphasizes that authentic being emerges only through the relational life revealed in the church. Creation becomes the stage upon which communion is realized rather than the primary locus of ontological significance. The danger of this shift is that the material world risks becoming ontologically secondary, important insofar as it mediates ecclesial communion but less clearly valuable in its own right. When read alongside ecological thinkers such as Chryssavgis, Kohn, Povinelli, and within Bulgakov's sophiological Christology this limitation becomes visible. If creation itself bears sacramental significance and participates in relational networks of meaning, then ontology cannot be grounded solely in ecclesial communion but must also account for the living, material world in which that communion unfolds.

## Agrarian Living

For Wendell Berry, *agrarian* does not name a political ideology, a nostalgic return to the past, or a narrowly rural lifestyle. It names a way of life ordered toward health through practices of care, restraint, memory, and responsibility. He writes of this old way of living as "focused upon its own local countryside and upon its own people, their needs, and their work."[18] Agrarianism is best understood as a lived standard, one that measures human flourishing by the mutual well-being of people and the places they inhabit. Berry consistently frames his agrarian vision around the hope that human communities might become a healthy people in a healthy land, a phrase that signals his refusal to separate social justice from ecological integrity. Agrarianism is thus not reducible to farming techniques or economic arrangements; it is a moral and cultural achievement sustained across generations.

At the heart of Berry's agrarian vision is what he calls "good farming," though the term should not be mistaken for technical efficiency or productivity maximization. Good farming names a long tradition of land-use shaped by cultural memory, skill, patience, self-mastery, and care. It presupposes intimate knowledge of places—their soils, seasons, limits, and possibilities—and it requires the cultivation of virtues that cannot be mechanized or outsourced. For Berry, the contrast between agrarian and industrial farming is not merely methodological but metaphysical. It is "wisely kind to the land and the people."[19] Agrarian farming understands land as an immeasurable gift, while industrial farming treats land as a resource to be extracted. In this sense, agrarianism begins with gratitude rather than control, reception rather than domination.

Berry insists that the conflict between agrarianism and industrialism is one of the most fundamental divisions in modern life because it represents two nearly opposite ways of understanding reality itself. Industrial civilization, he argues, is governed by the logic of the machine, where the machine becomes, more than a tool, an explanatory framework for life. When machines become the dominant metaphor for the world, living beings are understood mechanistically. And agriculture becomes a form of mining: soil is depleted, ecosystems are exhausted, and communities are hollowed out. Agrarianism, by contrast, begins from the givenness of life (i.e., land, water, animals, weather, hunger) and from the inherited knowledge required to live well within those conditions. It treats land not as inert matter but as a living partner in a shared economy of care.

Central to Berry's agrarian vision is a commitment to place and people, which is why such an approach and vision bring into focus a sacramental practice that extends the preferential option for the poor to the earth without losing sight of people. Berry writes, "The land and the people are here now. The present economic questions are about the work by which land and people might thrive mutually in the best health for the longest time, starting now."[20] Industrial economies, he argues, are fundamentally placeless and displacing. They treat land and people as interchangeable, applying standardized practices across vastly different ecosystems, cultures, and histories. This abstraction enables exploitation, especially when economic power is concentrated in the hands of those who are alien to the places they extract from and indifferent to the communities that bear the costs. Agrarianism, by contrast, depends upon local knowledge, local loyalty, and local love. It forms people who are native to their places, not necessarily by birth, but by long attention and responsibility, and therefore capable of genuine stewardship. Place and people, for Berry, are not a backdrop for economic activity; it is the context that makes moral accountability possible.

Berry also emphasizes that agrarian life is shaped by limits, and that these limits are not failures but gifts. Agrarian abundance does not arise from endless growth or technological escalation, but from renewal within boundaries. To farm well is to recognize finitude—of soil, water, energy, and human labor—and to work within those constraints in ways that sustain life over time.

This vision of life within limits also reshapes economic relations at the level of household and community. Berry argues that when people no longer participate in the making of their necessities, they lose both skills and responsibility, becoming dependent on distant systems they cannot see or influence. Agrarianism works in the opposite direction: It fosters thrift, neighborliness, shared labor, and local exchange.

Perhaps most radically, Berry insists that land cannot be truthfully assigned a fixed market value. Economies begin to lie, he suggests, the moment land is treated as just another commodity. Land is invaluable not because it is rare, but because it is the source of life itself. To treat land as sacred gift rather than economic asset is to place it beyond total market capture and to insist that human life remains accountable to realities that cannot be priced.

Importantly, Berry resists the idea that agrarianism requires universal land ownership or a wholesale return to rural life. To be "landed," in his sense, is not simply to own property but to be meaningfully connected to a home landscape through work, skill, and shared dependence. Agrarian responsibility can take many forms, including urban gardening, participation in local food economies, and intentional resistance to industrial consumption patterns. What matters is not geography but orientation: whether one's life is shaped by care for places and creatures, or by abstraction and mobility.

Taken together, Berry's account of agrarianism names a way of inhabiting the world that stands in sharp contrast to neoliberal capitalism. It resists abstraction, commodification, placelessness, and limitless growth. It affirms creaturely dependence, local knowledge, embodied labor, and gratitude for gifts received. In this sense, agrarianism is not merely an alternative economic model but a moral and spiritual posture, one that aligns profoundly with a sacramental vision of creation and prepares the ground for communities shaped by eucharistic practices of gift, limit, and shared life.

If the sacraments train the church to perceive the world truthfully, then an agrarian way of life can be understood as one of the sacraments' most concrete extensions. Agrarianism, as Berry articulates it, is not itself a sacrament in the technical sense, but it is profoundly *sacramental* in character: it forms communities to receive creation as gift rather than commodity, to inhabit place as holy rather than abstract, and to recognize human life as inseparable from soil, seasons, labor, and limits. In this way, agrarian life functions as a school of perception shaped by eucharistic logic.

At the heart of sacramental theology is the claim that grace does not bypass materiality but works *through* it. Bread and wine are not incidental to the Eucharist; they are theologically determinative. When the church blesses these elements, it confesses that salvation is not opposed to creatureliness but fulfilled within it. An agrarian posture extends this confession beyond the liturgical moment, refusing to treat food as a neutral commodity detached from its origins. To eat agrarianly is to remember that nourishment is always mediated through fragile ecological relations and communal labor. In this sense, agrarian life preserves the Eucharist from becoming an abstraction, an isolated ritual severed from the material realities it presupposes.

Capitalist economies train bodies toward disembodied consumption, where we eat without knowing where food comes from, labor without seeing its effects, and live without enduring attachments. Agrarian practices re-embed bodies in cycles of growth and decay, effort and rest, dependence and vulnerability. These practices cultivate humility, patience, and gratitude, virtues that the sacraments both signify and generate. The Eucharist teaches that life is received, not produced; agrarian life teaches the same lesson in soil and sweat.

This sacramental agrarian vision also clarifies how the preferential option for the poor must be extended to creation without displacing human concern. Agrarian sacramentality recognizes that wounded land and wounded people belong to the same economy of dispossession. To care for soil, water, and seed is not to neglect the poor but to defend the material conditions of their dignity. eucharistic communities that embrace agrarian practices enact a concrete form of solidarity in which justice is not abstractly proclaimed but materially sustained.

Thus, agrarian economies privilege use over accumulation, sufficiency over surplus, continuity over growth. These priorities mirror the eucharistic economy in which abundance appears not through hoarding but through sharing, and where what is most valuable cannot be bought or sold. In this way, agrarian communities embody a counter-economy, one that redirects desire away from consumption and toward communion.

Seen together, sacramental practice and agrarian life form a coherent pedagogy of liberation. The sacraments disclose the truth of creation as gift; agrarian practices teach communities how to live within that truth. The Eucharist gathers into a single act of thanksgiving what capitalism fragments: land, labor, body, and blessing. Agrarian life carries that gathering forward into time, space, and habit. What emerges is not nostalgia for a premodern past, but a disciplined hope: communities shaped by liturgical memory learning to inhabit the world otherwise.

In this sense, agrarian sacramentality does not oppose modern life from the outside; it converts it from within. It forms people capable of resisting abstraction because they have learned to love particular places. It resists commodification because it has learned to name what cannot be priced. And it resists despair because it knows that grace is already at work in soil, seed, and shared tables, waiting to be received.

To speak of liberation here is not to speak of the seizure of power or the acceleration of production; it is to speak of the restoration of creaturely freedom. Agrarian sacramental life liberates by retraining how bodies inhabit space, how communities understand time, how value is measured, and how desire is formed.

The sacraments are central to this liberation because they expose the lie at the heart of neoliberal subjectivity: that life is sustained by markets rather than by gift. In the Eucharist, the church confesses that life comes from what is received, not what is accumulated. Bread and wine appear not as commodities but as blessings, fruits of land and labor offered back to God and returned as communion. When this sacramental grammar shapes everyday life, agrarian practices become acts of resistance. Growing food, sharing meals, honoring seasons, and accepting limits all declare that survival does not depend on endless growth but on faithful participation in the givenness of creation. This way of life is liberatory precisely because it restores agency to bodies without romanticizing autonomy. Agrarian communities are not liberated because they are self-sufficient, but because they are rightly dependent on land, weather, neighbors, and God. Such dependence is not a failure of freedom but its condition. Liberation theology has long insisted that the poor are not liberated by being absorbed into the dominant system but by having their material conditions transformed so that life can flourish. Agrarian sacramentality extends this insight to creation itself, recognizing that land, water, and seed are also subject to regimes of extraction and must be released from them if human liberation is to be real.

Practicing the sacraments agrarianly also liberates time. The liturgical calendar trains communities to wait, to remember, and to hope without domination. Agrarian life mirrors this rhythm through planting and harvest, fasting and feasting, work and rest. Together, sacrament and agrarian practice free communities from the tyranny of urgency and productivity, allowing life to be lived at the pace of bodies and ecosystems rather than markets.

Liberation here is also spatial. Sacramental agrarian life reclaims place as holy without making it static or exclusionary. Fields, kitchens, tables, and sanctuaries become sites of encounter rather than nodes of exchange. This reorientation is deeply political: when land is known and loved, it cannot be so easily sold, poisoned, or abandoned. When communities are rooted, they are less vulnerable to displacement.

Importantly, this form of liberation avoids the false choice between human liberation and ecological concern. Agrarian sacramentality insists that the poor are not liberated *from* creation but *with* it. Industrial agriculture, environmental degradation, and climate collapse disproportionately harm the poor because they destroy the material conditions of life. By contrast, agrarian practices cultivate shared survival, local resilience, and mutual care. They enact what liberation theology has always claimed: justice must be material, communal, and structural, not merely symbolic.

Finally, agrarian sacramental life liberates desire. Capitalism preys on our dissatisfactions, presents us with continual novelty, and leads us toward excess. Sacramental agrarian communities learn to desire enough, to find joy in sufficiency, beauty in care, and abundance in sharing. This is not asceticism for its own sake but freedom from the compulsion to consume. credible by embedding it in daily practices of feeding, tending, and sharing.

To live this way is therefore not a retreat from liberation but to embody it. It is a refusal to accept the terms under which life has been made unlivable. Practicing the sacraments as agrarians forms communities that no longer mistake domination for freedom or consumption for fulfillment. It creates a people capable of imagining—and inhabiting—a world where land is cherished, bodies are honored, and life is received as gift. That is not merely an alternative lifestyle; it is a quiet, persistent, and deeply theological form of resistance.

## What is an Agrarian Practice of the Sacraments?

What, then, might it mean for the church to practice the sacraments agrarianly? The question does not call for a nostalgic return to premodern rural life, nor does it require that all Christians become farmers. Rather, it invites the church to recover the material, ecological, and social realities already embedded within sacramental practice and to allow those realities to shape communal habits. As Alexander Schmemann famously argued, the sacraments do not remove the church from the world but reveal the world's true vocation. The Eucharist, he writes, is the moment in which the church takes "the whole world as if it were one loaf and one cup and offers it to God," returning creation to its original purpose as thanksgiving and communion.[21] Sacramental life, therefore, presupposes land, water, labor, seasons, and human communities. When these realities are forgotten, the sacraments risk becoming detached from the world they are meant to transfigure.

An agrarian sacramental life begins with attention to the elements themselves. Bread, wine, and water are not neutral materials but the fruits of ecological and human relationships. Wheat grows only through soil fertility, rainfall, sunlight, and patient cultivation. Wine emerges from vines rooted in particular landscapes shaped by climate, pruning, fermentation, and care. Water flows through rivers, aquifers, rainfall cycles, and watersheds that sustain every living creature. These elements carry within them the histories of places and the labor of communities. To recognize this is already to see the sacramental depth of creation.

Baptism reveals this truth most immediately. In many contemporary churches, baptismal water appears detached from place, drawn from anonymous plumbing systems, and understood merely as a liturgical duty. Yet water is perhaps the most fundamentally ecological element in sacramental life. It binds together rivers, rainfall, oceans, and the bodies of living creatures. Schmemann insists that baptism restores water to what it was always meant to be: the element through which creation becomes transparent to divine life. "In baptism," he writes, "water is revealed as the image of life itself," the medium through which the world receives and sustains existence.[22] The sacrament does not introduce holiness into an otherwise neutral substance but reveals the depth of creation already given by God.

An agrarian practice of baptism simply refuses to forget this truth. Communities attentive to place recognize that the waters used for baptism belong to particular ecosystems, watersheds that sustain local life, rivers that nourish farms and towns, and rainfall that feeds soil and crops. When these waters are polluted or depleted, the damage is not merely environmental but sacramental. The health of rivers and aquifers directly shapes the material reality through which Christian life begins. In this sense, baptism quietly reveals the moral inseparability of ecological care and human flourishing.

This connection becomes especially clear when viewed through the lens of the preferential option for the poor. Across the world, it is the poor who most directly suffer from contaminated water, drought, and ecological collapse. Communities without access to clean water experience not only economic hardship but threats to the most basic conditions of life. Baptism, therefore, bears an implicit solidarity with the poor because it centers the church's sacramental imagination on the element most unequally distributed in a damaged world. To bless water without caring for the waters that sustain vulnerable communities would be a contradiction of the sacrament itself.

If baptism situates Christian life within the waters of creation, the Eucharist situates Christian nourishment within the fruits of land and labor. Bread and wine arrive at the altar carrying the history of fields, vineyards, weather, soil, farmers, and bakers. They are the culmination of seasons and human work. Schmemann emphasizes that in the Eucharist the church gathers creation into thanksgiving: "The Eucharist is always offered on behalf of all and for all," because the bread and wine represent the entire world restored to its vocation of communion with God.[23]

Yet modern economic systems obscure this gathering. Bread appears as an anonymous commodity purchased through global supply chains rather than the fruit of particular fields and communities. Agrarian eucharistic practice seeks to reverse this abstraction.

Congregations might source bread from local grain, partner with nearby farmers, or cultivate gardens connected to their worship. Such practices do not change the theology of the Eucharist but make its meaning visible. When the bread used at the altar is known to come from nearby soil or the wine from local vines, the eucharistic offering becomes the offering of a living landscape.

Schmemann's sacramental vision helps illuminate why all this matters theologically. For him, the Eucharist restores the fundamental truth of creation: that the world exists to become communion with God. "Man is what he eats," quoting Feuerbach, because humanity receives life through the food of the earth.[24] When bread and wine are offered in thanksgiving, the world itself becomes Eucharist. Agrarian practice simply extends this logic into daily life.

For communities shaped by the preferential option for the poor, this sacramental ecology carries urgent implications. The same systems that degrade soil and poison water are the systems that impoverish vulnerable communities. Agrarian sacramental life, therefore, refuses to separate ecological care from human justice. To defend the health of rivers, soils, and farms is also to defend the conditions under which the poor can live with dignity. In this way, the sacraments quietly train the church to recognize a deeper truth: that wounded land and wounded people belong to the same history of dispossession.

Agrarian sacramental practice therefore does more than enrich liturgy. It forms communities capable of inhabiting the world truthfully. Baptism teaches that life begins in waters shared with all creatures. The Eucharist teaches that nourishment comes from land cultivated through patience, labor, and gift. Together they reorient Christian life away from abstraction and toward gratitude, responsibility, and solidarity. The sacraments do not remove believers from the world's struggles. They teach the church how to live within them faithfully.

## Excursus: Place, Reconciliation, and Indigenous Sovereignty

Throughout this study, I have argued that Christian ethics must recover a theology of place capable of resisting the abstractions of neoliberal modernity. Such a recovery, however, cannot proceed as though place were merely a theological concept detached from history. Land is never simply sacramental; it is also political. Every landscape bears the marks of memory, conquest, migration, treaty, cultivation, displacement, and belonging. Consequently, any Christian retrieval of place must reckon honestly with the histories through which land has been claimed, contested, and inhabited.

Indigenous theologians and scholars have repeatedly reminded the church that appeals to creation and place cannot be separated from the concrete realities of colonization. Robin Wall Kimmerer argues that the central question is not simply how human beings inhabit a place but how they learn to become responsible for it. Drawing upon the Anishinaabe story of *Nanabozho*, the first human to walk the earth, Kimmerer observes that human beings do not arrive as owners but as newcomers. In the story, Nanabozho enters a world already inhabited by plants, animals, waters, and spirits, each of whom teaches him how to live well within creation. His first task is not to master the land but to learn the names of his neighbors, receive instruction from the more-than-human world, and discover the responsibilities that accompany every gift. The earth is not raw material awaiting development, but an older community into which humanity is graciously received. To become "indigenous to place," she writes, is to recognize that the land itself becomes our teacher, forming habits of gratitude, restraint, reciprocity, and care.[25] Yet Kimmerer carefully distinguishes this moral formation from Indigenous identity itself. Indigenous belonging is not something settlers can acquire by affection or longevity. Rather, those who inhabit colonized lands are called to become naturalized to place by relinquishing the logic of possession and learning instead to live as grateful guests who accept responsibilities before claiming rights.

Such a distinction carries significant theological implications. Throughout Christian history, appeals to creation have too often been detached from the political realities through which land has been taken, peoples displaced, and communities rendered strangers within their own homes. A theology of creation that celebrates the goodness of place while remaining silent about these histories risks becoming another abstraction. The church cannot proclaim creation as God's gift while ignoring the injustices through which that gift has been unequally distributed and violently defended. Nor can sacramental language become a means of spiritualizing land in ways that obscure the concrete claims of Indigenous peoples, treaty obligations, or historical responsibility.

At the same time, the church's response cannot consist merely in exchanging one account of ownership for another. The deepest theological question concerns the meaning of possession itself. Throughout this study I have argued that creation is fundamentally gift rather than commodity. Kimmerer's work presses this claim further by suggesting that gifts are inseparable from responsibilities. To receive land is simultaneously to receive obligations toward neighbors, waters, animals, plants, and future generations. Place, therefore, becomes not an object of possession but a community of mutual dependence in which every creature participates according to its own vocation. Christian theology should understand this not as an alternative to sacramental ontology but as one of its most profound expressions.

Such an account also reshapes the church's public witness. Congregations seeking to embody a theology of place cannot limit themselves to ecological stewardship understood narrowly as environmental management. Faithful participation requires attentiveness to the histories of the places they inhabit: whose lands they occupy, which treaties have been broken, what communities have been displaced, and how patterns of racial, economic, and ecological injustice continue to shape the present. Such practices need not produce identical political conclusions in every context. Rather, they cultivate the humility necessary for truthful discernment. Before asking what can be done with the land, Christians must first ask how the land—and the communities that have long belonged to it—have already been speaking.

This emphasis also guards against romanticism. Place is never simply innocent. The same attachments that cultivate memory, stability, and belonging may also generate exclusion, nationalism, and violence. Communities rightly love particular places, yet such love becomes idolatrous whenever belonging is secured through the denial of another's belonging. The church therefore receives every place as gift while remembering that no creature possesses creation absolutely. We dwell upon the earth not as owners but as guests whose citizenship is always ordered toward the Kingdom of God. Precisely because the earth belongs to the Creator, Christian belonging must always remain hospitable, repentant, and open to reconciliation.

Seen in this light, Indigenous sovereignty does not stand outside the theological concerns of this book but deepens them. The preferential option for the poor cannot be separated from the histories through which poverty has been produced by dispossession. Likewise, a sacramental account of creation cannot remain indifferent to the political realities that determine who enjoys secure access to land, water, and the conditions of communal flourishing. To receive creation as gift therefore requires more than ecological concern. It demands truthful remembrance, repentance for histories of domination, and a renewed commitment to forms of common life in which both people and place may flourish together before God.

## The Church as a Community of Holy Judgment

The practices proposed throughout this study should not be understood as a collection of ecclesial techniques capable of resolving every social, political, or ecological conflict. The church does not become sacramental because it possesses a flawless ethical program, nor does participation in Christ eliminate the tragic realities of history. Rather, the Eucharist forms a people capable of discerning faithfully within a world where genuine goods frequently stand in tension and where every available course of action may preserve certain goods while compromising others. Christian ethics, therefore, requires not only conviction but prudence.

This point is particularly important because the vision advanced throughout this study refuses to isolate the preferential option for the poor from the care of creation. The poor and the earth are not rival objects of Christian concern. Both belong to the one creation reconciled in Christ. Yet precisely because they belong together, situations inevitably arise in which their immediate claims appear to conflict. Ecological protections may limit employment within economically fragile communities. Industrial development intended to alleviate poverty may irreparably damage ecosystems upon which future generations depend. Affordable housing, Indigenous sovereignty, food security, labor protections, and environmental restoration frequently converge, but they do not always do so without tension. Christian communities, therefore, cannot assume that fidelity consists in the simultaneous maximization of every good.

The church's vocation in such moments is not the abandonment of theological conviction but the patient cultivation of practical wisdom. Stanley Hauerwas has long insisted that the primary task of Christian ethics is the formation of a people whose lives have been shaped by the story of Jesus Christ. Such formation does not eliminate disagreement, but it creates communities capable of asking the right questions before seeking immediate solutions. Character precedes strategy because only a people schooled in truthfulness, humility, forgiveness, and reconciliation can exercise judgment without reducing every conflict to calculations of efficiency or power. Rather than imagining ethics as the application of abstract principles to isolated dilemmas, Hauerwas understands the church itself as the social body within which the virtues necessary for faithful judgment are patiently cultivated.[26]

Luke Bretherton similarly reminds the church that faithful political engagement necessarily unfolds within pluralistic societies where no community possesses the power to realize the kingdom through political control. Christian participation, therefore, involves negotiation, coalition, compromise, and democratic deliberation without surrendering the theological convictions that give such engagement its distinctive character. The common good is not achieved through domination but through patient practices of listening, persuasion, hospitality, and shared responsibility among neighbors who frequently disagree about ultimate ends. Political participation thus becomes not an alternative to Christian witness but one arena in which disciples learn to pursue justice while acknowledging the legitimacy and dignity of those with whom they disagree.[27]

Samuel Wells deepens this vision by arguing that Christian faithfulness is fundamentally learned through presence before it is expressed through problem-solving. The church's first responsibility is not always to produce immediate solutions but to remain faithfully present with communities whose suffering resists easy resolution. Such accompaniment transforms ethical deliberation because the questions are no longer asked from a position of detached expertise but from relationships of mutual belonging. Communities discover what justice requires only as they learn to inhabit one another's lives. The church's most significant political witness therefore often consists less in solving social problems than in becoming a community capable of sharing life with those whom society has rendered invisible or expendable.[28]

Throughout this study, I have argued that neoliberalism, commodification, ecological degradation, and abstraction constitute pervasive structures that shape contemporary existence. Such realities can easily produce either despair or triumphalism. Despair concludes that meaningful resistance is impossible. Triumphalism imagines that sufficiently faithful communities can overcome these structures through moral resolve alone. Both misunderstand the nature of ecclesial action. Christian agency is neither absolute nor insignificant, as Oliver O'Donnell advises. It is participatory. The church acts faithfully not because it controls history but because it participates in the reconciling work that God has already begun in Jesus Christ.

Such participation necessarily remains modest. Congregations rarely possess the institutional power to transform global markets, reverse ecological collapse, or eradicate structural poverty. Yet they do possess the capacity to cultivate truthful forms of life that interrupt the logic of commodification. Communities learn to receive rather than possess, to accompany rather than dominate, to deliberate rather than manipulate, and to repent whenever their own practices unintentionally reproduce the very exclusions they seek to overcome. Faithfulness is measured less by the scale of visible success than by the integrity with which the church embodies Christ's reconciling presence.

This also requires acknowledging that even faithful action may generate unintended consequences. The history of the church repeatedly demonstrates that practices undertaken with sincere theological conviction have sometimes produced exclusion, paternalism, environmental harm, or new forms of injustice. Such failures do not invalidate Christian witness; they remind the church that sanctification remains an ongoing work of the Holy Spirit rather than a completed human achievement. The proper response to failure is therefore neither paralysis nor self-justification but repentance, renewed discernment, and deeper participation in the life of Christ.

Ultimately, the church's hope rests not in its ability to eliminate every conflict among competing goods but in the God who has entered those conflicts through the incarnation, cross, and resurrection. The Eucharist does not remove the ambiguities of history. It forms a people capable of inhabiting them without surrendering either hope or love. The practices described throughout this book should therefore be understood not as solutions to the crises of modernity but as schools of judgment through which Christians gradually learn to perceive, deliberate, and act according to the reconciled reality God has already inaugurated in Jesus Christ.

## Learning the Sacrament

A final clarification is necessary. Throughout this study I have argued that Christian theology offers a sacramental vision capable of resisting the abstractions of neoliberal modernity. Such a claim, however, should not be misunderstood to mean that the construction of a more adequate sacramental theology will itself resolve the crises of commodification, ecological degradation, or poverty.

Theology does not function as a technique capable of repairing social life through conceptual refinement alone. The church has possessed rich sacramental theologies for centuries while remaining fully capable of participating in slavery, colonialism, economic exploitation, environmental destruction, and the exclusion of the poor. Right doctrine alone has never guaranteed right perception.

The more fundamental claim advanced throughout this book is therefore the reverse. We do not first develop a sacramental theology and then learn to love our neighbors accordingly. Rather, it is in learning rightly to receive our neighbors, creation, places, and those rendered poor that we begin to discover what the sacraments have always meant. The Eucharist does not merely teach solidarity; solidarity discloses the Eucharist. Creation does not simply illustrate sacramental participation; participation in the giftedness of creation reveals the sacramental character of the world. The poor are not illustrations added to an already completed theology. They become the very place where the church is instructed into the truth of its own worship.

This reversal reflects the logic of the gospel itself. Jesus does not first offer a theory of communion before gathering disciples into a shared life. Nor does he explain the meaning of the Eucharist apart from the washing of feet, table fellowship with sinners, the feeding of the hungry, and ultimately the gift of his own body. The church learns the meaning of Christ's self-giving only as it is drawn into that same pattern of life. Sacramental theology is therefore not primarily speculative knowledge but a form of ecclesial perception made possible through faithful participation.

Such participation also guards against the temptation to treat the sacraments themselves as religious commodities. Whenever sacramental theology is detached from the practices of hospitality, reconciliation, care for creation, and solidarity with the poor, the

Eucharist itself risks becoming another object to be possessed, defended, or consumed. Ironically, a theology intended to resist commodification may itself become commodified if it is reduced to a system of ideas rather than a way of inhabiting the world.

For this reason, the practices proposed throughout this study should not be understood as applications of an already completed theology. They are themselves theological. The church comes to know the truth of the Eucharist by becoming a eucharistic people. It learns the meaning of creation by receiving creation as gift. It discovers communion by practicing reconciliation. It understands the preferential option for the poor only by allowing the lives of the poor to reorder its own life. Theology is therefore not simply the precondition for faithful practice; faithful practice is one of the Spirit's primary means of instructing the church in theological truth.

The deepest claim of this book, then, is not that sacramental theology offers a solution to commodification. It is that the church learns the sacramental character of reality only insofar as Christ continually reorders its loves. Wherever neighbors cease to be commodities and become gifts, wherever creation is received rather than possessed, wherever places become sites of hospitality rather than exclusion, and wherever the poor are encountered not as problems but as members of Christ's own body, there the church begins to perceive what the Eucharist has always been proclaiming: that all creation exists to participate in the inexhaustible gift of God's own life.

## Conclusion: Creaturely Liberation and the Recovery of Place

This chapter has argued that liberation theology cannot remain credible in the present moment without a sustained reckoning with creation. The preferential option for the poor, if it is to remain faithful to its own theological logic, must name the ecological conditions through which poverty is produced and endured. To draw creation inside the option for the poor is not to dilute liberation theology but to complete it. The suffering of the poor and the degradation of the earth arise from the same sacrificial logic, one that abstracts bodies, land, and communities into disposable units for accumulation. Any theology of liberation that fails to confront this logic risks sanctifying the very systems it seeks to resist.

Against both anthropocentric erasure and ecological reduction, the chapter has proposed *shared creaturehood* as a theological orientation capable of holding difference and solidarity together. Humans and nonhuman creatures are not identical, but neither are they ontologically opposed. They are bound together in finitude, dependence, and vulnerability within a world that is not self-grounding but given. This recognition resists the metaphysical assumptions that underwrite capitalist commodification, which thrives on denying creaturehood by rendering life cheap, interchangeable, and abstract.

The sacraments emerge within this framework not as inward religious acts but as counter-formative practices that re-train how life is perceived and inhabited. Eucharist, in particular, interrupts neoliberal economies of exchange by refusing abstraction: bread remains bread, land remains land, labor remains visible, and bodies remain irreducible. Sacramental space resists the flattening of place into empty extension, recovering the holiness of here rather than the mobility of everywhere. In doing so, sacramental practice exposes the violence of an economy that can only function by severing people from land, food from soil, and work from care.

Agrarian life, as articulated by Wendell Berry, names the social and ecological habits capable of sustaining this sacramental vision beyond the liturgy. Agrarianism is not an escape from modern life but a refusal of its most destructive abstractions. It cultivates limits, gratitude, locality, and responsibility, virtues that mirror eucharistic logic and resist the consumerist formation of desire. When communities live agrarianly, they enact a form of liberation that is quiet but structural: land is no longer merely owned, food is no longer merely consumed, and life is no longer measured primarily by growth.

To practice the sacraments as agrarians is therefore liberatory in the deepest sense. It restores agency without illusion, dependence without despair, and hope without domination. It refuses the false promise that freedom lies in endless choice or accumulation, and instead recovers freedom as the capacity to dwell rightly: with the poor, within creation, and before God. Such communities do not withdraw from history; they contest it by embodying alternatives that neoliberal capitalism cannot imagine.

What emerges is a vision of liberation grounded not in mastery but in fidelity: fidelity to land, to bodies, to shared creaturehood, and to a God whose grace is mediated through the very world capitalism teaches us to disregard. In an age of ecological collapse and economic abstraction, this is not merely an ethical option. It is a theological necessity, and a sacramental hope.

## Notes

1. Sallie McFague, *The Body of God: An Ecological Theology* (Fortress Press, 1993), 38.
2. McFague, *The Body of God,* 48.
3. Samantha Frost, *Biocultural Creatures: Toward a New Theory of the Human* (Duke University Press, 2016), 4.
4. Frost, *Biocultural Creatures,* 4.

5. Frost, *Biocultural Creatures,* 150.

6. Eduardo Kohn, *How Forests Think: Toward an Anthropology beyond the Human* (University of California Press, 2013), 21.

7. Kohn, *How Forests Think,* 224.

8. Elizabeth A. Povinelli, *Geontologies: A Requiem to Late Liberalism* (Duke University Press, 2016), 16.

9. John Chryssavgis, *Creation as Sacrament: Reflections on Ecology and Spirituality* (T&T Clark, 2019), 101–102.

10. John D. Zizioulas, *Being as Communion: Studies in Personhood and the Church* (St. Vladimir's Seminary Press, 1985), 17.

11. Chryssavgis, *Creation as Sacrament,* 7.

12. Chryssavgis, *Creation as Sacrament,* 19.

13. Kohn, *How Forests Think,* 9.

14. Povinelli, *Geontologies,* 4.

15. Frost, *Biocultural Creatures,* 3.

16. Zizioulas, *Being as Communion,* 15–17.

17. Zizioulas, *Being as Communion,* 18.

18. Wendell Berry, *The Art of Loading Brush: New Agrarian Writing* (Counterpoint, 2017), 30.

19. Berry, *The Art of Loading Brush,* 31.

20. Berry, *The Art of Loading Brush,* 37.

21. Schmemann, *For the Life of the World,* 15–16.

22. Schmemann, *For the Life of the World,* 45–47.

23. Schmemann, *For the Life of the World,* 34.

24. Schmemann, *For the Life of the World,* 11.

25. Robin Wall Kimmerer, "In the Footsteps of Nanabozho: Becoming Indigenous to Place," in *Braiding Sweetgrass: Indigenous Wisdom, Scientific Knowledge, and the Teachings of Plants* (Milkweed Editions, 2013), 207–31.

26. See Stanley Hauerwas, *A Community of Character: Toward a Constructive Christian Social Ethic* (University of Notre Dame

Press, 1981); Stanley Hauerwas, *The Peaceable Kingdom: A Primer in Christian Ethics* (University of Notre Dame Press, 1983); Stanley Hauerwas and William H. Willimon, *Resident Aliens: Life in the Christian Colony* (Abingdon Press, 1989). On the relationship between ecclesial formation, virtue, and truthful judgment, see also Samuel Wells, *Improvisation: The Drama of Christian Ethics* (Brazos Press, 2004), 45–87.

27. Luke Bretherton, *Christianity and Contemporary Politics: The Conditions and Possibilities of Faithful Witness* (Wiley-Blackwell, 2010); Luke Bretherton, *Resurrecting Democracy: Faith, Citizenship, and the Politics of a Common Life* (Cambridge University Press, 2015); Luke Bretherton, *Christ and the Common Life: Political Theology and the Case for Democracy* (Eerdmans, 2019). Bretherton argues that democratic participation should be understood less as the pursuit of political control than as the cultivation of institutions capable of sustaining common life among diverse communities.

28. Samuel Wells, *God's Companions: Reimagining Christian Ethics* (Blackwell, 2006); Samuel Wells, *A Nazareth Manifesto: Being with God* (Wiley-Blackwell, 2015); Samuel Wells and Marcia Owen, *Living without Enemies: Being Present in the Midst of Violence* (InterVarsity Press, 2011). Wells consistently argues that the church's vocation is fundamentally one of "being with" before "doing for," thereby locating Christian ethics within relationships of accompaniment rather than technical problem-solving.

CONCLUSION

# Wisdom Made Flesh: Communion, Place, and the Work of Liberation

This book has argued that the crisis confronting Christian theology today is not simply one of belief, doctrine, or ethics, but of *location*. We live within a world increasingly ordered by abstraction—abstract space, abstract value, abstract time, abstract exchange. Neoliberalism has not merely reorganized markets; it has reorganized our imagination. Land becomes real estate, bodies become labor, relationships become networks, and even salvation risks becoming a transferable good rather than a practiced way of life. Within such a regime, theology is tempted to mirror the world it seeks to critique, translating grace into mechanism, sacrament into transaction, and wisdom into system.

Against this backdrop, the work of this book has been a retrieval. It has not been a nostalgic work but an effort to present a *liberatory* grammar of life. At the center of that grammar stands Sophia, divine wisdom, not as an abstract principle but as a way of inhabiting the world truthfully. Sophia does not hover above history; she dwells within it. She delights in creaturely limits, takes pleasure in material dependence, and binds together God, humanity, and creation without dissolving their differences. Wisdom, in this biblical and theological sense, is never merely known. It is practiced, cultivated, and learned over time, through place, through labor, through shared meals, and through the slow disciplines of attention.

The chapters of this book have traced how this wisdom has been systematically obscured. Neoliberal political theology trains us to imagine freedom as mobility rather than belonging, value as accumulation rather than gift, and space as empty extension rather than sacred ground. In such a world, the poor are rendered surplus, the land is stripped of meaning, and the sacraments are reduced to private rituals detached from economic, ecological, and communal life. The preferential option for the poor, when severed from material practice, risks becoming a moral sentiment rather than a way of life capable of interrupting domination.

What has been proposed instead is not a single solution but a *reorientation*, a turning back toward creaturehood. To affirm creaturehood beyond anthropocentrism is to recognize that human life is never autonomous, never self-generated, never extractable from the web of relations that sustain it. We are earth-formed, land-bound, and place-dependent. Liberation, therefore, cannot be imagined solely in terms of human emancipation from constraint. It must also be named as reconciliation with the conditions of life itself, with soil, water, labor, seasons, and limits. Any theology that seeks justice while remaining indifferent to place ultimately reproduces the abstractions it claims to resist.

It is here that the practice of communion emerges not merely as a symbol, but as a site of formation and resistance. While *The Sacraments of Liberation* shares William T. Cavanaugh's concern that the Eucharist resists the abstractions and false desires generated by consumer capitalism, it departs from Cavanaugh's tendency to frame sacramental resistance primarily at the level of imagination, symbolic formation, and alternative ecclesial economy. As Antonio Eduardo Alonso notes in *Commodified Communion*, contemporary eucharistic theologies often presume that the Eucharist can function as a site of 'resistance' against commodification by generating alternative forms of desire and social imagination.[1] Alonso argues that even these resistance-oriented approaches can remain trapped within the same abstract logic they seek to oppose, insofar as they continue to evaluate sacramental practice according to its capacity to produce countercultural agency.[2]

Instead, this project argues that commodification cannot be resisted through sacramental imagination alone, but only through concrete forms of life practiced with and among the poor themselves. The sacraments do not merely produce an alternative symbolic economy; they bind communities to the material conditions of land, labor, bodies, water, and food through which poverty is produced and sustained. Thus, rather than presenting eucharistic practice as a conceptual antidote to neoliberal abstraction, this work insists that sacramental theology becomes liberative only when it is enacted within practices of shared creaturehood, agrarian locality, ecological responsibility, and solidarity with those rendered expendable by systems of extraction and exchange. In short, one does not merely take the sacrament to save the poor, but rather, only by living in and among the poor can one grasp the sacramental elements.

The Eucharist refuses the logic of exchange. It cannot be bought, scaled, optimized, or automated. It is given, received, and shared, or it ceases to be itself. In communion, bodies gather rather than circulate; bread is broken rather than hoarded; wine is poured rather than accumulated. The table interrupts the myth of scarcity not by denying limits, but by sanctifying them. Enough is discovered not through surplus, but through sharing.

Yet the Eucharist does more than reorder economic imagination. It *re-places* us. Drawing on phenomenological accounts of place, we have seen how modern abstraction evacuates space of meaning, rendering it interchangeable and disposable. Sacramental practice resists this by re-inscribing holiness into particular locations. Altars, tables, fields, kitchens, gardens: these become sites where heaven and earth are not fused, but held together. Communion teaches us that salvation does not occur nowhere. It occurs *here*. In bodies. In soil. In time.

From this eucharistic posture, agrarian life emerges not as an ideology or lifestyle brand, but as a concrete extension of sacramental wisdom. Following Wendell Berry, agrarianism names a way of living that honors limits, responsibility, memory, and care. It is attentive to how food is grown, how land is treated, how labor is shared, and how communities endure over generations rather than quarters. Agrarian life resists the violence of abstraction precisely because it binds people to consequences. One cannot extract indefinitely from land one must return to tomorrow.

When joined to sacramental practice, agrarian life becomes liberatory in a specific sense. It liberates bodies from total dependence on distant systems they cannot see or contest. It liberates land from perpetual exploitation. It liberates communities from the isolation produced by consumer individualism. And it liberates theology itself from the temptation to speak universally without remaining accountable locally. This is not a romanticization of rural life nor a denial of urban realities. It is a claim about orientation: liberation must be practiced where people actually live, eat, work, and die.

Sophia, liberation, place, agrarian life, and communion converge here as a single wisdom-practice. Together, they name a faith that does not seek escape from the world but reconciliation within it. A faith that does not spiritualize hunger, but feeds bodies. A faith that does not treat creation as a backdrop, but as a neighbor. A faith that does not await justice as future abstraction, but rehearses it weekly at the table.

## The Takeaways

The argument of this book has moved across several terrains. It has engaged sacramental theology, liberation theology, ecological thought, and critiques of neoliberal spatial imagination. Ultimately, it has sought to recover a vision of Christian life capable of responding to the intertwined crises of poverty and environmental devastation. Throughout these chapters, one claim has guided the inquiry: the sacraments are not merely liturgical moments within the life of the church but practices through which Christians learn how to inhabit the world. Water, bread, wine, land, labor, and community are not incidental to Christian theology; they are the material conditions through which God's grace becomes visible within creation.

To reclaim sacramental theology in this way is to confront the forces that have obscured this vision. Economic systems that treat the earth as expendable and human beings as disposable have reshaped our moral imagination, training societies to see the poor as burdens and the land as resource. Against this logic, the sacramental tradition insists that creation is not an object of extraction but a gift meant to be received, shared, and offered back to God in gratitude. When the church rediscovers this vision, the sacraments become practices that reorient communities toward solidarity with the poor and care for the earth.

The following reflections summarize the central theological insights of this work and gesture toward the practical implications of a sacramental theology committed to liberation. Together, they are steps toward a framework for imagining how Christian communities might recover their vocation to participate in the healing of both humanity and creation.

## 1. Sacramental Theology Must Be Reclaimed as a Practice of Liberation

This work has argued that the sacraments cannot remain abstract rituals detached from the social and ecological realities that shape human life. From the beginning of the Christian tradition, grace has been mediated through material realities—water, bread, wine, soil, and the fragile networks of life that sustain creation. When the sacraments are understood in this way, they inevitably confront systems that degrade both people and the earth. Sacramental theology therefore cannot remain confined to liturgical reflection. It must become a theological practice that reveals God's liberating presence within the material conditions of the world.

## 2. The Preferential Option for the Poor Must Extend to Creation

Liberation theology has long insisted that the God revealed in Jesus Christ stands in solidarity with the poor and oppressed. Yet the same systems that impoverish human communities also devastate the land, water, and ecosystems upon which those communities depend. The suffering of the poor and the suffering of the earth are not separate crises but intertwined realities. A sacramental theology attentive to the material foundations of life, therefore, expands the preferential option for the poor into an ecological horizon. To defend the poor while ignoring the destruction of creation is ultimately to undermine the conditions that make human flourishing possible

## 3. Recovering Place Is Essential for Recovering Moral Responsibility

Neoliberal modernity has reshaped the world into a totalizing abstract space, where environments are designed for efficiency, mobility, and extraction rather than for relationships and care. In such spaces, the poor appear as strangers rather than neighbors, and the earth appears as a resource rather than a gift. By contrast, Christian sacramental life is irreducibly rooted in place. Baptism occurs in the waters that sustain life, and the Eucharist gathers the fruits of land, labor, and community. These practices remind the church that salvation unfolds within particular places and relationships. Recovering the sacredness of place, therefore, becomes essential for recovering the ethical imagination necessary for solidarity with both the poor and the earth.

## 4. Agrarian Practices Help Restore the Sacramental Character of Creation

If sacramental theology is to be renewed, it must take concrete form in the ways communities inhabit the land. Agrarian practices, whether cultivating soil, caring for ecosystems, sharing food, and honoring the limits of creation, offer one way of restoring attention to the material foundations of life. Such practices do not romanticize rural existence but instead reconnect human communities with the ecological realities from which sacramental life emerges. When Christians attend again to the relationships between land, labor, and nourishment, the bread and wine of the Eucharist are recognized not merely as symbols but as gifts of the earth entrusted to human care.

## 5. The Church is Called to Participate in the Sacramental Healing of the World

The church does not celebrate the sacraments merely for its own spiritual benefit. Baptism and Eucharist form communities capable of participating in God's work of restoring creation. Through these practices, the church learns to recognize Christ among the poor, to resist the commodification of the earth, and to cultivate places where life can flourish. In an age marked by ecological devastation and economic inequality, the recovery of sacramental imagination is not optional. It is the means by which the church rediscovers its vocation: to become a community through whom the grace of God takes material form in the healing of both humanity and the earth.

Baptism and Eucharist remind the church that salvation unfolds within the material realities of water, land, labor, and shared life. When these practices are taken seriously, they form communities capable of resisting systems that exploit both the poor and the earth while cultivating places where life can flourish. A sacramental theology that extends the preferential option for the poor to creation, therefore calls the church not merely to believe differently, but to dwell differently, to inhabit the world as gift, to defend the vulnerable, and to participate in God's ongoing work of restoring the life of the world.

## Conclusion

The work of the church, then, is not to outcompete neoliberalism on its own terms, nor to offer symbolic critique while remaining materially complicit. It is to slowly, imperfectly, and locally practice a different world into being. The sacraments do not solve injustice. They train us to see it, resist it, and live otherwise in its midst. They school desire away from domination and toward communion. They teach us that wisdom is not mastered but received, not accumulated but shared. Thus:

> In a world organized by exchange, the church is called to remember gift. In a world that abstracts space, the church is called to sanctify place. In a world that consumes creation, the church is called to dwell with it.

This is not withdrawal. It is fidelity. And fidelity, practiced over time, is the quiet labor of liberation.

## Notes

1. Antonio Eduardo Alonso, *Commodified Communion: Eucharist, Consumer Culture, and the Practice of Everyday Life* (Fordham University Press, 2021), 40–41.
2. Alonso, *Commodified Communion*, 41.

# Acknowledgments

This book emerges from a long and often difficult struggle of mine to articulate a theology of the sacraments that does not collapse into the very thing it seeks to resist. What began as a set of questions about value, exchange, and the presence of God in material practices slowly became a more pressing concern: how to speak of grace without reinscribing the language and logic of profit that so often governs both our theological imagination and our common life. This project is, in many ways, an attempt to think against habits I have inherited, taught, and at times even defended. If it succeeds at all, it is only because of the patience and generosity of those who have allowed me to wrestle, revise, and begin again.

I am deeply grateful to Carl Bromley, whose constant support and quiet rigor have shaped my thinking in ways I am still discovering. He continues to remind me that theology, at its best, is never merely conceptual but always lively. I am also thankful for the team at Church Publishing, whose encouragement and care made this project possible. I am excited to be included in this new imprint series Divinity & Discourse, which is a gift beyond my wildest dreams. Their willingness to support a book that presses against familiar categories is a gift I do not take lightly.

This book is dedicated to my student and friend, Ellen Baker. She was brilliant in the truest sense; not simply intelligent, though she certainly was that, but perceptive, attentive, and alive to the world in ways that continually surprised me. She carried a kind of joy that was never naïve, a depth that was never heavy. She loved the outdoors, and there was something about the way she moved through creation that made it feel charged with meaning: ever abstract or distant, but always immediate and full.

I learned more from Ellen than I can adequately express. She had a way of asking questions that refused easy answers, of noticing what others overlooked, of holding together seriousness and delight. She listened well, spoke carefully, and lived with a kind of integrity that made those around her better. In many ways, this book bears the mark of those conversations, those questions, that shared pursuit of something true and good.

Ellen passed away on August 25, 2025, due to a tragic accident. She was 27 at the time of her death. I write now with her in mind. I try, in whatever small way I can, to live and work in a manner that she would have been proud of. If this book has any clarity, any attentiveness to what is often ignored or silenced, it is because I have learned—at least in part—from her example. Ellen had a way of making space for others, of seeing and naming what mattered, especially for those whose voices were not easily heard.

It is my hope that this work might do something similar: that it might speak, however imperfectly, for those who are silenced, and resist the systems that render them so. That, more than anything, is something Ellen did well.

# Bibliography


Agamben, Giorgio. *The Kingdom and the Glory: For a Theological Genealogy of Economy and Government.* Translated by Lorenzo Chiesa and Matteo Mandarini. Stanford University Press, 2011.

Alonso, Antonio Eduardo. *Commodified Communion: Eucharist, Consumer Culture, and the Practice of Everyday Life.* Fordham University Press, 2021.

Anidjar, Gil. *Blood: A Critique of Christianity.* Columbia University Press, 2014.

Arendt, Hannah. *The Human Condition.* 2nd ed. University of Chicago Press, 1958.

Aristotle. *Politics.* Translated by Carnes Lord. 2nd ed. University of Chicago Press, 2013.

Athanasius of Alexandria. "Sermon to the Newly Baptized." *Orthodox.net.* Accessed March 5, 2026. https://orthodox.net/gleanings/holy_communion.html.

______*On the Incarnation.* Translated by John Behr. *Popular Patristics Series 44.* St. Vladimir's Seminary Press, 2011.

______*The Works of the Spirit: Athanasius's Letters to Serapion on the Holy Spirit.* Translated by Mark DelCogliano, Andrew Radde-Gallwitz, and Lewis Ayres. Popular Patristics Series 43. St. Vladimir's Seminary Press, 2011.

Berry, Wendell. *The Art of Loading Brush: New Agrarian Writings.* Counterpoint, 2017.

Boff, Leonardo. *Cry of the Earth, Cry of the Poor.* Orbis Books, 1997.

Bonhoeffer, Dietrich. *Creation and Fall: A Theological Exposition of Genesis 1–3.* Vol. 3 of *Dietrich Bonhoeffer Works.* Edited by John W. de Gruchy. Translated by Douglas Stephen Bax. Fortress Press, 1997.

Bourdieu, Pierre. *The Social Structures of the Economy.* Translated by Chris Turner. Polity, 2005.

Bulgakov, Sergei. *Sophia: The Wisdom of God: An Outline of Sophiology.* Translated by Patrick Thompson. Lindisfarne Press, 1993.

______*The Lamb of God.* Translated by Boris Jakim. Eerdmans, 2008.

Brock, Rita Nakashima, and Rebecca Ann Parker. *Saving Paradise: How Christianity Traded Love of This World for Crucifixion and Empire.* Beacon Press, 2008.

Brown, Wendy. *Undoing the Demos: Neoliberalism's Stealth Revolution.* Zone Books, 2015.

Brueggemann, Walter. *Theology of the Old Testament: Testimony, Dispute, Advocacy.* Fortress Press, 1997.

Bretherton, Luke. *Christ and the Common Life: Political Theology and the Case for Democracy.* Eerdmans, 2019.

______*Christianity and Contemporary Politics: The Conditions and Possibilities of Faithful Witness.* Wiley-Blackwell, 2010.

______*Resurrecting Democracy: Faith, Citizenship, and the Politics of a Common Life.* Cambridge University Press, 2015.

Burgin, Angus. *The Great Persuasion: Reinventing Free Markets since the Depression.* Harvard University Press, 2012.

Bynum, Caroline Walker. *Holy Feast and Holy Fast: The Religious Significance of Food to Medieval Women.* University of California Press, 1987.

Casey, Edward S. *Getting Back into Place: Toward a Renewed Understanding of the Place-World.* Indiana University Press, 1993.

Cavanaugh, William T. *Being Consumed: Economics and Christian Desire.* Eerdmans, 2008.

______*Torture and Eucharist: Theology, Politics, and the Body of Christ.* Blackwell Publishing, 1998.

Chauvet, Louis-Marie. *Symbol and Sacrament: A Sacramental Reinterpretation of Christian Existence.* Translated by Patrick Madigan and Madeleine Beaumont. Liturgical Press, 1995.

______*The Sacraments: The Word of God at the Mercy of the Body.* Collegeville, MN: Liturgical Press, 2001.

Chrétien, Jean-Louis. *The Call and the Response.* Translated by Anne A. Davenport. Fordham University Press, 2004.

Collins, John J. *Introduction to the Hebrew Bible.* 3rd ed. Fortress Press, 2018.

Conzelmann, Hans. *1 Corinthians: A Commentary. Hermeneia: A Critical and Historical Commentary on the Bible.* Translated by James W. Leitch. Edited by George W. MacRae, S.J. Fortress Press, 1975.

Copeland, M. Shawn. *Enfleshing Freedom: Body, Race, and Being.* Fortress Press, 2010.

Charleston, Steven. *The Four Vision Quests of Jesus.* Morehouse Publishing, 1994.

Chryssavgis, John. *Creation as Sacrament: Reflections on Ecology and Spirituality.* T&T Clark, 2019.

Derrida, Jacques. *Given Time I: Counterfeit Money.* Translated by Peggy Kamuf. University of Chicago Press, 1992.

Eiesland, Nancy L. *The Disabled God: Toward a Liberatory Theology of Disability.* Abingdon Press, 1994.

Francis. *Laudato Si': On Care for Our Common Home.* Libreria Editrice Vaticana, 2015.

Friedman, Milton. *Capitalism and Freedom.* 40th Anniversary ed. University of Chicago Press, 2002.

Frost, Samantha. *Biocultural Creatures: Toward a New Theory of the Human.* Duke University Press, 2016.

Gebara, Ivone. *Longing for Running Water: Ecofeminism and Liberation.* Fortress Press, 1999.

Graeber, David. *Debt: The First 5,000 Years.* Melville House, 2011.

Gregory of Nyssa. "The Fourth Homily." In *Homilies on Ecclesiastes.* Edited by John Litteral. Translated by Richard McCambly. Litteral Christian Library Publication, 2014.

Gutiérrez, Gustavo. *A Theology of Liberation: History, Politics, and Salvation.* Rev. ed. Translated by Sister Caridad Inda and John Eagleson. Orbis Books, 1988.

Hall, Amy Laura. *Laughing at the Devil: Seeing the World with Julian of Norwich.* Duke University Press, 2018.

Hargaden, Kevin. *Theological Ethics in a Neoliberal Age.* Cascade Books, 2018.

Harvey, David. *A Brief History of Neoliberalism.* Oxford University Press, 2005.

______*Marx, Capital, and the Madness of Economic Reason.* Oxford University Press, 2018.

Hart, David Bentley. *The Beauty of the Infinite: The Aesthetics of Christian Truth.* Eerdmans, 2003.

Hauerwas, Stanley. *A Community of Character: Toward a Constructive Christian Social Ethic.* University of Notre Dame Press, 1981.

______*The Peaceable Kingdom: A Primer in Christian Ethics*. University of Notre Dame Press, 1983.

______*Matthew*. Brazos Theological Commentary on the Bible. Brazos Press, 2006.

Hayek, Friedrich A. *The Constitution of Liberty*. University of Chicago Press, 1960.

Holladay, Carl L. *Acts: A Commentary*. The New Testament Library. Westminster John Knox Press, 2016.

Isasi-Díaz, Ada María. *Mujerista Theology: A Theology for the Twenty-First Century*. Orbis Books, 1996.

Jennings, Willie James. *Acts*. Belief: A Theological Commentary on the Bible. Westminster John Knox Press, 2017.

Jenson, Robert W. *Systematic Theology, Volume 2: The Works of God*. Oxford University Press, 1999.

Johnson, Kelly S. *The Fear of Beggars: Stewardship and Poverty in Christian Ethics*. Eerdmans, 2007.

Julian of Norwich. *Revelations of Divine Love*. Translated by Elizabeth Spearing. Penguin, 1998.

Kant, Immanuel. *Groundwork of the Metaphysics of Morals*. Translated and edited by Mary Gregor. Cambridge Edition of the Works of Immanuel Kant. Cambridge University Press, 1996.

Käsemann, Ernst. "The Pauline Doctrine of the Lord's Supper." In *Essays on New Testament Themes*, translated by W. J. Montague, 108–135. SCM Press, 1960.

Kimmerer, Robin Wall. *Braiding Sweetgrass: Indigenous Wisdom, Scientific Knowledge, and the Teachings of Plants*. Milkweed Editions, 2013.

Kohn, Eduardo. *How Forests Think: Toward an Anthropology beyond the Human*. University of California Press, 2013.

Kotsko, Adam. *Neoliberalism's Demons: On the Political Theology of Late Capital*. Stanford University Press, 2018.

Kugel, James L. *How to Read the Bible: A Guide to Scripture, Then and Now*. Free Press, 2007.

Lefebvre, Henri. *The Production of Space*. Translated by Donald Nicholson-Smith. Blackwell, 1991.

Leithart, Peter J. *1 & 2 Kings*. Brazos Theological Commentary on the Bible. Brazos Press, 2006.

Levenson, Jon D. *The Hebrew Bible, the Old Testament, and Historical Criticism*. Westminster John Knox Press, 1993.

Lubac, Henri de. *Corpus Mysticum: The Eucharist and the Church in the Middle Ages*. Translated by Gemma Simmonds, Richard Price, and Christopher Stephens. University of Notre Dame Press, 2006.

Lysaught, M. Therese. "Liberating Theological Ethics from the Invisible Hand: Paul Farmer, the World's Poor, and the Quandaries of the Fortunate." *Journal of Moral Theology* 3, no. 1 (2014): 3–28.

Marion, Jean-Luc. *Being Given: Toward a Phenomenology of Givenness*. Translated by Jeffrey L. Kosky. Stanford University Press, 2002.

Marx, Karl. *Capital: A Critique of Political Economy. Vol. 1*. Translated by Ben Fowkes. Penguin Books, 1976.

Maximus the Confessor. *On Difficulties in the Church Fathers: The Ambigua*. 2 vols. Edited and translated by Nicholas Constas. Dumbarton Oaks Medieval Library. Harvard University Press, 2014.

______*On the Ecclesiastical Mystagogy*. Translated and edited by Jonathan J. Armstrong. Popular Patristics Series 59. St. Vladimir's Seminary Press, 2019.

McCarraher, Eugene. *The Enchantments of Mammon: How Capitalism Became the Religion of Modernity*. Belknap Press of Harvard University Press, 2019.

McFague, Sallie. *The Body of God: An Ecological Theology*. Fortress Press, 1993.

Milbank, John. *Being Reconciled: Ontology and Pardon*. Routledge, 2003.

______*Theology and Social Theory: Beyond Secular Reason*. 2nd ed. Blackwell, 2006.

Miller, Vincent J. *Consuming Religion: Christian Faith and Practice in a Consumer Culture*. Continuum, 2005.

Nietzsche, Friedrich. *On the Genealogy of Morals and Ecce Homo*. Translated by Walter Kaufmann and R. J. Hollingdale. Vintage Books, 1989.

O'Donovan, Oliver. *The Desire of the Nations: Rediscovering the Roots of Political Theology*. Cambridge University Press, 1996.

______*The Just War Revisited*. Cambridge University Press, 2003.

______*The Ways of Judgment*. Eerdmans, 2005.

Ohaneson, Heather. "Warp and Woof." *Syndicate Network*. March 27, 2026. https://syndicate.network/symposia/theology/divine-currency/.

Oliver, Kelly. *The Colonization of Psychic Space: A Psychoanalytic Social Theory of Oppression*. University of Minnesota Press, 2004.

Pervo, Richard I. *Acts: A Commentary*. Hermeneia: A Critical and Historical Commentary on the Bible. Edited by Harold W. Attridge. Fortress Press, 2009.

Pickstock, Catherine. *After Writing: On the Liturgical Consummation of Philosophy*. Blackwell, 1998.

Polanyi, Karl. *The Great Transformation: The Political and Economic Origins of Our Time*. Beacon Press, 2001.

Ramsey, Paul. *Basic Christian Ethics*. Charles Scribner's Sons, 1950.

______*Deeds and Rules in Christian Ethics*. Charles Scribner's Sons, 1967.

______*Who Speaks for the Church?* Abingdon Press, 1967.

Rivera-Pagán, Luis N. "Karl Barth and the Origins of Liberation Theology." In *Karl Barth and Liberation Theology*, edited by Kaitlyn Dugan and Paul Dafydd Jones, 15–31. T&T Clark, 2022.

Robinson, Cedric J. *Black Marxism: The Making of the Black Radical Tradition*. 3rd ed. University of North Carolina Press, 2020.

Rogers, Eugene F., Jr. "The Genre of This Book." *Syndicate Network*. February 2, 2015. https://syndicate.network/symposia/theology/blood/.

Schmemann, Alexander. *For the Life of the World: Sacraments and Orthodoxy*. St. Vladimir's Seminary Press, 1973.

Shenon, Philip. *Jesus Wept: Seven Popes and the Battle for the Soul of the Catholic Church*. Knopf, 2021.

Siedentop, Larry. *Inventing the Individual: The Origins of Western Liberalism*. Belknap Press of Harvard University Press, 2014.

Singh, Devin. "A Reply." *Syndicate Network*. March 24, 2026. https://syndicate.network/symposia/theology/divine-currency/.

______*Divine Currency: The Theological Power of Money in the West*. Stanford University Press, 2018.

Slobodian, Quinn. *Globalists: The End of Empire and the Birth of Neoliberalism*. Harvard University Press, 2018.

Sonderegger, Katherine. *Systematic Theology, Volume 2: The Doctrine of the Holy Trinity: Processions and Persons*. Fortress Press, 2020.
Spaulding, Henry Walter III. *The Just and Loving Gaze of God with Us: Paul's Apocalyptic, Political Theology*. Wipf and Stock, 2019.
Swinton, John. *Becoming Friends of Time: Disability, Timefulness, and Gentle Discipleship*. Baylor University Press, 2016.
Taylor, Charles. *A Secular Age*. Belknap Press of Harvard University Press, 2007.
Tinker, George E. *Missionary Conquest: The Gospel and Native American Cultural Genocide*. Fortress Press, 1993.
Tuan, Yi-Fu. *Space and Place: The Perspective of Experience*. University of Minnesota Press, 1977.
Verhey, Allen. *Remembering Jesus: Christian Community, Scripture, and the Moral Life*. Eerdmans, 2002.
Weheliye, Alexander G. *Habeas Viscus: Racializing Assemblages, Biopolitics, and Black Feminist Theories of the Human*. Duke University Press, 2014.
Weinberg, Robert. "The Blood Libel in Eastern Europe." *Jewish History* 26 (2012): 275–285.
Wells, Samuel. *A Nazareth Manifesto: Being with God*. Wiley-Blackwell, 2015.
______*God's Companions: Reimagining Christian Ethics*. Blackwell Publishing, 2006.
______*Improvisation: The Drama of Christian Ethics*. Brazos Press, 2004.
Wells, Samuel, and Marcia Owen. *Living without Enemies: Being Present in the Midst of Violence*. Downers Grove, IL: InterVarsity Press, 2011.
Williams, Delores S. *Sisters in the Wilderness: The Challenge of Womanist God-Talk*. Orbis Books, 1993.
Williams, Rowan. *Christ the Heart of Creation*. Bloomsbury Continuum, 2018.
Winner, Lauren F. *Still: Notes on a Mid-Faith Crisis*. HarperOne, 2012.
Wirzba, Norman. *The Paradise of God: Renewing Religion in an Ecological Age*. Oxford University Press, 2003.
Wolfe, Patrick. "Settler Colonialism and the Elimination of the Native." *Journal of Genocide Research* 8, no. 4 (2006): 387–409.
Wood, J.D. (2018), "Creation is Incarnation: The Metaphysical Peculiarity of the Logoi in Maximus Confessor." *Modern Theology*, 34.1: 82–102. https://doi.org/10.1111/moth.12382
Woodley, Randy S. *Shalom and the Community of Creation: An Indigenous Vision*. Eerdmans, 2012.
Yong, Amos. *The Bible, Disability, and the Church: A New Vision of the People of God*. Eerdmans, 2011.
Zizioulas, John D. *Being as Communion: Studies in Personhood and the Church*. St. Vladimir's Seminary Press, 1985.

# Index

www.ingramcontent.com/pod-product-compliance
Lightning Source LLC
LaVergne TN
LVHW020953010926
846999LV00032B/416
* 9 7 8 1 6 4 0 6 5 8 9 4 3 *